Yankees in the Afternoon

To all the brave young men, and indeed, all the brave young women,
who have ever felt and responded to the bite of the *gusano*,
every ambitious kid who has ever faced the horns,
basked in the warmth of triumph, or choked upon the humiliation of failure,
and especially to those whose illusions of destined glory
have been pounded into the dust, spirited away by the deadly winds,
or answered upon the point of an anxious horn,
this book is gratefully dedicated.

And especially
to the memory of John Fulton,
matador and friend.

Yankees in the Afternoon

An Illustrated History of American Bullfighters

Lyn Sherwood

foreword by Barnaby Conrad

McFarland & Company, Inc., Publishers
Jefferson, North Carolina, and London

Acknowledgments: The author would like to thank Roy Badillo, Diego O'Bolger, Tony Brand, Walter de La Brosse, Wally Burdge, Dra. Lee Burnett, Ed Byerley, Toni Christian, Ed Cohn, Harry Conner, Salvador Contreras, Richard Corey, Pat Cunningham, Paul Dobson, Muriel Feiner-Alaez, Bette Ford, Dick Frontain, John Fulton, Tony Galvez, Paul Gray, "El Güero" Guerra, Bruce Hutton, Don Joslyn, Pepe López Hurtado, Jay Manrique, Juan Martinez, Raquel Martinez, Patricia McCormick, Mike McMahon, David Moss, Daniel Muñoz, Wayne Pearce, Alfonso Ramirez "El Calesero," Jeff Ramsey, Barbara Renk, David Renk, Fred Renk, Bill Robinson, Pete Rombold, Robert Ryan, Fred Sayeg, Roy Shiflett, Alex Sonek, Bill (Guillermo) Torres Lira, Pepe Luis Vásquez, Jim Verner, Charlie Zavala—and anybody else whose name belongs here except that the author forgot to include them—whose kind assistance is gratefully acknowledged.

And very special thanks to this author's heroes, Barnaby Conrad and Budd Boetticher, who have done more to nurture North American interest in bullfighting than has anybody else in history, including Ernest Hemingway. And, especially to Constantine Mengason, who provided several photos for this book, but of greater importance, kept my computer up and running, so that I could write it.

The present work is a reprint of the illustrated case bound edition of Yankees in the Afternoon: An Illustrated History of American Bullfighters, *first published in 2002 by McFarland.*

Library of Congress Cataloguing-in-Publication Data

Sherwood, Lyn, 1937–
Yankees in the afternoon : an illustrated history of American bullfighters / Lyn Sherwood ; foreword by Barnaby Conrad.
p. cm.
Includes bibliographical references and index.

ISBN 978-0-7864-3769-6
softcover : 50# alkaline paper ∞

1. Bullfighters—United States—Biography. 2. Bullfighters—United States—Pictorial works. 3. Bullfights—United States—History. I. Title.

GV1108.A1 S54 2008
791.8'2'092273—dc21 2001044778

British Library cataloguing data are available

On the cover: Bullfighter confronts bull (photograph by the author)

Manufactured in the United States of America

McFarland & Company, Inc., Publishers
Box 611, Jefferson, North Carolina 28640
www.mcfarlandpub.com

Contents

Section III: The Women Bullfighters

Section IV: The Novilleros

Foreword

by Barnaby Conrad

It has happened to me, often, over the years. The last time was the other day, at a cocktail party in Beverly Hills.

"Oh, Mr. Conrad," gushed the hostess. "You just have to meet this gentleman, over here. He used to be a bullfighter, an American matador!"

I was introduced to a tall, graying man.

"I understand that you used to fight bulls," I said.

"Yes. A long time ago."

"When?"

"In the forties and fifties."

"Where?"

"Mexico."

"Ah, then you must have known Arruza."[1]

He hesitated. Then, he said, "Spell it."

I walked away, without saying anything. But, that was before I had seen Lyn Sherwood's marvelous book. Now, when some phony tries to tell me that he was a bullfighter, all I have to replay is, "OK, buster, what page of the book are *you* on?"

Because, you may be an American, or you may be a matador. But, if you aren't included in this comprehensive book, you are not, and never were, an American matador.

Many Americans have had a one-time go at bullfighting — or, rather, cowfighting — at tientas[2] in Spain or Latin America. It can be a memorable experience and not to be sneezed at. As Gary Cooper told me, after an encounter at (Matador) Luis Miguel Dominguín's ranch:

[1]*Carlos Arruza was, perhaps, Mexico's greatest matador. His story is recounted in Barnaby Conrad's* My Life as a Matador, *published in London, by Hutchinson.*

[2]*Frontain, Dick,* How to Enjoy a Bullfight, *pp. 6–7, Hooper Press, Phoenix, Arizona, 1966.*

"I've been around dangerous livestock, all my life. Cattle, broncs, Brahma bulls. But, I've never known such pure fear as I felt in that arena, walking out with nothing but a cape, toward that horned animal. A few minutes before, in the corral, it had looked so small and tubercular, and now it looked like a Greyhound bus! I took an awful beating, but I also managed to do a couple of adequate passes and got some *olés*. And, that was better than any Hollywood applause that I've ever received."

But, one encounter with a calf does not a matador make. Nor a hundred. Most people don't realize what a monumental task it is to become a real matador, no matter what one's nationality may be.

The current star, "El Juli,"[3] studied at the Madrid bullfighting school, from the time that he was 10, until he was 14, living, thinking, working, every day, at nothing but bullfighting. Then, at 15, he became an "overnight sensation" in Mexico.

The odds against a Spanish boy becoming a star matador are huge. The odds against an American becoming even a successful *novillero,*[4] much less a senior matador, are astronomical.

Lyn Sherwood knows all about those odds, having been on both sides of the *barrera* (red fence, surrounding the arena) for decades. One of the reasons that he takes such great photos is that, knowing so much about the Art of Cúchares,[5] like the renowned Spaniard, Paco Cano,[6] he knows exactly when to press that little button.

Now, he has done the taurine world an enormous favor by straightening out the myths that have surrounded Yankee toreros and giving us the facts on every single one, from Harper B. Lee to Bong Way Wong, to Conchita Cintrón, whose mother is American, her father Puerto Rican, born in Spain, and her great grandfather an American Yale professor.

In these pages, you'll find the true story of Sidney Franklin a rather different one than the Hemingway version. And, you'll find out a whole lot more in this highly readable aficionado's treasure trove.

There should be future editions of *Yankees in the Afternoon* because there will be future Yankee toreros, as long as the challenge of *La Fiesta Brava* is out there, beckoning to gutsy Americans.

As for this book: *orejas y rabo!*[7] And, OK, *una pata*[8] for this splendid achievement.

[3] *Spanish Matador Julián López, "El Juli," had great success as a* novillero *(apprentice matador) in Mexico during the 1997–98 seasons. He became a full matador, in the summer of 1998, at only 16 years of age.*

[4] *A* novillero *is an apprentice matador who, although a professional, has not yet received the Doctorate of Matadorship.*

[5] *The Art of Cúchares: bullfighting.*

[6] *Paco Cano is recognized as the world's greatest bullfight photographer.*

[7] *Ears and tail, awards to a matador for a grandly successful performance in the arena.*

[8] *Hoof. The maximum awards. Carlos Arruza cut the first hoof in bullfight history, in 1940, in Cieza, Spain.*

Section I

America's Fascination with Bullfighting

Introduction

La Fiesta Brava. La Fiesta Nacional. The Art of Cúchares. La Corrida de Toros. The Bullfight.[1] By any name, it's a subject that fascinates Americans. However, because of diametrically opposed cultural mores—exemplified by the term "politically correct"—most citizens of the United States find bullfighting very difficult to comprehend or appreciate.

American children are inspired by the courage of *The Little Engine That Could* and Bible stories of Joshua and David and Goliath. We play cowboys and Indians, and cops and robbers. At the movies and on television, we applaud windmill-tilting heroes. In school, we learn of the hardships of the pioneers and the patriots of the American Revolution. We are impressed by images of Abraham Lincoln, Daniel Boone, Martin Luther King, Jr., Amelia Earhart, John Glenn, and other explorers, revolutionaries, astronauts, leaders, presidents, athletes, and innovators, men and women who dared to dream impossible dreams and who invested enough true grit and tenacity to eventually feast on the spoils of success.

In such beloved cinematic morality plays as *Mr. Smith Goes to Washington, It's a Wonderful Life, Sergeant York,* and *Forrest Gump*, the good guy is always a clean-cut, honest, courageous, somewhat naïve character who is dedicated to truth and the red, white, and blue-blooded American Way, while the villain wears a hat as black as his heart and delights in throwing starving widows and their children out into the snow.

In such conflicts of good vs. evil, nefarious vs. virtuous, there are no question marks, no gray areas, no room for debate or exception. The good guy always plays fair and never takes advantage of a weaker opponent. The bad guy always plays dirty and can be counted on to kick the good guy in the crotch.

[1] *Kehoe, Vincent J-R,* Aficionado, *p. 14, Hastings House, New York, 1959.*

Rooting for the "Underdog"

Ours is a very sports-minded nation that loves to see a "Cinderella team" stand up to smite the heavily-favored champion, or the 98-pound weakling force the big bully to back down.

Likewise, we are a nation of animal lovers. *Lassie, Rin Tin Tin, Black Beauty, Bambi, Willy,* and *Flipper* make us laugh and cry. We cannot tolerate anything that seems to inflict cruelty on any animal, especially if it's physically attractive, even more so if it's cute. If baby Harp seals looked like tarantulas, nobody would care about them.

Default Assumptions

In 1997, K.C. Cole,[2] science writer for the *Los Angeles Times*, wrote a series about the human brain and its relation to prejudice. The feature focused on biases against racial and ethnic minorities, but it also revealed something about the vociferous, anti-bullfight stance of animal rightists.

Cole wrote of *default assumptions*, by which the brain "uses past experience to jump to the most likely conclusions." In other words, our expectations often influence that which we perceive. And, sometimes, those perceptions are grossly inaccurate. Cole maintained in his study that patterns of perception are active processes, in which people see that which they expect to see. Such perceptions are particularly acute when the perceived evidence is ambiguous. People watching a 3-D film will usually duck when a rapidly-moving object seems to be targeted at their heads, even though they know that it's simply an illusion. Stereotypes, based on preconceived notions, are, therefore, inevitable.

As bullfighting is foreign to our culture, the majority of uninitiated Americans consider it to be cruel and unfair. In spite of the reality that the bull has lethal weapons growing from its head, it rarely survives its encounter in the arena. Thus, to the average observer, the bull is the pure-of-heart underdog. Such a conclusion places tauromaquía into the context of sport. But, a sport is a match or competition between supposed equals, to an undetermined goal. The word "bullfight" fails to convey what is involved in La Fiesta, for there is no competition, per se, between man and bull, no archetypal battle of brain vs. brawn, no contest.[3] Man and bull are far from equal. And, except in those rare instances in which a bull demonstrates such outstanding bravery that its life is spared, via the *indulto*, the goal is determined and constant.

In fact, bullfighting is a sport only in the context that figure skating and gymnastics are sports.[4] In all three events, accomplishment is secondary to method. Figure skaters, gymnasts, and toreros perform stylized, ballet-like rituals in which specific disciplines must be demonstrated. One performer uses a cape and muleta; another uses skates; while the third works on parallel bars, rings, and other equipment. The torero does *lances* and *muletazos*; the figure skater does lutzes and axels; while the gymnast does handstands and flips. Each engages in a complicated, intimate dance in which individual identities are melded within swirling illusions of geometric precision and deep emotion. Each, in cadence with the music and in response to the cheers of the crowd, attempts to weave and link the aesthetics of his/her own art into a beautiful, ethereal, albeit temporary, tapestry. Each

[2] *Cole, K.C.,* Los Angeles Times, *July 11, 1997.*
[3] *Llovet, Enrique,* Bullfighting/Tauromachy, *pp. 7–9, Art et Industrie Paris, 1957.*
[4] *Lyn Sherwood's* Bullfight World *column,* La Prensa San Diego*: Sept. 7, 1997.*

Mexican Matador César Pastor offers the classic *Verónica*.

maneuver, each discipline, has a name and must be done according to established patterns. The form of the body, the degree of difficulty or risk involved in each maneuver, the flow, the grace, the plastic symmetry, the personality, and the mastery of technique, are the primary elements.

Winning and Losing

Yet, even after explaining all of this, the average uninitiated Anglo will still ask, "But, why doesn't the bull ever win?"

Winning and losing is a concept that is impossible to apply to bullfighting just as it cannot be applied to ballet. The figure skater doesn't compete with the ice, the dancer doesn't compete with the stage, the gymnast doesn't compete with the parallel bars, and the matador doesn't compete with the bull.

To be a genuine aficionado, one must first be a lover of animals. The real aficionado looks upon *Toro Bravo* as the principle player in the tragic taurine drama, and will tolerate no degradation or humiliation of the animal's body or dignity.

Nevertheless, the majority of Anglos subscribe to a default assumption that has led them to a conclusion that they are convinced is reasonable and rational. Thanks to K.C. Cole, we understand why ignorance, intolerance, and social prejudice are so sadly common to the human psyche.

Sentient Creatures

Perhaps, an example of the debate can be discovered in a 1993 episode of *Star Trek: Deep Space Nine.*[5] A creature, "Tosk," was fleeing the "Hunters" from his planet.

[5]Star Trek: Deep Space Nine, *1993*

Not unlike the flowing lines of figure skating discipline, the natural symmetry of the classic *Verónica* is demonstrated, here, by Matador Luis Segura, in Plaza de Las Ventas, Madrid. This, obviously, is no sport, but a performing art, as aesthetically pure as any formal ballet.

Commander Sisko asks one of the Hunters, "You say that this whole thing is a hunt, and Tosk is the prey?"

"Have you nothing similar in your society?" the Hunter asks.

"Centuries ago, people of my world engaged in blood sports, for pleasure. A few cultures still do. But, even they wouldn't consider hunting a sentient being," Sisko responds.

To which the Hunter replies, "He [Tosk] is sentient, because we have made him sentient. He has been bred for the hunt. His entire reason to exist is the hunt, to make it as exciting and interesting as he can."

"I have no tolerance for the abuse of any life form," counters Sisko.

"Abuse? We *honor* Tosk. They are the symbol of all that is noble and courageous. They condition themselves, all their lives, for this event. They're proud of their role in our culture," counters the Hunter.

Later, when Chief O'Brien advises the Tosk to ask for asylum and protection by the Federation, the creature responds, "I am Tosk, The Hunted. ... I live to survive, until I die with honor. I will not deny my existence as Tosk."

Later, as Tosk leaves the space station, he tells O'Brien, "Die, with honor."

With the caveat that lower animals, such as bovines, aren't sentient—that is, they aren't aware of living and dying—the entire episode is analogous to the most important cultural difference between aficionados and bullfight antagonists. Americans fear death, while citizens of most other countries accept it as a fact of life, indeed of celebration. The essence of the debate is not that a man or a bull dies. Dying is dying. But, dying with honor is noble. That which is important is not the fact, but the manner, of death. Had Manolete died of a heart attack, would anybody remember him?

The bullfight upholds the dignity and bravery of the fighting bull by affording it a privileged life and an honorable death, something quite more dignified than the ignobility of the slaughterhouse. Until one comes to grips with that most basic concept, appreciating or even understanding the Fiesta of the Bulls is impossible.

The Dangers

Make no mistake. While neither gymnasts or figure skaters face the potential of dying for their arts,[6] bullfighting is very, very dangerous to toreros. The horns can rip and tear, destroying flesh, breaking bones, and rupturing arteries. And they do it, frequently. When a bull gores a torero, it will always raise its massive head, driving the horn deeper. The animal shakes its head, attempting to free it of the weight of the impaled torero, and in the process, makes internal trajectories. A goring may have an entry of only a few inches; but, inside, the horn can produce many, much larger, life-threatening trajectories.

The average matador, during a career that normally spans 15 to 20 years, receives the last rites of his church six times.[7] He suffers dozens of lesser, non–life-threatening gorings and injuries. Dressed in a bathing suit, the average torero resembles a walking scar. Nevertheless, the death rate is comparatively low. Every major plaza de toros has a well-equipped infirmary. Surgeons who specialize in repairing horn wounds claim that in 90 percent of the cases, if the man is still breathing when he arrives at the infirmary, they can save his life. There are countless cases in which toreros have suffered disembowelments, or ruptures of the femoral artery, and have not only survived, but returned to the rings.

Except in those cases in which the wound is so profound that death is nearly instantaneous, the greatest danger from a goring is not the wound itself but the potential of infection. Bulls' horns are not solid bone, but layers of bone. Beneath the layers are dirt and bacteria. Surgeons must open and cleanse every centimeter of every wound. Even one tiny overlooked horn splinter can fester into gangrene, usually resulting in either amputation or death. Outside the most important bullring in the world, Madrid's *Plaza de Las Ventas*, there

[6]*Shay Oag:* In the Presence of Death/Antonio Ordoñez, *pp. 211–212, Coward-McCann, New York, 1968.*
[7]*Conrad, Barnaby,* La Fiesta Brava, *p. 33, Houghton Mifflin, Boston, 1959.*

Here, Spanish Matador Marcelino Librero receives two gorings, one from either horn. He survived, but his career took a downhill plunge.

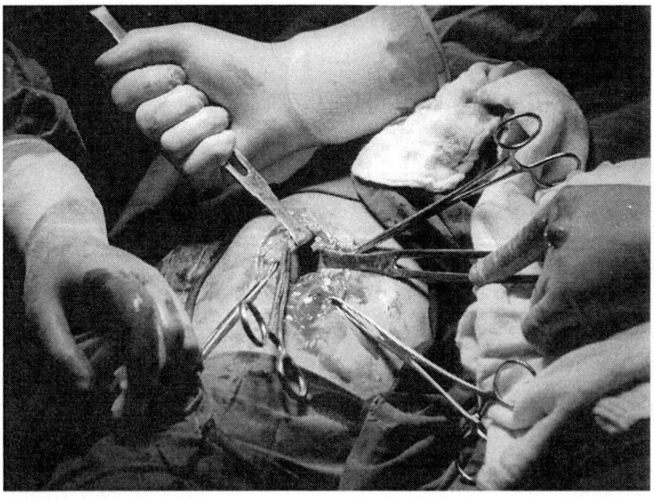

Surgeons probe the depths of a severe goring in a torero's thigh.

is a monument to Sir Alexander Fleming, the bacteriologist who developed penicillin.

Critics charge that toreros understand the dangers when they choose *toreo* as a profession, while the bull is afforded no choice in the matter. They say that there is no team of talented veterinarians, well-appointed surgical facilities, antibiotics and penicillin standing by to patch up the bull so that it can live to fight another

Here, Mexican Matador "El Callao" is gored in the groin and stomach.

day. They seem to have a valid argument, albeit a default assumption, until one realizes that no bull is ever fought more than once. In its 20 minutes in the plaza, Toro Bravo learns the ways of the torero and the futility of attacking the cloth lure. And, he remembers. Stepping into the ring with him again would be simple suicide. Art would be impossible.

In *Death in the Afternoon*, Ernest

Mexican Matador Pepe Luis Vásquez enters to kill his bull, in spite of the blood that erupts from a ruptured femoral artery in his left leg. Although he nearly bled to death, he dispatched the bull before being carried to the plaza infirmary. He became history's first matador to survive the severing of the femoral artery twice! With an open wound, Pepe Luis performed in the same arena, only 30 days later.

Hemingway wrote that in the 17th century, in Valencia, Spain, one bull was fought in the ring, many times. During a five year period, it killed 16 men and boys, and badly wounded over 60 others.

So, if the bulls weren't killed in the ring, what should be done with them? Would you want to take one home, as a house pet? Put them out to stud, you say? One *semental* (stud bull) can keep 100 or more cows happy and pregnant, while those bulls being raised for the plaza de toros are never allowed the presence of a cow, a reality that undoubtedly contributes to Toro Bravo's negative disposition. Being a semental is a great job, but it's a hard one to get. The truth is, were the bulls not killed in the arena, they would be afforded the ignoble death of slaughterhouse steers. Without the bullfight, an entire species of animal would quickly disappear.

His Majesty, Toro Bravo

Toreros aside, the most misunderstood character in the bullfight is its principal element: the brave bull.

Bos Taurus Africanus. Bos Taurus Ibericus. Toro Bravo. Toro de Lídia. Known

Toro Bravo isn't raised in a muddy pen, shoulder to shoulder with his castrated brothers, but rather as a wild animal, on acres of rolling hills and pasture, denied nothing except the presence of a cow.

Above: The bull of brave blood only remotely resembles his domestic cousins. Look at his massive neck and his lean hindquarters. *Opposite:* At the sorteo, where the matadors draw lots to see which bulls they will face, the witnesses, above, are quiet, but the bull, below, isn't the least bit happy about being removed from his graze.

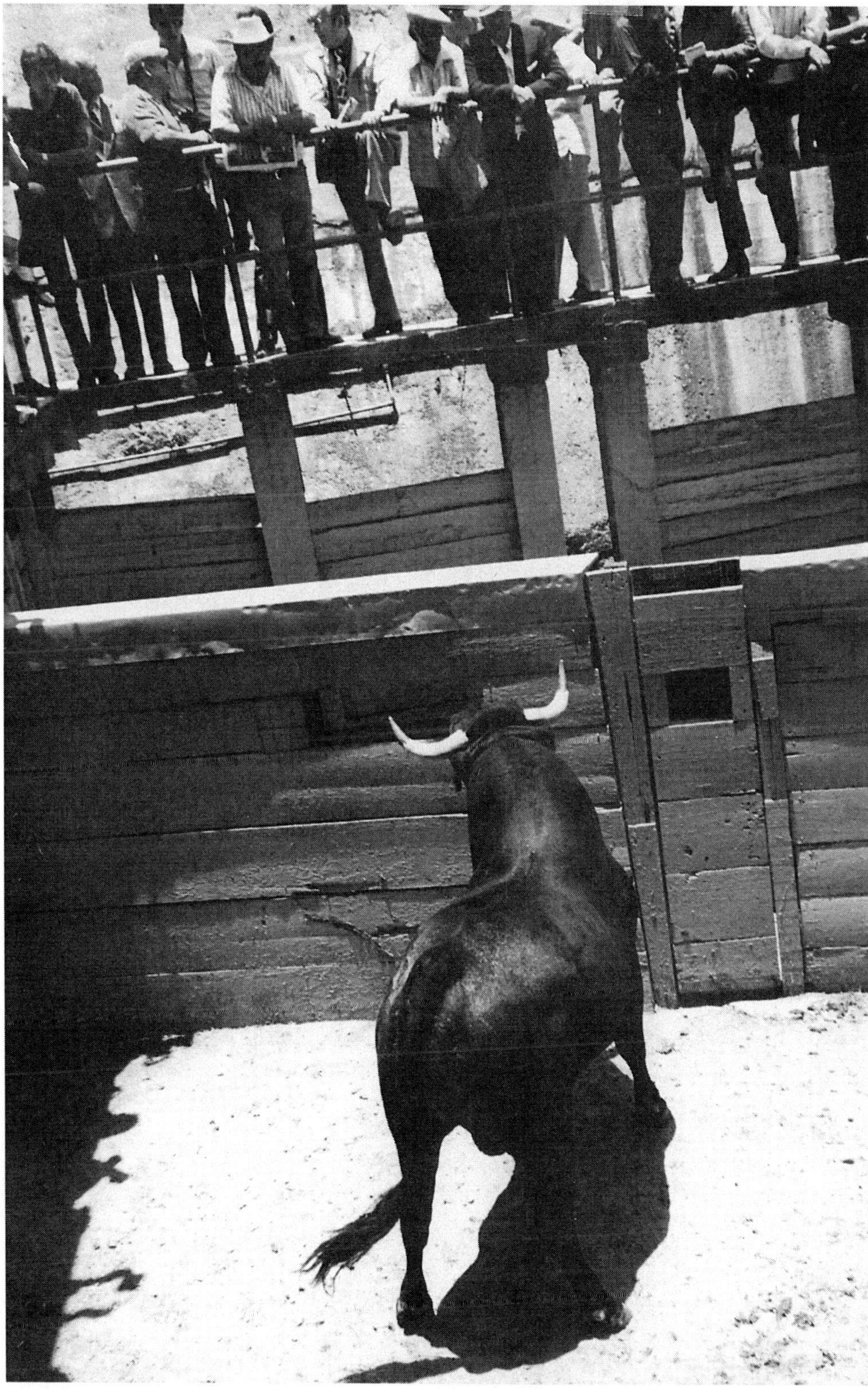

In a group, the bulls are comparatively docile. They must arrive at the ring at least a week before the corrida, for on the road, they will neither eat nor drink. They must be allowed time to recuperate with plenty of food and water.

by many names, the fighting bull is a magnificent creature, an animal which, according to Ernest Hemingway, "is to the domestic bull as the wolf is to the pet dog."[8] The behemoth is described in the Book of Job thusly:

His majestic snorting is terrible. He paws in the valley and exults his strength ...
He laughs at fear and is not dismayed ...
His sneezings flash forth light ... His eyes are like the eyelids of dawn.
Out of his nostrils comes forth smoke, as from a boiling pot and burning rushes.
His breath kindles coals, and a flame comes forth from his mouth.
In his neck abides strength, and terror dances before him ...
When he raises himself up, the mighty are afraid ...
Though the sword reaches him, it does not avail ...
Upon earth, there is not his like, a creature without fear.
He beholds everything that is high.
He is king over all the sons of pride.[9]

Was the behemoth, as some religious scholars maintain, some kind of hippo-

[8]*Hemingway, Ernest,* Death in the Afternoon, *p. 44, Charles Scribners, New York, 1932.*
[9]The Holy Bible, *chapters 30, 40, and 41, the Book of Job.*

Toro Bravo rushes into the arena. From a standing start, he can outrun any quarterhorse for 100 yards; he can catch a leaf in midair; raise his own weight above his head; or pick up a leaf from the ground.

potamus? Or, was it the aurochs, the direct ancestor of the modern fighting bull?[10]

Ancient cave drawings in Altamira,[11] in northern Spain, and in Les Trois-Frères and Lascaux,[12] France, reflect the fear and respect that Paleolithic man held for the aurochs, the horned devil-beast. Representations of animals were supposed to give power to the hunter in facing and overcoming his enemies. It was tantamount to sticking pins in the clay images of one's enemies.

Julius Caesar described the aurochs[13] of 65 B.C. as follows: "In size, they are but little inferior to elephants, although in appearance, colour, and form, they are bulls."[14]

Skeletal remains of aurochs, discovered in Spain, demonstrate that they were some six feet tall. Their progeny, according to taurine historians, eventually evolved to become the contemporary fighting bull.

Sumerian culture worshipped the bull as a deity, while other societies feared it as a creature of evil. The *sign of the horns* and the *evil eye* (thumb and pinkie), demonstrate the kind of ethereal malevolence that

[10]*Macnab, Angus,* Fighting Bulls, *p. 5, 1959, Harcourt, Brace, New York.*
[11]*Fulton, John,* Bullfighting, *pp. 28–29, Dial Press, New York, 1986.*
[12]*Fraser, Allan,* The Bull, *p. 8, Osprey Publishing, Berkshire, England, 1959.*
[13]*Fraser, Allan,* The Bull, *p. 10, Osprey Publishing, Berkshire, England, 1959.*
[14]*Macnab, Angus,* Fighting Bulls, *p. 5, 1959, Harcourt, Brace, New York.*

Graceful, agile, and athletic, Toro Bravo is a magnificent creature to behold.

ancient peoples invested, and some contemporary societies still invest, in the bull as a dark, satanic monster and a temptress of sin.

In A.D. 447, the Council of Toledo defined the devil as "a large, black, monstrous apparition, with horns on its head, cloven hoofs, hair, fiery eyes, terrible teeth, an immense phallus, and a sulphurous smell."

In Catholicism, a common icon depicts the Virgin Mary, seated upon a half

Toros Bravos are athletes, too. This splendid example leaps into an offered cape.

moon. The half moon, according to Greek mythology, was the sign of the horns. To the ancient Greeks, the thunder was the bull's bellow; the lightning was the sun, glinting off the bull's horns; and the rain was his seed, spilling upon the ground, to fertilize the crops.

Mythology[15] would have suffered without the Minotaur, the Bull of Macedon, and the unnatural passion of Pasiphaë and

[15]*Fraser, Allan,* The Bull, *p. 67, Osprey Publishing, Berkshire, England, 1959.*

Toro Bravo blasts into the plaza, looking for something to kill. The sign above the toríl gate announces that the bull's number is "1"; the matador's name is Flores; the bull weighs 465 kilos; and the bull's name is Canastilla.

the Egyptian Apeis. Hinduism and Christianity accepted the bull cult as their own.

As recounted in John Fulton's excellent book, *Bullfighting*, Gilgamesh, a mythical character of ancient Babylon, spurned Ishtar, the goddess of fertility. The bull-god Anu sought revenge by sending a heavenly bull to destroy him. Gilgamesh slew the creature.

Zeus, in the form of a bull, seduced Europa, who then bore Minos, the Bull God King of Crete.

Public awe and worship of the bull was also evidenced in Mesopotamia, Egypt, and India, where it was the symbol of power and fertility. Bull-worshipping cults flourished among the Phoenicians, Hebrews, Hittites, and the citizens of Levant. The domestic cow is still worshipped in India.

A traditional sport or spectacle in Minoan Crete, as demonstrated via the representations in the Palace of Minos, involved the leaping over the horns of a charging bull. Although some historians claim that the Greek legend of Theseus and the Minos involved the throwing of hostages to a monster half man/half bull, others insist that such hostages voluntarily attempted to leap over the horns, and in the process, many were killed.[16]

Another aspect of the spectacle involved the touching of the horns, bringing virility to men and fertility to women.

The most basic maneuver, *La Verónica*, gets is name from an old painting of St. Veronica, holding a cloth, to wipe the face of Christ at Calvary, in the same manner by which the matador offers his cape to the bull.[17]

In the Roman Colosseum, gladiators often challenged the fighting bull. They marched into the arena and saluted Caesar, in much the same way that modern toreros make the *paseillo* into the arena and salute the judge of the plaza. Christians were thrown to bulls in the Colosseum, long before lions got into the act.

Mithraism, a Sun-Bull religion, introduced by the soldiers of Pompeii, dominated the Roman Empire. In Mithraic baptisms and other rituals, bulls were sacrificed.[18] The eating of the bull's flesh and the drinking of its blood would bring salvation to the soul. But, following Emperor Constantine's conversion to Christianity, a compromise was reached. The blood of the lamb — a common reference in contemporary Christianity — was substituted for that of the bull.

In addition to being an historically and religiously important creature, the central character in the passion play of the *corrida de toros* is nature's most ferocious, graceful, and beautiful natural-born killer. Toro Bravo will attack anything that moves, without provocation, kill for lust, and never attempt to devour the subject of its wrath. There are many stories on record of fighting bulls killing themselves, attacking freight trains or trucks that seemed to have invaded their territory.[19]

Throughout the centuries, Toro Bravo has been matched against lions, tigers, and even elephants. In frontier California, imported fighting bulls were frequently pitted against grizzly bears. For the much heavier bear, it was considered a cruel fate. Sometimes, one of the bull's hooves would be staked to the ground, in order to give the bear a better chance. From such combats came the bull and bear stock market symbols.

Nevertheless, in spite of its long history, of all the performing arts, bullfighting is the most controversial and misunderstood. Literally for centuries, animal protection agencies have waged war against bullfighting.

Early Bullfights in America

Marshall Hail did extensive research of early, bloodless bullfights in the United States. In the introduction to his book, *Knight in the Sun*, Hail wrote that, in 1641, in the Massachusetts Bay Colony, it was

[16]*Magnab, Angus,* Fighting Bulls, *pp. 6–7, 1959, Harcourt Brace, New York.*
[17]*Fraser, Allan,* The Bull, *p. 89, Osprey Publishing, Berkshire, England, 1959.*
[18]*Fraser, Allan,* The Bull, *p. 97, Osprey Publishing, Berkshire, England, 1959.*
[19]*Hemingway, Ernest,* Death in the Afternoon, *p. 41, Charles Scribner's, New York, 1932.*

decreed that "no man shall exercise any Tiranny or Cruelties toward any brute Creatures which are usually kept for man's use."[20]

In the late 1860s, Hail wrote, Mexican troupes presented bullfights, of a sort, in Los Angeles and San Francisco. A bloodless bullfight was scheduled, in 1880, in a makeshift arena at Broadway and 168th Street, in New York. But because of pressure from Henry Bergh, Jr., founder of the American Society for Prevention of Cruelty to Animals (ASPCA), the planned function was a bust that developed into a riot.

Hail's research revealed that Albert Braniff, cousin of the founder of Braniff International Airways, was an amateur torero. And, that when Ireland-born Ernest Carleton Bass moved to the United States, he dubbed himself "the only Anglo-Saxon matador." In his debut in Mexico, Bass was booed out of the arena. In 1903, he reappeared in Mexico, but was too frightened to perform. He again appeared in 1904, in St. Louis, as part of the celebration of the Louisiana Purchase Exposition.

Although the St. Louis Humane Society pleaded with the Missouri governor to "avert this flagrant outrage upon the civilization of the State of Missouri and of the United States," promoter Richard Norris sold 7,000 tickets. But, before the toreros could enter the arena, they were arrested. The crowd became a rioting mob that burned the arena to the ground and wrecked nearly all of the other buildings on the midway, Hail wrote.

In Gillette, Colorado, according to Hail, a bullfight was held, August 24, 1895, featuring Mexican matadors and ornery, but nonetheless domestic, bovine stock. The county sheriff yelled, "Stop the fight! Shoot the bull!" But, Matador José Marrero Báez dispatched it with his sword.

Hail related an interesting story that took place on July 4, 1884, when a bullfight, complete with kills, was presented in Dodge City, Kansas. The former mayor, A.B. Webster, concerned over Eastern writers who were describing Dodge City as "tamed down," was searching for some kind of Independence Day weekend spectacular that would restore Dodge City's reputation as a rough-and-tumble town. He convinced the town council to present a weekend of two authentic bullfights, with six bulls per day.

News of the planned event spread even to New York City and Washington, D.C. As he had done in New York City, Henry Bergh, Jr., put pressure on the federal government to stop the fights. Subsequently, the U.S. Attorney's office telegraphed Webster, warning him that bullfighting was illegal in the United States. Webster reportedly replied, "Hell, Dodge City ain't in the United States!"

A herd of 12 domestic bulls was given such colorful names as "Cowboy Killer," "Long Branch," "Lone Star," and "Doc." Five Mexican bullfighters, led by one Captain Gregorio Gallardo, were contracted to fight and dispatch the bulls. But, due to the lack of spirit in the domestic bovines, it wasn't exactly an artistic affair.

However, that wasn't the end of bullfighting in Dodge City. In the 1980s and '90s, several Independence Day celebrations have been highlighted by bullfights, of the bloodless variety, but at least with purebred Mexican fighting bulls.

The Protesters

In recent times, extremist zealots who comprise the memberships of "animal rights" organizations have waged vociferous anti-bullfight campaigns. One such

[20]*Hail, Marshall,* Knight in the Sun, *pp. 14–16, Little, Brown, Boston/Toronto, 1962.*

group even bills itself as Friends of Islero. Islero was the bull that killed Manolete.

Such groups picket bullrings, hand out pamphlets, and make appearances on radio and television shows, in campaigns every bit as vociferous as the so-called pro-lifers. They successfully intimidate newspaper and magazine editors, threatening to boycott advertisers who sponsor any printed article or television program that concerns bullfighting.

The problem is that those who conduct such campaigns have resorted to distortions and blatant lies. They claim that the bulls are sandbagged, that Vaseline is rubbed into their eyes, and that knitting needles are stabbed into their testicles. To which, knowledgeable aficionados respond, "Who does these things? And, what is the bull doing about it?" Can you imagine a 1,000-pound brave bull, standing still for such indignities?

Another question is "why"? No matador would want to face a bull that has had its strength depleted, for it would be defensive and unpredictable. Likewise, no matador would want to face a blinded bull. The bull's eyes are on the sides of its head, affording it excellent peripheral vision, but poor center vision. By offering the lure to the outside eye, the matador can lead the bull through each pass. But, any bull that has been blinded by Vaseline wouldn't be able to see the lure.

Morality

Nevertheless, aficionados must concede that, purely on contemporary moral grounds, bullfighting is an indefensible anachronism. Taking the life of a magnificent animal, purely for the entertainment of a paying crowd, cannot be morally justified, in spite of the fact that the meat is consumed.

In his book, *To the Bullfight*, English author John Marks wrote, "Bullfighting is not a cruel sport, but a cruel method of achieving plastic beauty."[21]

But, moralists can take some consolation in the fact that domestic cattle are raised shoulder-to-shoulder in muddy corrals. At approximately 18 months of age, they are castrated. Six months later, they're sent to ignoble, and often sloppy, painful slaughter.

But, Toro Bravo is a noble thoroughbred which, for hundreds of years, has been raised as a wild animal, on ranches designed exclusively for that purpose. During his four or five years of life, Toro Bravo is afforded abundant food and water, and endless acres upon which to roam. He is denied nothing, except as previously noted, the company of cows.

To live as a wild animal and to die with dignity and honor is the only reason for Toro Bravo's existence.[22] When Toro Bravo is sent to the plaza de toros, his exposure to man on foot has been only minimal. As pointed out by Barnaby Conrad,[23] in *Gates of Fear*, from a standing start, Toro Bravo can outrun any quarter horse for 100 yards. He is so accurate with his horns, he can pick up a postage stamp from the ground, or catch a leaf in midair. He is a regal, noble beast, and the Fiesta of the Bulls is the stage upon which his royalty is proclaimed.

Judging Toro and Torero

In the bullring, Toro Bravo is judged by three precepts: bravery, nobility, and

[21]*Marks, John,* To the Bullfight, *Alfred E. Knopf, 1952.*
[22]*Daley, Robert,* The Swords of Spain, *p. 68, Dial Press, New York, 1966.*
[23]*Conrad, Barnaby,* Gates of Fear, *p. 70, Bonanza Books, New York, 1957.*

strength. Bravery inspires the attack; nobility causes it to be honest and true; and Toro Bravo's stamina must be great enough to allow him to make at least three honest entries to the picadors' horses,[24] and still maintain his strength, throughout all three acts of the *lídia*.

The matador is, likewise, judged by three precepts[25]: *parar*, to hold his feet and legs steady, to not surrender ground; *mandar*, to not just take advantage of the bull's normal line of attack from Point A to Point B, but to *impose* upon the animal, to direct its attack, to lead it from Point A to Point C; and *templar*, the most difficult of the precepts, is that which separates genuine toreros from common bullfighters. To demonstrate temple, or timing, the matador must perform with a rhythm and tempo that match the bull's speed of attack. In low passes, the bull's horns must never touch the red *muleta*.

And, while we're on the subject, the matador's sword is not a defensive instrument. During the third act, most matadors use wooden or aluminum swords. Only when he is ready to kill, at the end of his third act performance, does the matador exchange the ersatz sword for a real one.

When Toro Bravo is brave and noble, and when the matador is honest and courageous, both seem to be working with each other in slow motion. It isn't a fight; it's a ballet, a ballet of death. The whole thing seems to be choreographed. There is nothing violent, forced, or superfluous in the matador's style.[26]

The Hot Dog Toreros

However, new aficionados should beware of the "hot dog" matador, the character who makes the whole thing seem like a kamikaze affair. Such toreros are known as *tremendistas*, and they are usually frauds. *Tremendismo* is to real *toreo* as pornography is to erotica. They dishonor the bull and take advantage of the gullibility of the unsophisticated tourist or otherwise neophyte crowds.

As Robert Daley pointed out in his book *The Swords of Spain*, "A beautiful bullfight is never scary, and a scary bullfight is seldom beautiful."[27]

Toro Bravo must become the confidant of the matador, a partner, rather than an adversary. Toro Bravo's courage and killer instinct must never be emasculated. When a strong, brave bull and a talented, honorable matador come together, the sands of the plaza become a confessional, in which truth is naked and bold. Toro Bravo's death becomes a penance, to be celebrated as the tragic but essential culmination of the life drama.

True bravery need not be proclaimed. It is a quiet, deliberate, dignified, and personal thing. It's the discipline of integrity that inspires a man to attempt, under difficult circumstances, to persevere when others would surrender, to enter honestly with the sword, and to never belittle either the martyrdom of Toro Bravo or the deadly seriousness of the taurine drama.

Within the context of those precepts, a proper amount of showmanship is welcome, indeed necessary. The plaza de toros is a theatre-in-the-round. But showmanship must be incorporated as an exclamation point, punctuating a treatise of artistry. Only then is it acceptable.

However, when *tremendismo* is used as the entire taurine essay, when it deceives the crowd and suffocates the performance

[24]*Macnab, Angus,* Fighting Bulls, *p. 222, Brace and Company, New York.*
[25]*Llovet, Enrique,* Bullfighting/Tauromachy, *p. 199, Art et Industrie, Paris, France.*
[26]*Cossío, José María,* Los Toros, *Volume III, p. 111, Dirección General de Turismo, Madrid, Spain, 1963.*
[27]*Daley, Robert,* The Swords of Spain, *p. 207, Dial Press, New York, 1966.*

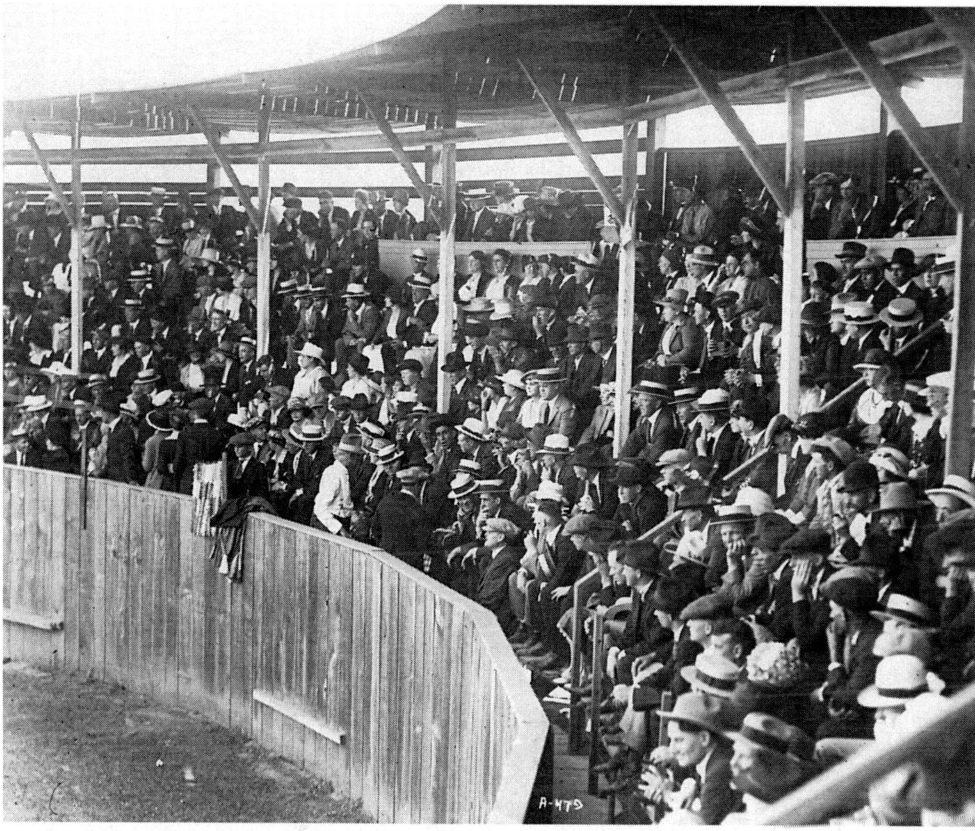

Spectators at a Tijuana bullfight, near the turn of the century. (Photograph courtesy of the Historical Collection of Title Insurance and Trust Company, San Diego, California.)

in overt gutsmanship, it becomes a parody of the drama. It emasculates and belittles the tragedy of Toro Bravo's sacrifice and threatens the honor and dignity of La Fiesta.

When a matador ignores the meaning of the play, when he projects the image of the ham, the tourist-pleasing con man, he cannot assume the role of a prince, only that of a court jester. For such an ignoble peasant to assume the Power of Death is to denigrate the tragedy into a farce, and the plaza de toros into a noisy, outdoor brothel. And, those who applaud such fraudulent hucksters do not deserve the title of *aficionados*. They are nothing more than voyeurs, lasciviously witnessing and encouraging the rape of art.

The ability to distinguish between showmanship and tremendismo is that which separates the genuine aficionado from the common bullfight fan.

The corrida de toros is a complicated, intense, formal ritual, a ballet in three acts, in which the brute force of Toro Bravo and the grace and artistry of the matador do not clash, but meld. The torero does not *fight* the bull; he *dances* with it. Toro Bravo is the torero's unwitting dance partner, the mysterious Mr. X. All of the toreros have scripts; they know their roles in the drama. But, the bull has never appeared on this stage of sand. How he responds is the big question mark.

Nevertheless, considering all of its history and its complicated, esoteric

El Cordobés was the biggest bullring attraction since Carlos Arruza. Here, during a Tijuana appearance, he performs an *estatuario*, also known as a statue pass, or a pass of death.

nature, is it really any wonder that bullfighting is so foreign to Anglos and so difficult for them to understand?

The Fame Spreads

Still, we are intrigued by the bullfight. Much of the credit for that interest can be attributed to the publishing, broadcasting, advertising, and entertainment industries.

The flash point was realized in the 1960s, with the emergence of Spain's Manuel Benitez "El Cordobés," whose story was related in the book *Or, I'll Dress You in Mourning*. Projecting the rebellious spirit of the Beatles and the charisma of Bobby Kennedy, he appeared on the cover of *Life* magazine, which dubbed him "Spain's Beatnik Bullfighter."

In terms of impact and popularity throughout the world, El Cordobés was the most successful matador in history. He was also, at the time, the world's highest paid athlete. He earned $25,000 per afternoon, and he performed in more than 100 afternoons per year.

The publishing industry has contributed mightily to the tremendous wave of American interest in bullfighting. Since Hemingway's *Death in the Afternoon*, 48 nonfiction, English language bullfight books have been published. Among them are some genuine classics, including Barnaby Conrad's *La Fiesta Brava, Matador,*

Bullfight crowds at plazas de toros along the U.S.-Mexican border are up to 50 percent from the American side.

Gates of Fear, The Death of Manolete, How to Fight a Bull, and *The Encyclopedia of Bullfighting*; Peter Buckley's *Bullfight*; Vincent J-R Keyhoe's *Aficionado* and *Wine, Women and Toros*; Kenneth Tynan's *Bull Fever*; Angus McNab's *Fighting Bulls*; John Marks' *To the Bullfight* and *To the Bullfight, Again*; Robert Daley's *Swords of Spain*; Marshall Hail's *Knight in the Sun*; John Fulton's *Bullfighting*; and many others. All have enjoyed outstanding sales success.

And, too, some questionable bullfight books and novels have been published, including *The Last Serious Thing*, by Bruce Schoenfeld, a nonfiction work that was published by Simon & Schuster. Schoenfeld is a fine writer, but he bit off more than he was capable of chewing when it came to writing a serious book about bullfighting.

In fiction novels, huge publishing triumphs have been recorded by Peter Viertel's *Love Lies Bleeding*; Tom Lea's *The Brave Bulls* (now in its 16th printing); Luis Spota's outstanding *The Wounds of Hunger*; and Earl Shorris' hilarious satire, *The Boots of the Virgin*, the story of Saul "El Sol" Feldman, which asks the question, "Can a young, Jewish boy find true happiness as the world's greatest bullfighter?"[28]

Bloodless Bullfights in the USA

Literally hundreds of bullfight features have been published in prestigious magazines, including *Reader's Digest*. And, although of the bloodless variety, bullfighting has caught on in a big way in the United States. In one series of such presentations,

[28]*Shorris, Earl,* The Boots of the Virgin, *Delacorte Press, New York, N.Y., 1968.*

Those who are opposed to the use of picadores should realize that bulls frequently dump the mounted man onto the ground. With armor on his right leg, he must usually wait for the other toreros to lead away the bull. *Note:* In more than 40 years with the bulls, the author has seen only one picador's horse killed. It isn't pretty, but it doesn't happen very frequently.

in the Houston Astrodome, 107,000 spectators watched four afternoons of bullfighting, featuring Antonio Ordoñez, who was the world's leading matador and the subject of Hemingway's *The Dangerous Summer.*

Since then, bloodless bullfights have been successfully presented in Washington, D.C.; Dodge City, Kansas; Las Vegas; Philadelphia; Detroit; and on almost a weekly basis in northern California and in Santa Fe Springs, near Los Angeles. Today, bloodless bullfights are popular, especially among the Portuguese community, throughout California. In several locations, purebred fighting bulls are bred and raised for the affairs. Their locations are purposely not listed here.

Border Bullfights

Bullfights along the U.S.-Mexico borders consistently attract crowds that are 40 to 50 percent American. In Tijuana there are two first-class bullrings, one of which is the world's second largest. Every summer, an average of a quarter million Americans spend $15 million to attend the bullfights along the border.

In bloodless bullfights, picadores (one is shown above) aren't used. Thus, the bull's strength isn't tempered, and its head remains high, thus making performances by the toreros very different from those in countries in which picadores are used.

Even in Spain, South America, and France, especially during the big summer fairs, in which good seats are scalped for as much as $500 apiece, Americans account for an impressive percentage of the audiences.

In 1998, in Spain, France, and Portugal, some 1,000 corridas and 624 *novilladas* (in which novilleros, professional aspirants who have not yet attained the doctorate of matadorship, perform) were held. In Mexico, 394 corridas and 269 novilladas were celebrated,[29] while South American rings presented another 150 bullfights.

Aficionados clubs can be found in Detroit; Chicago; New York City; Denver; El Paso; San Francisco; Phoenix; Chula Vista (near San Diego); McAllen, Texas; and Los Angeles. In 1999, the Los Angeles club celebrated its 50th anniversary. Nevertheless, the club in McAllen, La Peña Taurina del Valle de Texas, claims to be the first, for it was established three months earlier than Los Aficionados de Los Angeles.

The National Association of Taurine Clubs (USA), a united front representing most of the bullfight clubs in the United States, has an annual week-long convention in Mexico, Spain, or France. In many of the NATC's conventions, amateur Yankee toreros perform, just for the fun of it. They are not paid, and usually have to purchase their own bulls.

Clarín, the English language bullfight magazine, was published beginning in 1966 and enjoyed a distribution of 10,000, most of which was in the United States. *Clarin* folded in 1988.

Nearly every aspect of American life

[29]*Newsletter of Los Aficionados de Los Angeles taurine club, May 1999.*

has been affected by the bullfight. Taurine skits have been used on many television sitcoms and variety shows, including such contemporary hits as *Friends, Just Shoot Me, Frasier*, and *The Carol Burnett Show*. Questions concerning bullfighting are frequently asked on *Jeopardy*.

El Chicano's gold record, *Viva Tirado*, written by American jazz maestro Gerald Wilson, for Mexican Matador José Ramon Tirado, spent several weeks on the Top 10 charts. Wilson's "Torero Impressions in Jazz" series includes *Paco*, written for Matador Paco Camino. It became *Playboy* Jazz Poll's Number One. Wilson's *Carlos*, which utilizes jazz to tell the story of Matador Carlos Arruza, is the first cut on Wilson's hit album, *The Golden Sword*. He has recorded several other hits, dedicated to particular toreros and capturing their styles.

The advertising industry utilizes taurine themes to sell everything from new cars to beer and laundry detergents. American Motors produced the *Matador* model. American Express, Merrill-Lynch, United California Bank, GTE, the Carnation Company, Federal Express, Ford Trucks, Chevrolet Trucks, Target Sports Wear, Hershey's "Kisses," KPMG stock brokers, Blue Cross/Blue Shield, and other major companies have used bullfight themes to help sell their products. Everybody is familiar with the Schlitz Malt Liquor bull, which was designed by American Matador John Fulton.

Bugs Bunny, the Roadrunner, Laurel & Hardy, and Abbott & Costello films, comic strips, as well as political cartoons, have all used bullfight stories or theme lines. In the film *Fail Safe*, the president of the United States has nightmares about ferocious bulls. Running with the bulls in Pamplona opened the Oscar-winning Billy Crystal film *City Slickers*.

The fashion industry incorporated bullfight motifs in *torero pants* and women's jackets with embroidered shoulder epaulets.

Professional basketball teams often utilize that which has come to be known as the *matador* defense. Even *Monday Night Football* has incorporated bullfighting as a theme.

Indeed, in spite of the controversy that it almost always provokes, bullfighting is big among Anglos. Therefore, it is only natural that a few of those individuals would attempt to seek careers on the stages of the Bullfight World.

The following are their stories.

Chapter 1

Hollywood's Love Affair with Bullfighting

Gilbert Roland, Manolete, and Ernest Hemingway.

How many film stars can you spot in these photographs?

Budd Boetticher's *The Bullfighter and the Lady* holds the record for being the most frequently shown feature film on television. Shown are Gilbert Roland, Joy Paige, and Robert Stack.

Prior to 1932, with the publishing of Ernest Hemingway's *Death in the Afternoon*, only a small handful of Americans could speak knowledgeably of the national passion of so many countries. Most of them had been influenced by the first *Blood and Sand* film, starring Rudolph Valentino.

In the years that followed, Hollywood's glamorous upper echelon discovered that becoming involved in bullfighting was another way to demonstrate one's own celebrity. Randolph Scott, Rita Hayworth, Ava Gardner, Gilbert Roland, Lana Turner, John Wayne, Kirk Douglas, Peter Graves, Debra Paget, Andy Williams, Herbie Alpert, Sammy Davis, Jr., Peter Brown, Frank Sinatra, Richard Boone, Lee Marvin, Joseph Cotten, Rock Hudson, Anthony Quinn, Glenn Ford, and Orson Welles frequently occupied expensive, front row, shady-side seats in *plazas de toros* from Madrid to Tijuana.

In more contemporary times, those Hollywood figures have been replaced by Robert Redford, James Coburn, and Charlie Sheen, among many others. Being photographed with a well-known matador is a status symbol. Before becoming a sweetheart of the animal rightists' set, Stephanie Powers was an avid bullfight fan, and even performed as an *aficionada práctica* (amateur torera).

But, the Hollywood set couldn't forever hold an exclusive on attending bull-

Famed film director Budd Boetticher (right, standing) receives the dedication of a bull, during a corrida in Tijuana.

Carlos Arruza was a great matador, the prime rival to Manolete in the 1940s.

Arruza invented several disciplines. Here, he does *El Teléfono*, with his left elbow resting on the bull's forehead.

fights. Tremendous public interest was ignited in 1941, with the remake of *Blood and Sand,* this one with Tyrone Power. It won an Oscar. Then, in 1947, international headlines proclaimed that the great Manolete had been killed by a bull, in Linares, Spain. That tragedy would eventually be chronicled by Barnaby Conrad in his book, *The Death of Manolete*, and a Playhouse 90 television production, which, although a truly awful production, opened the gates to a veritable tidal wave of American curiosity about the romantic taurine drama.

As an interesting footnote, somebody in the Lamborghini automobile family was or is, obviously, an aficionado. Among the Lamborghini automobiles have been the Espada, the Islero, and the Miura. *Espada* translates to the swordsman or the sword. And, *Islero,* from the Miura ranch, was the name of the bull that killed Manolete.

In 1950, Tom Lea's book, *The Brave Bulls*, was put to film. Although it was a disaster of a movie, it attracted huge crowds. The excellent novel has since enjoyed 16 reprints.

Shortly thereafter — with John Wayne as producer — famed director and renowned aficionado Budd Boetticher, who had been technical director on the remake of *Blood and Sand,* directed *The Bullfighter and the Lady*, the film that launched Robert Stack to stardom. That film provided the catalyst for intensified American interest in bullfighting, not just in Hollywood, but throughout the nation. Even today, *The Bullfighter and the Lady* holds the record for being the most frequently-run movie on television.

All Yankee aficionados owe a great deal to Boetticher, who has been involved in practically every major bullfight film produced in the United States. In 1955,

Arruza retired three times. On his third return to the rings, he performed not as a matador, but as a rejoneador, performing astride exceptionally well-trained horses.

John Wayne was an admirer of Carlos Arruza and made him a member of the cast of *The Alamo*.

Boetticher, himself a fine amateur torero, on foot as well as an amateur *rejoneador* (horseback, Portuguese-style torero), followed up with *The Magnificent Matador*. It wasn't a great movie, but it was very successful at the box office.

In the mid–60s, at approximately the same time that Spain's "El Cordobés" was dominating the bullfight world, Boetticher was completing his cinematic masterpiece, *Arruza*, which would, as it turned out, become the final chapter in the life of one of the world's greatest toreros. The "Mexican Cyclone," Carlos Arruza, had retired as a matador, then returned to the rings, but in the role of a rejoneador. Boetticher had invested many years and a small fortune in the film, which was almost completed when disaster struck. Carlos Arruza was killed, May 20, 1966, in an auto accident.

In spite of having invested all of his money, wrecking his marriage to Debra Paget, nearly destroying his health and his career, and ending up in jail and finally in a Mexican insane asylum,[1] Boetticher still managed to complete *Arruza*. It attracted international accolades and became a cult film for American aficionados.

This author interviewed Boetticher at the Equestrian Center of San Diego Country Estates, where he and his wife, Mary, breed and train *rejoneo* (Portuguese-style bullfighting) horses.

[1]*Boetticher, Budd,* When in Disgrace, *p. viii, Neville, Santa Barbara, Calif., 1997.*

Arruza performed many years as a rejoneador, until his death, May 20, 1966, in an automobile accident in Mexico. He had faced 2,000 bulls in his career, any one of which could have crushed his chest as easily as did the bus into which his car crashed.

Tell me about the first bullfight film on which you worked.

In 1940, I was technical director for *Blood and Sand.* Producer Rouben Mammoulian was out of his element, making a bullfight picture. He didn't know anything about it. And, he didn't make a very good picture. Some call it a classic, but it wasn't. Technically, it was so wrong.

Who selected Tyrone Power as the lead?

The world! He was the number one box office. He was the most beautiful man you ever saw in your life. All Mammoulian wanted to do was make the most beautiful color picture that had ever been made. And, he did. He won the Academy Award for color cinematography. But, I thought, "I'll bet I can make a better picture. I love and understand bullfighting. Now, if I can just learn to direct, I'll make *The Bullfighter and the Lady.*" I suddenly realized that I wanted to be a director, and I became one, four years later, in 1944.

How about The Magnificent Matador? *Was it a successful film?*

Yes. It did fairly well at the box office, and it had good reviews. But, of greater importance, that which I wanted the most, it established Anthony Quinn as a genuine star.

Tell us about Arruza.

I wanted to make the definitive picture of bullfighting, at least as far as *rejoneo* is concerned. With the combination of Carlos Arruza and his beautiful horses, I had the best of *Black Beauty* and *Blood and Sand.*

But, you never made any money out of it.

Not a penny! Let me tell you what *Arruza* cost me. I was averaging $300,000

Tyrone Power in ***Blood and Sand.***

a year in Hollywood. *Arruza* took seven years to film. That's $2,100,000 that I didn't make, plus I invested $250,000 of my own money.

What a shame that Arruza was killed before the film was finished. He never got to see it.

Ah, but he did! At least, he saw the most important part, that final performance in *La Plaza México.* [For that particular section, the nail-biting climax of the film, six cameras—including one that was installed at ground level, in the middle of the arena—recorded Arruza's

Budd Boetticher, giving a nice *derechazo* to a well-armed *novillo,* on Carlos Arruza's Pastejé ranch.

final triumph. The footage is absolutely spectacular.] I arranged a private showing, at Churrubusco Studios. Afterward, when the lights came back on, Arruza stood up and said, "Budd, that's better than I am!"

Bullfighting has certainly changed in the past two or three decades.

Unfortunately, what's happened in this country isn't good. When I became interested in bullfighting in 1938, it was glamorous. It enhanced your life and your career. Hemingway became an authority because it was something that he really loved, and because he was Hemingway. It made many new aficionados. Today, the animal rights people have said so many absurd things, you know that they've done absolutely no studying at all.

What's the biggest problem involved in Americans enjoying bullfighting?

People who don't know bullfighting cannot understand how a bullfighter can love a bull. Well, I love horses, but the fighting bull is the most noble animal in the world. The truth is, everything that's bad about bullfighting is really bad. And, everything that's good about it is great! As Matador John Fulton put it, "An aficionado is someone who knows all about bullfighting, but likes it, anyway."

According to reliable sources, Frank Sinatra was taken with Manolete's story and inves-

tigated producing a film about the matador's life, casting himself in the lead role. Those sources insist that, somewhere, there are photos of "Old Blue Eyes," in suit of lights and Manolete makeup, complete with the late torero's deep facial scar.

He was an aficionado. Ava was a devout enthusiast, as you know. And, that was Frank's kind of life. It was romantic. He looked great, in those days. If I had directed Frank Sinatra as Manolete, it would have been one hell of a picture. [Note: When contacted, a year before his death, Sinatra declined to comment.]

How much influence did Manolete's death have on American interest in bullfighting?

It's hard to tell. Barney's [Barnaby Conrad's] book was wonderful. But, the Playhouse 90 production, using Jack Palance as Manolete, was a disaster. If they had used Frank Sinatra, they would have had something authentic.

There's a movement in Spain to ban bullfighting.

Oh, for the last forty years, at least, there has been a movement in Spain to ban bullfighting. But, they're never going to do it. You know, bullfighting is very easy to criticize. You see a bad bullfight and you can't believe that such things go on. But, if you see a great one, like I did the first time, you'll go back, as long as you live. I never discuss bullfighting with people, unless they really want to learn something. The anti-bullfight people are as violent as the anti-abortion-choice people.

Why has there been no truly successful American Matador?

Well, they're handicapped, to start with. It's extremely difficult for an American to be accepted in Tauromaquían society. John Fulton was put through hell. He gave it more than all of the other American toreros, put together. And, he was technically a good bullfighter. He did everything right. He was extremely, fanatically, brave. I loved John. He was a dear, dear friend of mine. If John couldn't make it big, no American can.

How many other Yankee toreros have you seen?

Very few. I saw Sidney Franklin, at the end of his career. He was very brave, very clumsy, and a despicable son of a bitch. I saw John Fulton fight, way past his prime. Jeff Ramsey's sweetheart lived in the same condominium that I did, just before I left to make *Arruza*. I gave Jeff his first *traje corto* [informal outfit, worn in bullfight charity festivals]. A few years later, I saw him working a young *novillo*, and he was wonderful. I was delighted. And, he became a very good *aficionado práctico* [amateur torero]. I never saw him fight formally, in suit of lights, but I saw him in the ring, with me, and he knew what he was doing.

What about your own activities in the ring?

Had I stuck with it, I think I could have become a successful Matador de Toros. My parents were wealthy, so I wouldn't have had to scrounge around to get fights. But, these kids, today, who start from scratch, broke, trying to eat and make it as toreros, well it's almost impossible.

Section II

The Yankee Matadors

Chapter 2

The First Yankee Matador

"Harper B. Lee was a brilliant torero and very brave."
—Rodolfo Gaona[1]
(late, great Mexican matador)

If contemporary aficionados could travel back to turn-of-the-century Mexico, during the last years of the Porfírio Díaz regime, they would probably be shocked by the style of bullfighting that was in vogue. Agility of foot was an attribute of successful toreros. Slow, aesthetic bullfighting was still several years away. The great innovator, Spanish Matador Juan Belmonte—whose gimpy legs forced him to revolutionize bullfighting by relying upon his arms and wrists, rather than clever footwork—didn't achieve stardom until about 1918.

As the mattress-like *peto* had not yet been invented, picadores' horses weren't protected from the horns. It wasn't unusual for a half dozen or more horses to be gored to death during the course of just one corrida de toros. It had to have been a very ugly scene.

The awarding of ears and tails[2] for triumphant performances had not yet become a custom in Mexico, and had only recently been initiated in Spain. Applause, music, and turns of the ring were the only public rewards for the matadors of the

[1]*Most of the research for this section was gleaned from: Hail, Marshall,* Knight in the Sun, The First Yankee Matador, *Little, Brown, Boston, 1962.*
[2]*Fulton, John,* Bullfighting, *p. 185, Dial Press, New York, 1977.*

Mexico Matador Rodolfo Gaona took his alternativa in Spain, May 31, 1908. He retired in 1925.

time. Determining which matador was the most triumphant of any particular afternoon was totally subjective.

Transportation and communications were in their infancy. Matadors and their subalterns would perform in one city, then endure several long days and nights of hot, uncomfortable travel, usually by train, to their next appointments in the arena. Pole-vaulting over bulls— a common practice in ancient Crete — was a popular discipline in the repertoire of many top-ranked matadors, as was standing upright, or sitting in a chair, motionless, in the center of the ring, and refusing to move, even when the bull threatened to attack. The theory was that bulls will not attack a stationary figure. But, on many occasions, somebody forgot to reveal that idea to the bulls.

Perhaps, the most ominous reality, at least from the standpoint of the toreros, was that medicine and surgical techniques were pure horse-and-buggy. Today's toreros survive wounds that would have proven fatal in those early days. Likewise, nowadays, we have penicillin, which has saved the lives of many gravely-gored toreros.

But, it was within that rather rustic, turn-of-the-century environment that Harper B. Lee became the first Yankee matador.

He was born James Harper Gillett, September 5, 1884, in Ysleta, a border suburb of El Paso, Texas. Lee's father, James Buchanan Gillett, was a Texas Ranger, and according to Marshall Hail's *Knight in the Sun*, was a "high toned Christian gentleman who never swore, told smutty stories, drank whiskey, or used tobacco," at least not in the presence of women. Nevertheless, he spent plenty of time socializing with his Texas Ranger friends in El Paso's saloons and bawdy houses.

Lee's grandfather, James S. Gillett, was a lawyer, legislator, soldier in the Mexican and Civil wars, friend of Sam Houston, and adjutant general of Texas. Lee's mother, Helen, was a daughter of Gillett's company commander, George Whythe Baylor, whose uncle, R.E.B. Baylor, founded Baylor University.

Helen didn't have much luck with husbands. Charging adultery, she divorced Lee's father, early in 1889, and changed her son's name to Harper Baylor Gillett. But, she apparently had a taste for Texas Rangers, for she married another one, Captain Frank Jones, who was subsequently ambushed and slain by horse thieves, before he could meet his first son, Frank Taylor Jones, who was born prematurely and would become a prodigy of musical comedy. The boy died at 15 years of age, from congenital heart disease.

According to Marshall Hail's book, in 1895, Helen married Samuel M. Lee and changed the names of both of her sons. Frank became Francisco Baylor Lee, while his older brother became Harper Baylor Lee. The family then moved to Guadalajara, Mexico, where Samuel Lee was employed by a railroad construction firm.

As a child, Harper's favorite books were *Don Quixote* and *Ivanhoe*. Such romantic literature provided the perfect breeding ground for the *gusano*, the imaginary worm of taurine passion that lives in the belly of every torero.

In Guadalajara, Harper and his school friends played bullfighter games. Before long, rather as a lark, he was participating in amateur bullfights in dusty pueblos. After Harper's mother died, in 1903, the youngster began performing in charity *novilladas*, the taurine equivalent of minor league baseball games. After seeing Harper torear in such a function, Jalisco Governor Miguel Ahumada encouraged him to turn professional.

So, Harper became a full-fledged *novillero*, performing as such throughout Mexico. He became well-known for his risky style of placing *cortas* (short *bander-*

illas, the paper-decorated, barbed sticks, placed during the second act). He would break the 29-inch banderillas in half, then place the abbreviated sticks in the dangerous *al quiebro* (to the feint) style. He would hold his ground as the bull attacked, then make a quick feint to one side or the other. As the bull changed direction in order to intercept the apparently-escaping target, Harper would quickly return to his original position, then place the cortas on top of the powerful shoulders of the animal as it lumbered by.

Harper was also famous for performing that which is now known as the *Puerta Gayola*, a deceptively simple, yet always exciting, maneuver. The torero places himself on his knees, in front of the *toril* gate, through which the bull enters the ring. Waiting for the gate to open, the man spreads his magenta and yellow *capote* on the ground, in front of himself, thus forming a semi-circle on the sand. He holds both sides of the cape with a palms-up grip.

The crowd becomes silent, holding its breath. The *toril* gate opens. Then, as the bull thunders into the arena, the torero challenges it. The animal charges. Then, at the last heart-in-throat second, as the bull bears down on the kneeling torero, the man lifts either the right or left side of the cape, but usually the right, inverting it to show its reverse, yellow side, and swings it over his opposite shoulder, leading the bull mere inches from the torero's face. Timing is everything. Lifting the cape a fraction of a second too early or too late has proven disastrous.

After several successful performances in the provinces, Lee was invited to make his debut in *Plaza El Toreo*, of Mexico City, at that time the most important bullring in the republic. A crowd of 20,000 was in the stands, on that May 16 of 1909, when the population of the Aztec capital was only 400,000.

Harper captured the Mexico City crowd with his *capote, banderillas*, and *muleta* work. But, while attempting to kill, he was violently caught and tossed. Uninjured, but furious, Harper jumped up and ran at the bull, cocking his arm, as if preparing to hit the animal in the nose. But, before he could throw the punch, the bull dropped dead, from the sword. Some observers insisted that the sight of the onrushing torero caused the bull to die of fright, Hail related.

The Yankee novillero also triumphed with his second bull, inspiring the screaming aficionados to leap onto the sand, pick up Harper Lee, and carry him upon their shoulders, all the way to his lodging house, five blocks away. The headlines of Mexican newspapers proclaimed the triumph of Lee, making much of the fact that he was a *gringo*.

On his second Mexico City performance, May 30, 1909, in front of another near-capacity crowd, Harper triumphed, but suffered a goring in his right leg. In his third appearance in *Plaza El Toreo*, he suffered another small goring, this time in the thigh. Next, came a huge triumph in a Mexico City charity performance.

Once again, the Mexican press reported Harper's performances as a phenomenon. Harper performed, several times, in Juárez, once with Francisco Alonso "Paquiro," the matador father of the late actor Gilbert Roland.

In his several Juárez appearances, Harper had hoped that his natural father would show up to watch him. But, as the elder Gillett considered his son's bullfighting activities to be a blight on the family name, he never saw Harper in the arena.

After completing 28 novilladas, Harper decided to seek the *alternativa*, the formal ceremony in which the man graduates from the level of novillero to that of Matador de Toros. The event was set for the following January. But, on October 10, 1909, in San Luis Potosí, while placing banderillas, he received a huge goring in the groin. According to Marshall Hail, the wound was "sixteen centimeters into the upper part of the right exterior groin muscle, downward obliquely, eight centimeters, beneath the Poupart ligament, terminating three centimeters from the spine of the pubis."

The wound, wrote Hail, required 147 stitches. Harper endured three surgeries, one of which involved the removal of one of his testicles. When informed of Harper's injuries, his crusty, Texas Ranger father replied that, for having brought disgrace to the family, it would have been a good thing had Harper been killed.

During his two-month hospital stay, Harper fell in love with a 15-year-old visitor, Roxa Dunbar. They entered a long distance romance that would last many years, with Roxa remaining true, but refusing to marry Harper as long as he continued bullfighting.

Harper returned to action, Jan. 10, 1910, in Guadalajara. Because of the goring and his recuperation, he had missed his alternativa date in Mexico City. But, he was offered the opportunity to receive the doctorate in Monterrey, where the famous Mazzatinito—whose brother had been killed by a bull—would be his sponsor. Thus, on Feb. 20, 1910, Harper B. Lee was granted the title of Matador de Toros.

Harper's plans to perform in Spain were interrupted by still another injury. The horn opened the wound from his San Luis Potosí goring, causing 18 inches of his intestines to protrude. But, he refused to be carried to the infirmary. He shoved the intestines back into place, then killed his bull.

A few months later, Harper reappeared, in Tampico. But, suddenly, opportunities for the Yankee matador became scarce. The Mexican Revolution was beginning to percolate. Throughout Mexico, there was growing anti–American sentiment. In Mexico City, mobs trampled the American flag. Reviews of Harper's performances began to reflect a distinctly nationalistic attitude.

Juárez fell to the revolutionaries. Two weeks later, the central government was overthrown. All bullfights were temporarily canceled. Transportation and communications lines became undependable, at best. The top Mexican stars, such as Rodolfo Gaona, went to Spain.[3]

On October 15, 1911, in Saltillo, Lee was gored in the right leg. He was transferred to San Luis Potosí, where he recuperated in Mrs. Dunbar's home and renewed his romance with Roxa. Infection developed in the wound, and the doctors seriously considered amputating the matador's leg, but Harper refused. It was late in December before the Yankee matador could walk without pain.

In all, Harper B. Lee had spent five years as a novillero and a little over three years as a matador. He had killed 100 bulls in 52 afternoons in 24 Mexican cities. He had suffered three serious gorings and 30 comparatively minor ones. He had earned as much as $1,000 in one afternoon, a veritable fortune in those days.

But, at 27, Harper had to face reality. He was in pain, broke, and in love. He announced his retirement.

Tradition dictates that a retiring matador make one final tour, ending in Mexico City, where the *coleta* (pigtail) is cut from the back of his head. But, Harper could not bear to perform again, knowing that to do so would awaken his sleeping *gusano* and re-ignite his desire to continue in the profession that he so much loved. So, on Sunday, December 3, 1911, in the Dunbar home, Roxa cut Harper's pigtail. He never again faced a bull.

[3]*Luján, Néstor,* Historia del Toreo, *pp. 278–279, Ediciones Destino, S.L., Barcelona, Spain, 1954.*

With a new Mexican Revolution going on, all around them, the Dunbars moved to San Antonio, Texas. Harper and Roxa were married on April 21, 1915, in St. Mark's Episcopal Church. Disinherited by his father, Harper worked a number of jobs. For a while, he was a construction superintendent. Later, he sold insurance and was employed by an oil company. Finally, Harper and Roxa began a poultry ranch.

In 1937, Harper developed cancer on his lower lip. The malignancy spread. Five years later, on June 26, 1941, he died. The couple left no children.

I always think of Monterrey as the place where the greatest American bullfighter took his alternativa. Sidney Franklin? No, the lesser known, but greater, Harper B. Lee. Many people consider him to have been the finest non–Latin to try the *Art of Cúchares.* ... Harper was very brave, had a large repertoire, and placed his own banderillas. He was not a truly great matador, but he was a highly competent one, and that is quite miraculous, considering his background and nationality.— Barnaby Conrad[4]

[4]*Conrad, Barnaby,* Gates of Fear, *pp. 280–284, Bonanza Books, New York, 1957.*

Chapter 3

The Bullfighter from Brooklyn

The second Yankee to attain matadorship was Sidney Franklin. But as he was such an outrageous braggart and egomaniac, it is almost impossible to validate his own, overblown assessments of his accomplishments. His celebrity overwhelmed his career. Judging by his accounts of his performances, one would have to conclude that he was either the greatest torero in history, or a legend in his own mind. Anybody reading his autobiography should have a large shaker of salt nearby.

Yet, nobody can deny the reality that he became a matador, and that some knowledgeable critics considered him to possess genuine talent.

On June 8, 1922, the 17-year-old kid who would later dub himself the "Bullfighter from Brooklyn" boarded the S.S. *Monterrey*, heading for Mexico. Seeking a career as a torero was the farthest thing from his mind. He just wanted to get away from a difficult home life, made so by his brutish father.[1]

In Mexico City, he saw his first bullfight, which featured two historic names, Rodolfo Gaona and Marcial Lalanda. In those days, the picadores' horses weren't protected by padding, and although Sidney claimed to be sickened by the sight of slain horses, he was nevertheless fascinated by the grace and courage of the matadors, and especially by the adulation that the crowd heaped upon them.

From that point, forward, Sidney claimed, he became an instant, phenomenal success as a torero. He befriended Gaona, who— for whatever reason — agreed to train the greenhorn Yankee.

Franklin's first experience in the ring was at the Xochitl (now Xajay) ranch of

[1]*Franklin, Sidney,* The Bullfighter from Brooklyn, *pp. 18–19, Prentice Hall, New York, 1952.*

brave bulls, near Mexico City, where he participated in the testing of brave-blooded cows to determine which would be allowed to breed. (The fighting bull inherits its size and bulk from its father, but its killer instinct is a gift from the fighting cow.) And, although he was tossed and badly beaten up several times, he managed to accomplish some decent cape lances and discovered the special joy of performing.

A week later, according to Franklin, never having lifted a sword, never having used a *muleta*, never having worn a suit of lights, and possessing only the experience gained, training with small cows at Xochitl, a promoter, who Franklin identified as "Don Ramón," arranged for the young New Yorker's debut in a small Mexico City ring.

Reading Franklin's account of his inaugural performance, one must conclude that he was either born with remarkable abilities, or he lived in a fantasy world of self-delusion. He wrote: "There wasn't a soul present who remained unaffected by what he had seen. They were gasping for air. Red Cross nurses were administering first aid to those who had fainted."[2]

As if recounted in a supermarket tabloid, not only was Franklin's debut a resounding success, he killed with a full sword placement, and the crowd carried him upon their shoulders, 10 miles, to his home. Mexico must have been very hungry for toreros in those days because Franklin claimed that he was immediately contracted for a three-month tour. Of his first performance in Villahermosa, Franklin wrote, "The bulls and I seemed to be in tune ... I couldn't do anything wrong. Before my second bull was actually dead, the fans swarmed into the arena and carried me, on their shoulders, to the hotel."

In 1929, Franklin wrote, he went to Spain, where his first novillada was in Sevilla's *Plaza de la Maestranza*, which was a great deal more than a remarkable accomplishment for an unknown foreign novillero. He killed his first bull with what he described as "one of the most perfect sword thrusts" of his life, and the public demanded that he take five turns of the ring. Upon the death of his second bull, Franklin was carried through "The Prince's Gate," an honor reserved for masterful performances, and which had been afforded on only four previous occasions. The governor of the province sent a 24-motorcycle escort to accompany Franklin to the governor's mansion. Thereafter, the empresarios of *La Maestranza* agreed to preposterous terms to sign the Yankee novillero to work four Sundays in a row, all according to Franklin.

"I was given the ears and tail of every bull I killed. And, I would have been carried out, each time, on the shoulders of the crowd, except that it was now prohibited," he related in *Bullfighter from Brooklyn*.

On one occasion, using a chartered plane to transport him between towns, he fought in three different bullrings on the same day, Franklin asserted. The following was a Sidney Franklin performance in San Sebastián, Spain, as seen through his eyes: "I made him pass me in thirty-one connected passes ... all in about a yard and a half of ground. ... I'd make a pass with my right hand and then repeat it with my left. Then, I'd do the same thing on one knee and then on the other. Then, I'd do it with both knees on the ground," Franklin wrote.

Sidney claimed that, after killing the bull with one sword thrust, the fans swarmed into the ring and carried him all over town, until late that night. When he appeared on the street, after that, his presence "caused a traffic jam."

[2]*Franklin, Sidney,* The Bullfighter from Brooklyn, *p. 88, Prentice Hall, New York, 1952.*

Sidney, far right, kept in training by participating in tientas. Here he is shown with a Mexican bull breeder. (Photograph by Constantine Mengason.)

Franklin's debut in Madrid ignited a total sellout of the plaza, he claimed. Tickets that would normally sell for 25 pesetas were priced at 500 pesetas. At one point in that first Madrid performance, he was caught and dragged all over the sand. When the bull finally loosed him, Franklin "sauntered casually" back to the *barrera* (red fence, surrounding the arena), where he poured water on his head, then casually combed his hair, while his sword handler held a large mirror for him.

Thereafter, he claimed, wherever Franklin traveled, the king's uncle, a duke, accompanied him in a caravan of about 20 cars. In each city in which he was to perform, the duke reserved a floor or two in the swankiest hotel. Sidney even had his own personal chef accompany him, because his stomach couldn't handle the constant diet of rich banquets. But, the story is a rather big bite for aficionados to stomach.

He wrote that, one morning, while sitting at a sidewalk cafe on Madrid's major boulevard, he was approached by a seedy-looking man who hadn't shaved and who needed a haircut. He wore a shabby suit, which looked as though it had "forgotten what a tailor's iron felt like." He wore battered bedroom slippers.

Franklin assumed that the guy was a beggar. The fellow approached, very meekly, and in a small voice, asked, "Are you Sidney Franklin?"

And, who was this meek, humble, shabbily-dressed bum? Ernest Hemingway—who wasn't known for being shy, meek, or, especially, humble.

"EL TOREO DE TIJUANA"

CATORCEAVA GRAN CORRIDA DE LA TEMPORADA

DOMINGO 30 DE AGOSTO

a las 16:00 horas

Previo permiso de la autoridad y si el tiempo no lo impide, se lidiarán a muerte a la usanza Española

8 Finos y encastados toros de la ganaderia de **Garfias y Las Huertas 8**

Para ser lidiados por los Espadas:

SYDNEY FRANKLIN

Unico matador Norte-americano con alternativa en Madrid quien presenta y dara la alternativa a su discipulo

BARON CLEMENTS

Alternando con los matadores Mexicanos:

JAIME BOLAÑOS Y CHARRO GOMEZ

Con sus cuadrillas completas de Picadores y Banderilleros.

Completo servicio de Plaza, Juez de Plaza y Cambiador de Suertes los que designe la autoridad.

Médico de Plaza: Dr. Angel Ruiz y Fernández A.

PRECIOS DE ENTRADA EN DOLARES:

	Sombra	Sol
PALCO CON 4 ASIENTOS	32.00	28.00
BARRERA 1a. FILA	11.50	8.00
BARRERA 2a. FILA	10.00	7.50
BARRERA 3a. FILA	9.00	7.00
BARRERA 4a. FILA	8.00	6.50
BARRERA 5a. FILA	7.00	6.00
TENDIDO NUMERADO:		
Primeras cinco filas (1 al 5)	6.00	5.00
Siguientes cinco filas (6 al 10)	5.00	4.00
ENTRADA GENERAL	4.50	3.50

Niños en barreras y tendido numerado pagarán boleto entero.

Niños menores de 10 años en entrada general, media paga.

NOTAS: No hay toros de reserva. Una vez lidiado el primer toro si la corrida se suspende por fuerza mayor, no hay derecho a devolución. Estrictamente prohibido tirar botellas y cojines al ruedo. Orden de la Policía.

Toda persona que se siente en otro asiento que el que cubre su boleto será cobrada la diferencia.

TIJUANA Bull-Ring "EL TOREO"

FOURTHEENTH GREAT BULLFIGHT OF THE SEASON

SUNDAY AUGUST 30th. - 1959

Exactly at 4:00 p.m.

Previous permit from the authorities and weather permitting there will be fought to death in the Spanish fashion

8 Fine, pure bred, fighting bulls from Breeding Farms **Garfias & LasHuertas 8**

TO BE FOUGHT BY

SIDNEY FRANKLIN

The only American bullfighter with alternativa in Madrid who wil present and give the alternativa to his pupil

BARON CLEMENTS

alternating with the Mexican Matadores

JAIME BOLAÑOS & CHARRO GOMEZ

With their complete troupe of Picadores and Banderilleros

Presiding Judge and Technical advisor to be named by the Municipal Authorities.

Medical Service: Dr. Angel Ruiz and Fernandez A.

ADMISSION PRICES U. S. CURRENCY

	Shady Side	Sunny Side
BOX WITH 4 SEATS	32.00	28.00
BARRERA 1ST. ROW	11.50	8.00
BARRERA 2ND. "	10.00	7.50
BARRERA 3RD. "	9.00	7.00
BARRERA 4TH. "	8.00	6.50
BARRERA 5TH. "	7.00	6.00
RESERVED GRADE SEATS		
FIRST 5 ROWS (1st to 5th.)	6.00	5.00
SECOND 5 ROWS (5th. 10th)	5.00	4.00
GENERAL ADMISSION	4.50	3.50

Children in reserved seats will pay full price.—Children under 10 years in general admission half price.

Above prices include all taxes paid to the Mexican Government.

NOTES: There are no reserve bulls. Once first bull has been fought if the fight is stopped due to causes beyond our control there will be no refund Strictly prohibited to throw bottles or cushions into the ring. Police regulations.

Any person using other than the seat covered by his ticket is subject to an overcharge, or fined by the police.

Sidney bestowed the alternativa on Baron Clements, an unknown truck driver. His doctorate was never recognized by the Mexican matadors union.

"When he offered to get me some of his books, I told him I wasn't interested. I had read so many pieces of tripe in English by people who said they were authors of repute that I had better use for my time."

When Franklin agreed to allow Hemingway to accompany him on his bullfighting tour, the famous author's eyes watered and it "appeared that he would burst into tears."

Thereafter, even though he had not yet graduated to matadorship, Franklin boasted that he was the highest-paid torero in Spain and powerful enough to insist on selecting bulls from his favorite ranches. And, he could dictate which other novilleros would be on cards with him.

"The moment my name appears on a card, you can't find a ticket," he claimed.

Sidney eventually got around to reading *The Sun Also Rises* and *A Farewell to Arms*. Thereafter, Sidney said that Hemingway couldn't write fast enough to keep him satisfied. He claimed to have assisted Hemingway in writing *Death in the Afternoon*.

During only a four-month period in 1929, Franklin maintained that he performed in 58 *novilladas*, although Cossío's *Los Toros* (the bible of Spanish bullfighting) lists him as having appeared in only 14, but at least all of them were in major plazas de toros.

Sidney wrote that he had to hire three different teams of subalterns, located all over Spain, because one team would never

Sidney (left) and Clements, posing before the corrida in which the latter received his alternativa.

have been able to keep up with him and "probably wouldn't have been able to stand the strain."

It was on March 9, 1930, that Sidney professed to have introduced the *peto*, the protective padding on the picadores' horses. Thereafter, thanks to Sidney Franklin, the peto became mandatory throughout the bullfight world, and bullfighting became more palatable to the public. He also claimed to have invented *La Verónica*, the most basic cape lance.

He received his first goring, from a Murube bull, in Madrid. The bull's left horn entered just below the tip of Franklin's spine. In other words, he was gored in the buttocks. Only five weeks later, Franklin returned to the rings.

During his next appearance in Madrid, Franklin recalled that he accomplished a rather unusual way to crown a series of cape lances. After completing a set of Verónicas, he dropped his cape and grabbed the bull's tail with his right hand, while sticking his left hand into the animal's mouth and grabbed its tongue. He then sauntered cockily away, holding both hands high for the fans to see. He held a fist full of long hairs in his right hand, and his left hand was covered with the bull's slobber.

In the third act, Franklin went to the center of the ring, where he tied his ankles together with a handkerchief and did 15 consecutive muleta passes.

But, complications from the Madrid goring resulted in four more surgeries. The doctors advised Franklin to recuperate for a while. So, he went to New York City, where, he claimed, he was installed in the presidential suite of the Hotel Astor, as guest of the city for a week of official functions that included a motorcade up lower Broadway and the official presentation of the key to the city, on the steps of City Hall.

Returning to Mexico in 1930, Franklin suffered another goring, which he described as a wound that passed almost completely through his right leg, extending from the knee to the ankle. But, he didn't feel any pain, so he ignored pleas for him to go to the infirmary, and continued fighting. It wasn't until later, back at the hotel, that Franklin realized that he had received a serious wound.

After his recovery, Sidney fought in Colombia and Panamá, then decided to take some time off to see the 1932 Olympic Games in Los Angeles, where naturally, Hollywood received him as if he were a visiting monarch. Even Sam Goldwyn, Charlie Chaplin, Douglas Fairbanks, Sr., and Eddie Cantor fussed over him. Sidney was contracted as technical director on Cantor's latest film, *The Kid from Spain.*

Thereafter, Franklin and Ernest Hemingway made plans to build a 20,000-capacity plaza de toros in Havana and to introduce bullfighting to Cuba. But, the Spanish Civil War broke out, and Hemingway was contracted to cover it for the North American newspaper *Alliance.* At Hemingway's insistence, the *Alliance* also agreed to contract Sidney Franklin — as the author's assistant — at 50 cents per word for his written impressions of the Spanish conflict.

Such would be excellent pay for a field journalist, sixty years later. For that era, it was more than slightly difficult to believe, as was all of the clandestine, Robert Ludlum–style spook business that Sidney described, involving his secret entry to Spain from France and his subsequent exploits during the war.

When the war ended, Sidney returned to New York, where he performed, in bloodless style, in the World's Fair.

In 1945, the Yankee novillero returned to Spain, where he finally received his alternativa in Madrid's Plaza de Las Ventas. Twenty-two years after he had begun, separated by a mere 12-year hiatus, Sidney Franklin was a Matador de Toros.

Again, referring to Cossío's *Los Toros,*[3] Franklin's alternativa was recorded, July 18, 1945, with bulls of Sánchez Fabrés. The bull of his doctorate was named *Tallealto.* Cossío described Franklin's performance as "not exactly picturesque." He added that, on August 10, 1952, in Tangier,

[3]*Cossío, José María de,* Los Toros, *Dirección General de Turismo, Madrid, Spain, 1960.*

When an alternativa ceremony is scheduled, the sponsoring matador, the graduating novillero, and at least one witnessing matador exchange greetings, next to the red barrera. Therefore, it is difficult to understand why only Sidney and Clements are pictured, here, exchanging muletas in the center of the El Toreo de Tijuana plaza de toros.

with bulls of Miura, Franklin was unable to kill his first bull, which was removed, alive, from the ring. He came close to enduring the same fate with his second bull, Cossío wrote.

On August 30, 1959, in Plaza El Toreo de Tijuana, Sidney bestowed the alternativa on Baron Clements, a truck driver apparently known only to his immediate family. It had to have been a strange ceremony, for neither of the other two matadors on the card chose to serve as a witness to the historic event. One of them, Eliseo "El Charro" Gómez, recalled the afternoon: "It was hilarious! Right in the middle of his performance, Franklin's toupee came loose and flapped in the breeze, while the crowd responded with tremendous laughter."

In any case, Clements failed to kill *any* bull, that afternoon. And, no record reflects that he ever performed, anywhere, either before or since his "alternativa." Several years later, Franklin, who had suffered a stroke and was confined to a wheelchair, died in New York City.

How much of his story can be believed? Even Ernest Hemingway later recanted what he had previously written of Franklin. One thing is for certain. If Sidney Franklin wasn't the greatest torero in history, he was, at least, the most colorful. And, he obtained the greatest mileage from a very short career.

Chapter 4

The Bittersweet Career of John Fulton

"The American Matador has no country.
He's not understood in his own,
and not accepted in the others."
— *John Fulton,*
Matador de Toros

In spite of shabby treatment by those who were in positions to determine the success or failure of anybody who dreams of facing bulls for a living, Philadelphian John Fulton (Short) left an indelible mark on bullfighting.

It was very early in his career when Fulton discovered the most painful truth of bullfighting: aside from a privileged few — mostly sons of famous matadors or bull breeders — it's hard for any hopeful torero to get a chance. The stereotypical story of "poor boy makes good as torero and saves sister from whorehouse" is romantic fiction, reserved for paperback novels. And, for the torero whose veins run with neither Mexican tequila nor Spanish sherry, it's an almost impossible task.

A handful of matadors in each bullfighting country earn the big money, while the rest hungrily gobble up the crumbs and leftovers. Contracts are reserved for the very best, or at least, the very suicidal. And, if in his desperation, one of those invisible "also appearing" guys — one of the sad multitudes who never get enough opportunities to become good toreros — is gored or killed, well that attracts even more ticket buyers.

By the mid–'50s in Mexico, several

The bullfight capital of the world is Madrid's Plaza de Las Ventas, home of the most critical, sophisticated aficionados in the world.

Yankee toreros had already appeared upon the scene, but few had inspired great interest, and only two had attained the title of Matador de Toros. Inspired by the Tyrone Power film *Blood and Sand*, John Fulton began his training, as have most Yankee aspirants, on Mexican bull-breeding ranches.

In 1956, John Fulton, realizing that Spain was the promised land of toreros, initiated his professional career on the Iberian Peninsula. In Spain, at least in the '50s, Yankee toreros were novelties who attracted crowds of the curious. But, the Machiavellian politics of bullfighting are harsh. In spite of registering some outstanding triumphs, the overwhelming majority of Spanish impresarios never took him seriously. And, when, years later, he forced them to admit that he was a genuine torero, capable of becoming a star, they shut the doors, firmly, in his face.

He appeared in his first formal Spanish novillada on June 29, 1958, and according to Cossío, in his eight-volume work, *Los Toros*, Fulton acquitted himself quite well. Nevertheless, throughout the latter part of the '50s, Fulton fought mostly on throw-away cards, with other obscure novilleros, facing culls, rejects, and bulls that had become too old to be presented to major-name matadors. Such modest cards don't attract huge crowds, but being comparatively inexpensive to organize, they're still profitable, at least for the promoters.

In the summer of 1961, after performing in the tiny pueblos for several years, Fulton finally received an opportunity to make his debut in the supremely-important Plaza de Las Ventas in Madrid. As he hadn't fought in several months, and as a good showing in Madrid was so vital to his career, he got a warmup fight in Puerto de Santa María. He triumphed, winning the afternoon's only ear and leaving upon the shoulders of the crowd. But,

John Fulton made his home in Sevilla, the most Spanish of all Spanish cities.

one of his bulls had stepped on and severely sprained Fulton's foot. Three days later, performing in Las Ventas, he could hardly walk. The afternoon was a disaster.

"Most of the critics used that failure as proof that North Americans have no business in Spanish bullrings, and should be banned, by law," Fulton said.

But, the intrepid Fulton would not be discouraged. He continued to *torear* in the sticks, and only occasionally in decent plazas. In the process, he impressed such

An example of a superb *derechazo* by John Fulton in Madrid. (Photograph by Martin Santos.)

top stars as Antonio Ordoñez and Jaime Ostos. Even the great, retired Spanish Matador Juan Belmonte was convinced that, given the chance, Fulton could become a *figura* (star). John's tenacity finally paid off.

On July 18, 1963, in Sevilla's magnificent Plaza de La Maestranza, Fulton received his alternativa, becoming only the third Yankee Matador de Toros, behind Harper B. Lee and Sidney Franklin. (Fulton pointed out that Baron Clements was actually the third Yankee matador, but Clements' alternativa, in Tijuana, was dubious, at best.)

John's first bull, that of his alternativa, weighed 503 kilos. Fulton showed some good work, but won no ear. The notoriously demanding Sevilla public remained unconvinced. But, when his second bull blasted into the arena, the fans gasped. Weighing 576 kilos, it was a genuine Toro Toro, the largest and most vicious animal to be seen in many years in that plaza.

No, Fulton didn't register a triumph. He cut no ears. But, he had demonstrated that he was a matador who could handle the largest bulls.

Tradition dictates that every Spanish or Mexican matador who performs in the other's country must confirm his doctorate in both Madrid and La Plaza México. In truth, very few matadors of either country have confirmed in both bullfight capitals.

Four more years passed—six years since his first Madrid appearance, as a novillero—before Fulton was again afforded a chance in Las Ventas. On Oct. 12, 1967, he confirmed his alternativa in the world's most important bullring. On that after-

A nice *derechazo* by John Fulton. (Photograph by Jesus, Madrid.)

noon, he earned the respect of many knowledgeable aficionados.

He appeared three more times in Sevilla, and on one memorable afternoon, won the only ear of the day, from a six-year-old Miura bull. He was carried on shoulders through the Prince's Gate, a very rare honor that has been bestowed on only a small handful of toreros. The fact that it was a bull from the Miura ranch, which produces the most deadly of all Spanish fighting bulls, made the triumph even more impressive. (It was the Miura bull *Islero* that killed the great Manolete, in 1947.)

That great success, which should have paved the way for more contracts, instead marked the last time that John Fulton would ever perform in La Maestranza. The Yankee had evolved to being a torero who could compete with Spain's finest. And that reality, it seems, could not be allowed to continue.

"If an American from Philadelphia could triumph with a Miura in Sevilla, it meant that he must either be a damned good torero, or the Miuras ain't what they used to be, two things that are just about impossible for the Spanish, at least those who run the business, to admit. My triumph, the one that all matadors dream about, worked against me. The aficionados of Sevilla wanted to see me in the feria with the Miuras. The empresario did not want to give me that opportunity and risk my repeating my triumph and establishing me as a true torero, capable of handling bulls," Fulton told the author.

Some of Fulton's greatest successes occurred as adjuncts to the *Feria de San Fermín*, in Pamplona. In those comparatively informal affairs, the toreros are anonymous. There are no handbills or posters announcing their names. All of the toreros dress alike, in the traditional *Navarese* garb of white shirt and trousers, red beret, scarf, and sash. Nationalities are obscured. On several occasions, Fulton was awarded ears and tails in such presentations.

ENRIQUE

Above: Fulton received his alternativa in Sevilla's Plaza de la Maestranza, one of the most beautiful, and certainly one of the toughest, plazas de toros in Spain. ***Opposite:*** Fulton (center) confirmed his alternativa in Madrid, becoming the only Yankee to do so. (Photograph by Enrique, Madrid.)

In this charity performance, Fulton was awarded ears and tail, rewards for having triumphed over a rather large bull.

Fulton had the Madrid confirmation and he was determined to be the first Yankee matador to confirm in La Plaza México. In the back of his mind was a plan to do so with his first bull, and officially retire with his second.

But, while the Spanish prejudice is usually subtle, that of Mexico can be blatantly cruel. Dr. Alfonso Gaona, the first empresario of the world's largest bullring, promised Fulton the Mexican confirmation. But, he would first have to prepare himself by working in the provinces. Gaona sent Fulton all over Mexico, where the Yankee matador would encounter only tough, leftover bulls.

He even faced the last three herds of *Casablancas*, the Mexican counterparts of the Spanish Miuras. The Casablancas were so vicious and tough, no top-rated Mexican matador would even dream of fighting them. For that reason alone, Casablanca eventually folded its tents. But, Fulton did well against those that he faced.

But, politics would not be denied. Even after risking his life in the pueblos, where medical facilities were very limited and accommodations were somewhat less than elegant, it became obvious that the powers-that-be were firmly aligned against allowing John to confirm his alternativa in Mexico City. So, finally admitting defeat, Fulton retired.

As recounted in the September 1994 edition of the *Los Aficionados de Los Angeles* newsletter, on that farewell afternoon in San Miguel de Allende, Mexico, Fulton's first bull was a teratoid that hooked to both sides and refused to offer an honest attack. Sixty-year-old John Fulton worked hard, but could not encourage a clean attack from the ignoble animal.

But, his second bull, from the Santa Cecilia ranch, offered an opportunity, and

Opposite: **Fulton also performed in numerous charity festivals with some of Spain's biggest stars, including Antonio Ordoñez, who was at that time the world's número uno matador.**

JOHN FULTON

Plaza de Toros de NERVA
Domingo 2 de Abril de 1961 - PASCUA DE RESURRECCION
¡GRANDIOSO ACONTECIMIENTO TAURINO!
5 Hermosos NOVILLOS, 5
Pepe Luis VAZQUEZ
Manolo VAZQUEZ
Antonio ORDOÑEZ
JOHN FULTON
Aurelio GONZALEZ

In this charity festival, Fulton dedicated his bull to Ambassador Adlai Stevenson (far right).

Fulton was always a good swordsman. Here, he delivers a perfect *estocada*. The photograph is autographed to aficionado/author/photographer Dick Frontain. The dedication translates to: "For Dick Frontain, as a remembrance of my debut in Nogales [Mexico], a matador with evil ideas and a bull with worse ones." (Photograph by Dick Frontain.)

Fulton was determined to either triumph, or die, trying. His cape work was slow and elegant. And, in the third act, with the red muleta, John ran the hand long, incorporating excellent wrist action, as he performed series after series of excellent right- and left-handed passes. The *olés* and music reverberated throughout the plaza.

Then, he raised the sword. The music stopped and the crowd became silent. All of Fulton's good efforts depended on this, the most important and deadly moment. John profiled, then dived over the horns, burying the blade. It wasn't a perfect placement, but it was effective. The animal stood only seconds, then dropped to the sand, dead. White handkerchiefs undulated throughout the stands, and the plaza judge ordered both ears to be cut for Fulton.

After taking his noisy, delicious turn of the ring, retrieving flowers and wineskins that the crowd had thrown to him, John Fulton went to the center of the arena and raised his arms over his head, in one last salute. His adopted son, Federico, then removed the pigtail that was pinned to the back of John's head, symbolically announcing the matador's formal retirement.

A visit to Fulton's art studio in Sevilla was an absolute must for visiting aficionados.

John Fulton had faced and triumphed with the last bull of his career. And, prejudice and politics be damned, on that April 2, 1994, all of the dignity and pride of all the toreros who have ever faced the horns was vividly proclaimed.

In addition to his taurine talents, Fulton was an outstanding artist and illustrator. His dramatic depictions of bulls, painted in their own blood, became valuable collectors' items, throughout the world. He designed the Schlitz Malt Liquor bull logo. He conceived extraordinary suits of lights, and even created magnificent jewelry from semiprecious stones.

Stopping by Fulton's art studio in Sevilla was a must for every visiting aficionado. And, although he smiled and greeted everybody who visited, behind his charismatic facade was a heart that deeply, even bitterly, lamented the glory that might have been, *should* have been, his, but which was denied him. Not by the bulls, but by the omnipresent politics, which can be even more formidable.

Fulton wrote and illustrated *Bullfighting*, perhaps the most intellectual and artistic journal ever written on the subject. Tom Lea, whose own outstanding novel, *The Brave Bulls*, has been reprinted 16 times, reviewed *Bullfighting* for the *Los Aficionados de Los Angeles* newsletter. The following is an excerpt from that review.

> It may be the most remarkable book about bullfighting ever written in English, Spanish, or any other language ... John Fulton has given us a Tauromachy in the old, classic instructional tradition of Hilo or Montes. ... It is entirely illustrated by drawings (by Fulton) ... The

Some of Fulton's most popular works were of bulls, painted in bulls' blood. "I gauge friendship by the reaction that I get when I ask if I can store blood in somebody's freezer," Fulton said. "After all, the cave man depicted his enemy, the aurochs, on cave walls, so I really haven't hit upon anything truly original," he added.

book is an extraordinary performance by a triply-gifted man.

In an interview with this writer, John Fulton spoke of the frustrations that marked his career.

> I believe that the single most outstanding factor that has prevented Americans from becoming genuine figuras in Spain and Mexico is the belief of the Spanish that no one but a Spaniard, and in particular an Andalucian, can be a great matador. The Spaniard may be able to bring himself to admit a foreigner's bravery, but is often quick to label it as suicidal, rather than of the serene valor attributed to a Spaniard. The foreign torero will never receive from the crowd the unconditional support, or the unbridled passion, that even the most incompetent, lackluster Spanish kid would automatically get.

Nevertheless, nobody can dispute the history that Fulton made. He was the only Yankee to receive and confirm his alternativa of matadorship in Spain. He accomplished the seemingly impossible, and he did it on his own terms.

On February 7, 1998, John Fulton suffered a series of severe heart attacks. He slipped into a coma. Then, he developed pneumonia. On February 20, he died.

Although the empresario of La Maestranza strenuously objected, the mayor of the city proclaimed that Fulton had been adopted by Sevilla and was thus entitled to the same treatment that would be afforded any Sevillano matador.

Fulton's body was cremated, and following a last turn of the ring, upon the shoulders of his friends and admirers, his ashes were spread upon the sands of La Maestranza. At last, John Fulton had returned to that magnificent plaza de toros. And, nobody will ever be able to deny that the sands of the most beautiful bullring in the world are the final resting place of a man who deserved as much glory in life, as he had in death.

Qué en paz descance. (Rest in peace.)

CHAPTER 5

Robert Ryan: The Classy Matador from California

Clark Kent had nothing on Robert Ryan. The 5' 10", 135-pound native of Inglewood, California, is thin, easy-going, and soft-spoken. Such a mild-mannered demeanor would seem to contradict the image of his chosen profession. But, when Ryan dressed in the suit of lights and emerged from his personal phone booth, assuming a look of steely confidence and determination, he was 100 percent torero.

Ryan's understated courage was a reflection of his deep, quiet, and dignified personality. Nobody could ever accuse him of being a crowd-pleasing showboat. He was an intense, deeply serious, classical torero, a man who had profound respect for the bulls, for the art of tauromaquía, and for his own professional responsibilities in the ring.

In addition to his talents in the arena, Ryan is a fine artist. He discovered bullfighting as a child and began depicting its fluid moments on canvas. The emotions of the deadly ballet flowed naturally from Ryan's brushes. And he read constantly of the glories of La Fiesta. It seemed only natural that his sensitivity and artistic talents would eventually be translated to his becoming an interpreter of the taurine arts. But, he wanted to be more than an artist on canvas. He told his parents that he wanted to become a torero. But, as in other cases of kids who make such radical announcements to their parents, they didn't take him seriously. However, after seeing his first corrida de toros, in Tijuana, Robert was hooked. He would become a matador. Nothing could prevent him from realizing his dream.

He was befriended by one of Mexican history's most important retired matadors, Pepe Ortiz, who was to Mexican bullfighting as was Juan Belmonte to Spanish bullfighting, the originator of a "school," or style, of toreo.[1] Ortiz took Ryan into his home, treated him like a son, taught him how to deal with bulls, and was instrumental in launching his career. Ryan spent every school vacation at the Ortiz ranch, training and working toward his goal. Under Ortiz' tutelage, 15-year-old Robert Ryan killed his first novillo.

During a novillada in Acapulco, Ryan dedicated a novillo to one of his personal heroes, the internationally-famous matador, Carlos Arruza. At the end of the afternoon, Arruza — who wasn't prone to giving *coba* (false praise) — commented, "I've seen dozens of Americans in the ring and in *tientas*. Robert Ryan is the only one I've seen who can make it to the top. He can become a *figura*."

Thereafter, the young Yankee impressed aficionados throughout the bullfight world. On August 7, 1966, the Yankee novillero was presented in the world's largest bullring, La Plaza México, alternating with Antonio Lomelín and Salvador Santoyo. But, it wasn't an easy debut. With only a couple of exceptions, the bulls lacked strength and were defensive. Ryan did well with his first novillo, but his usually-reliable sword failed him and he was limited to polite applause.

But, he tore them up with his second animal. Greeting the novillo with a pair of *faroles de rodillas* (kneeling cape lances), he brought the crowd to its feet. However, while performing a set of *Gaoneras*, he was caught and tossed, although he escaped serious injury.

In the third act, during a series of *naturales* (left-handed passes), Robert was again caught and trampled. This time, he was taken to the infirmary. But, as they lay him on the operating table, he jumped up and ran back into the ring, where he killed with the best sword placement of the afternoon. The plaza band reacted by playing "Stars and Stripes Forever," an event that set off intense debate among the Mexican aficionados, who resist any foreign intrusion on their national pastime.

The reviewers were full of praise. Although Ryan hadn't cut ears, he had left a powerful impression. The fans, not believing it possible for a foreigner to show such depth of emotion, were surprised by his elegant, classic style.

In the spring of 1963, with influential help from Carlos Arruza, Pepe Ortiz, and Ryan's manager Pablo Lozano, the Yankee torero made his debut in Spain. He had been contracted to perform in ten novilladas, of the type known as *económicas*, in which beginning Spaniards get their first experience. In such presentations, the bulls are younger and smaller, and there are no picadores. But, upon Ryan's arrival in Spain, it was ruled that foreigners could not perform in económicas. Ryan had to immediately face the larger, older bulls, in *novilladas picadas* (with picadores).

Spanish bulls are generally much tougher and more difficult than are Mexican bulls. Nevertheless, Robert was successful. He made his presentation in Segovia. Three weeks later, he was strongly applauded in Aranjuez. Then, in Alcalá de Henares, he cut two ears. In Mora de Toledo, he won ears and tail. He continued to perform throughout Mexico, Spain, and Portugal, and was hailed as a prime candidate for future matadorship.

In 1966, Ryan re-appeared in La Plaza México. He had a fine afternoon, followed by still more triumphant performances in Monterrey, Chihuahua, and San Miguel de Allende. He appeared four times in La Plaza México. In five years as a novillero, Ryan performed in more than 40 novilladas.

Then, on a sunny afternoon in the

[1]*Kehoe, Vincent J-R,* Wine, Women, & Toros, *p. 36, Hastings House Publishers, New York, 1962.*

Robert Ryan salutes the plaza judge prior to entering the third act on the day of his alternativa in Tijuana.

summer of 1967, in Plaza El Toreo de Tijuana, Novillero Robert Ryan became a Matador de Toros.

The fourth Yankee to receive the Doctorate of Matadorship, Ryan was, perhaps, the only North American matador to be accepted and respected by the other toreros in all of the countries in which he performed. On four occasions, he worked *mano a mano* (two matadors, competing against each other, each facing three bulls) with Mexico's Alfredo Leal. The tall, darkly

A near perfect placement of banderillas by Ryan.

handsome Leal, whose elegance and manners were true reflections of his sobriquet, "The Prince of Bullfighting," would never have performed in competition with any torero for whom he did not have enormous respect.

While registering a clamorous triumph, one afternoon, in Plaza Monumental de Tijuana, which is dubbed "The Beautiful Bullring by the Sea," Ryan inspired bullring owner Major López Hurtado to excitedly exclaim to this observer, "At last! Your country has a genuine torero!"

The taurine arts seemed natural to Ryan. He was especially good with the banderillas and the sword. But, likewise with the muleta, he had the ability to create poetry on the sand. His biggest problem, he later admitted, in an interview with the author, was his eyesight. He wore contact lenses, and the dust and sand of the bullring were irritating, sometimes making him nearly blind.

"I couldn't admit that to anybody, because if it were known, they might not have allowed me to continue," he told me.

Finally, in 1972, Ryan had gained enough celebrity to be presented in Madrid, a city whose aficionados have, historically, been particularly hostile to for-

Ryan dedicates his banderillas placements to the capacity crowd in Tijuana.

eign, especially Yankee, toreros. On that afternoon, in Plaza Vista Alegre, Robert Ryan greatly impressed the fans and the critics. But, he also suffered a horrible, near-fatal goring in the stomach.

Wrote Spanish journalist Rafael Campos de España: "While placing a pair of banderillas, the sixth bull caught him in a spectacular and anguishing manner. The horn was stuck in the back of the torero's

[2]*de España, Campos, Rafael,* ABC *(newspaper), p. 7, June 11, 1972, Madrid.*

A complete *faena* requires the matador to perform a variety of linked passes in series. Here Ryan offers a right-handed chest pass, climaxing a series of *derechazos* or *naturales*.

jacket, and [the bull] tossed him back and forth, for several seconds. The bull gored him in the stomach, and there was great hemorrhage."[2]

Ryan was a fan of ballet, and particularly of the beautiful French ballerina Marie France, whom he had seen perform on television. In 1972, he had the opportunity to meet the dancer, in person, and discovered that she was a knowledgeable bullfight aficionada. Five months later, Robert and Marie France were married. And, more than a quarter of a century later, they were still a happy couple.

Ryan's intense desire and his style of pure artistry caused him to sometimes insist, when discretion might have been wiser. As a result, although he was never gored as a novillero, he suffered six gorings as a matador. He appeared four times as a matador in Plaza Monumental de

Opposite, top: **For the matador, the most dangerous moment in any performance is the kill. It requires the matador to offer his own body to the bull, as he lunges over the horns and buries the sword into a space no larger than the palm of one's hand. Robert Ryan was an excellent killer.** ***Opposite, bottom:*** **Working to both sides is a requisite for any performance. Here Ryan runs the hand long in a perfect *natural*.**

Grimacing as he plunges over the horns, Robert Ryan gave new meaning to the expression "Moment of Truth."

Juárez, and on each occasion, it was a case of feast or famine. Twice, he left on shoulders. On the other two afternoons, he left in an ambulance. But, he was philosophical about his injuries.

"If you're scared in the ring, that's the time that you should quit. Ninety-nine percent of the time, when a bullfighter is gored, it's his own fault, either by mistakes, or by attempting to obtain more than is possible with a particular bull. With the exception of the goring that I received in Torrejón de Ardoz [Spain], all of my wounds have been my

In triumph, Ryan accepts the cheers of the crowd as he takes a turn of the ring on the shoulders of his fans.

mistakes. The one in Torrejón happened because of high winds. It's impossible to fight in the wind. Oh, I could have run away from the bull, but I'm a Matador de Toros, and that title carries heavy responsibilities," he said.

Ryan didn't encounter the same brand of prejudice that other Yankees have met in Spain. Indeed, he was a highly respected matador, of whom the Spanish press wrote very complimentary reviews. He had a more rational and realistic reason for his difficulties in obtaining a greater number of contracts.

Robert Ryan suffered numerous gorings and other injuries during his career. Here, he is caught, tossed, and knocked unconscious. But, he recovered and recorded a triumph with the bull.

"Spain, Mexico, France, and South America have their *convenios* [exchange agreements]. Mexicans are afforded contracts in Spain, so that Spaniards can perform in Mexico. But, there are no authentic bullfights in the United States, thus no convenio, thus, no obligation by any bullfighting country to contract North American toreros," he surmised.

As most other aspirants who have attempted to overcome the many roadblocks placed in the paths of all toreros, and especially those of foreigners, Ryan's initial success in Mexico didn't automatically pave the way to more contracts. After becoming a full matador, he was typecast as a torero who should perform exclusively in plazas de toros along the Mexican-U.S. border. He could never convince enough Mexican *empresarios* to give him new opportunities, as a matador, in the important interior plazas de toros, where he had registered so many outstanding triumphs as a novillero.

"As a matador in Mexico, the empresarios kept me in the border plazas, where a lot of North Americans would buy tickets. I was stuck. They wouldn't allow me to advance," Ryan reflected.

His final performance was in April of 1982, in San Miguel de Allende, where he won the ears of a bull from San Tomás, the ranch owned by his new manager, Tomás Valles. Then, tired and prematurely gray, Ryan retired from the rings, in order to dedicate full time to painting, writing, and remembering the successes that were his and the realities of the politics that kept him from realizing even greater ones.

But, his taurine achievements outside the rings have been equally as impressive, and even more enthusiastically reviewed. His artworks gained celebrity throughout

Robert Ryan's intense desire sometimes resulted in severe gorings. He received six major gorings in his career. In Madrid, he was gored in the stomach.

the world. Following a particularly successful exhibition in Mexico City, Fernando Gamboa, former director of that city's Museum of Contemporary Art, wrote: " Few artists have better defined their true circumstances, or more accurately ignored the inhibitions of culture. ... He has attained in taurine art an unprecedented level of expression. ... His work is distinguished by an elegance of line and a reality of depth: the contemplation of the poet, eloquently expressed in precious images."[3]

Such words effectively captured the inner persona of Robert Ryan, who is as much a philosopher as an artist. And, as a dedicated aficionado, he is obsessed with the true king of beasts, the central character around him, and around which the ancient art of tauromaquía revolves: Toro Bravo.

Ryan's emotional sensibility and his depth of feeling for the taurine arts are perfectly reflected in his central philosophy: "The fiesta *taurina* is of sun and happiness. Mine, that which interests me, is the shade that surrounds the bull, his beauty, and also his life, which is a tragedy, the same tragedy which, for the man, is life."

That poetical analysis of the taurine ballet is brilliantly reflected in Ryan's artworks. Ryan's long, narrative poem, *Vestigios de Sangre* (Vestiges of Blood)—which American aficionada/writer Muriel Feiner, who is married to a torero, described as "an artistic and almost poetic autobiography"—won the coveted Díaz Cañabate award, in Madrid, as the best taurine book of 1987.

Taurine journalist Serge Montes, wrote in the 1987 edition of *El Clarín de La Busca*, "Anyone who has read *Vestigios de Sangre* will be no stranger to the evocative imagery, here reflected in visual art, instead of word pictures ... the juxtaposition of the real and surreal strike me, profoundly."[4]

Ryan's most celebrated art exhibitions have taken place in Madrid, the same city in which some of history's most famed artists have shown their works. Ryan's artistic expressions have included etchings, lithographs, and scratch boards, including portraits of brave bulls and elaborate embroidery patterns of suits of lights.

José María Alvarez del Manzano, Madrid's mayor, wrote in the July 1987 edition of *Diario* magazine, "Madrid recognizes and honors artistic merit and, at the same time, with this exhibition, is honored that its customs and festival of bulls should be the source of lifelong inspiration to an artist of the quality of Robert Ryan."

In the same edition, taurine journalist Ignacio Alvarez Vara, the most distinguished of contemporary Spanish critics, wrote: "of all the North American toreros of this century, Ryan has been the one of the most class. ... A master of a magnificent, sonorous Castillian Spanish, Ryan is an excellent writer, whose *opera prima*, the beautiful book of poetry, *Vestigios de Sangre*, is a masterpiece."

In the prestigious taurine magazine, *Toros*, Juan Antonio Gómez Angulo, organizer of some of the most important taurine art exhibits in Madrid, said of Ryan's 1995 exhibition: "Robert Ryan does not consider himself a taurine painter, but rather a torero who paints. Robert Ryan paints the bull as he has lived it, from very close up, face to face. Or, as he has dreamed it. Bullfighting is an intimate dream; it corresponds to the intimate shadows, against which all artists must struggle."

Ryan's *El Toreo de Capa*, his salute to

[3]*Gamboa, Fernando,* Mundo Taurino *(newspaper), Sept. 10, 1985, p. 3, Madrid.*
[4]*Montes, Serge, article in* El Clarín de La Busca, *November 1987.*

the art of the *capote*, published in 1996, in a limited edition of 1,500 copies, is a hard bound, gold embossed book which is covered in silk, of the color used in silk capes of the 19th century.

For Robert Ryan, as for every other person — especially North Americans— who has ever dreamed of glory in the planet of the bulls, it is a world of struggle. Yet, very few have done it as well, or accomplished as much, as has Robert Ryan, artist, writer, gentleman, and a genuine, honest torero.

CHAPTER 6

Diego O'Bolger: The Clothing Model Who Became a Matador

Handsome and personable Jim Bolger looked like a school teacher, an insurance salesman, or possibly a C.E.O. for a major corporation. It took a rather wide stretch of imagination to picture him in the plaza de toros.

Indeed, during the week, the Tucson, Arizona, resident led a somewhat conventional life. When he wasn't working as a public relations man for Pedro Domecq, the wine and brandy people of Spain and Mexico, he was modeling fine clothing. But, on Sundays, an amazing metamorphosis took place. Jim Bolger shed his gray herringbone tweed, donned a handmade suit of silk and gold, and became Diego O'Bolger, Matador de Toros. In either venue, he was dressed to kill.

He was born in Buffalo, New York, but his family moved to Tucson when he was very young. He was raised Catholic and was even an altar boy. When he was 10 years old, he saw his first bullfight, in the old Nogales bullring, at the Mexico/Arizona border. American torera Patricia McCormick and two young Mexicans performed that day.

"I don't remember much about Patricia," he reflected. "But, those two boys were trying so hard not to be outdone by

Opposite, top: **In his debut in La Plaza México, the world's largest plaza de toros, Diego O'Bolger surprised everybody by cutting an ear. Here, he performs a cape lance, *La Chicuelina*. *Opposite, bottom:* While placing the short banderillas, O'Bolger wasn't even aware that the bull had hooked the torero's faja, the silk sash that goes around the waist. Luckily, the bull then pulled its horn out of this very dangerous position.**

Brinde
con

BACARDI

JOSE
Tequila

Reno

her, I was really impressed. I decided that I could do that, too."

Later, as a kid, selling the *Tucson Citizen* newspaper, Bolger's thoughts kept returning to the bullring. Upon graduation from high school, he was offered a scholarship to the University of Arizona. But, he had discovered another profession that interested him more than anything he could learn in college. Bolger saved his money, bought a motorcycle, and rode it to Mexico City, where he hoped to find someone who would teach him to fight bulls. The motorcycle was quickly stolen and his money was soon gone, but neither event dampened his enthusiasm.

As had other hopefuls of the profession, he sought opportunities along the borders. But, Diego's professional debut, August 11, 1963, in Nuevo Laredo, was a disaster.

"I did everything wrong," he admitted to this author. "And, I began to learn the truth. Bullfighting isn't a battle of strength, but of wits. Timing and distance are everything. If the matador can keep his cool and understand the bull, he can deal with it. The fighting bull is a violent, noble animal that has a tremendous instinct to attack and kill. The matador must transform the bull's brute power into something slow, graceful, and seemingly choreographed.

"The paradox is that to be a torero, or for that matter even a bullfight aficionado, it's essential that you love animals. I have had all kinds of pets, including an opossum, a sloth, and an ocelot. Once, I had a black bear and a lion, plus all kinds of dogs and cats. But, the most beautiful animal of them all is the fighting bull."

In spite of, or perhaps because of, his initial failure, Bolger honed his talents and began to show some genuine promise. He received more contracts. He changed his name, legally, to Diego O'Bolger.

In his important first appearance in La Plaza México, Mexico City, the Yankee novillero amazed the critics by cutting an ear, rather a serendipity for an inexperienced *gringo*. In all, he fought eight times in La Plaza México. One afternoon, the other two novilleros were seriously gored, leaving Diego O'Bolger to fight and kill all six novillos. At the end of the afternoon, he was a very tired, yet very happy, young man.

With assistance from famed bull breeder Don Luis Barroso Barona, Diego received his alternativa of matadorship in Tijuana, in 1969, and did very well. O'Bolger was only the fifth Yankee in history to become a Matador de Toros.

Six feet tall and wearing a trim 157 pounds, Diego had the perfect build for a torero. And, although he trained constantly, he never dieted. He is one of those rare people who can load up on tacos and enchiladas, yet never gain a pound.

At his peak, O'Bolger was one of the best Yankee toreros. He was competent with the capote and very good with the muleta. He was especially talented with the banderillas and the sword. He had courage, determination, personality, and style. But, the politics! There's that word, again. After taking the alternativa, the powers that control bullfighting gave him precious few opportunities in the big, important plazas, where he had recorded such impressive triumphs as a novillero, consigning him instead to the border plazas, where the crowds from the United States are in abundance and the pay is usually rather less than generous. Diego O'Bolger's full potential was never achieved, as he was not afforded the opportunity to have his talents evolve toward genuine success.

Opposite, top: **During O'Bolger's alternativa performance in Tijuana, he placed banderillas that were only 12" long.** ***Opposite, bottom:*** **O'Bolger prepares to kill the bull of his alternativa.**

Diego O'Bolger offers a classic *pase de pecho* (chest pass), leading the bull up and under the torero's left arm pit.

O'Bolger performed for the better part of a quarter century, throughout Mexico, achieving a reputation as a dominator. And, he may have been one of the few of his profession who utilized preperformance self-hypnosis to temper his concentration and assuage his fear. Some considered him a mystic.

Although he laments never having become a genuine star, he has no regrets about the many years that he spent in the bullrings.

"I gave it my best. I had some good afternoons and a lot of fun. At least, I received only one bad goring. And, I enjoyed every minute in the ring. I love bullfighting. Perhaps, in another life..."

Chapter 7

The Virginian

There are, basically, two types of toreros: the deeply serious, classical types whose courage is expressed in a quiet, dignified, deadly serious, highly artistic style; and the *tremendistas*, the triumph-at-all-costs, suicidal lunatics who always seem to be teetering between death and disaster, but who in actuality substitute simple, crowd-pleasing antics for honest toreo. They con the crowds. With such toreros, the bull becomes a secondary player in a farcical drama. And, La Fiesta becomes less an art and more a contest to be *won* by whoever has the most courage, man or bull. And, that is not what tauromaquía is supposed to be.

But, there are exceptions. There are *tremendistas* whose courage is sincere and absolute. And, although they may not inspire comparisons to Antonio Ordoñez, Paco Camino, or the current heroes, Enrique Ponce and Julián López, "El Juli," neither do they resort to the simple tricks that fool tourists and neophyte aficionados. They put their gonads on the sand and dare the bulls to step on them.

Richard Corey of Charleston, West Virginia, was of the latter cut. Although he was frequently labeled a *tremendista*, his courage was honest and sometimes outrageous. He received six gorings and literally hundreds of tossings during his nine-year career. Yet, his successes in the rings cannot be denied. He was better received in Mexico and Spain than were many of his Yankee predecessors. Corey's only fear was of failure.

Yet, lurking within all of his blackboard-scratching, let-it-all-hang-out courage was, likewise, a torero capable of art. With the muleta, he could run the hand long, seemingly leading the bull from Guadalajara, Mexico, to Guadalajara, Spain. He was a paradox, a torero who mystified serious critics. They couldn't condone his rather peculiar interpretation of the taurine arts, but neither could they ignore his apparent willingness to die in the ring, in quest of success.

Richard Corey chose a very dangerous method of attracting the public spotlight. During a corrida in Mexico City, Corey, who was only a spectator, jumped into the arena and managed to perform some very fine muleta passes before being manhandled out of the arena by police. (Photograph by Carmona, Mexico City.)

Corey's major deficit was inconsistency with the sword. But, that criticism could be leveled against many toreros, including some of the genuine masters of the art. The most dangerous and difficult moment in the entire *lídia* (the three acts of any bullfight) is the kill, and few have been consistently good at it.

Corey grew up as a typical Southern "good ol' boy," to whom a bull was merely something used to impregnate cows, which would bear the calves that would grow up to either become members of dairy herds or star in Sunday afternoon pit barbecues.

But, in 1964, at 22 years of age, Corey's life was irrevocably changed. He saw his first bullfight, in Tijuana, at the Mexico-California border and was immediately filled with enthusiasm. Two years later, he made his professional debut in the arena.

He did his homework. After receiving preliminary training in Southern California, from former novillero Rafaél Larrea — who had also initially trained Matador Robert Ryan — Corey headed to Aguascalientes, Mexico, and the life of a typical, struggling *maletilla*. Literally translated, maletillas are luggage carriers. But, in the world of bullfighting, they are a legion of usually-hungry, always-anxious dreamers who are willing to do practically anything for opportunities to perform. Except for those privileged, well-connected few, most toreros begin their careers as maletillas, traveling from bull ranch to bull ranch, sleeping in barns or on the ground, hoping to gain confidence, experience, reputation, and possibly the attention of a manager or other benefactor who could focus the public spotlight on their talents and further their ambitious careers

In those early years, Corey spent

In Monterrey, Corey suffered his first grave goring. Here, the bull impales the novillero in the right side of the groin, then lifts its head, driving the horn deeper.

much of his time in the Aguascalientes slaughterhouse, where he practiced killing bulls, some of which were brave-blooded animals that, for whatever reasons, were disqualified from being presented in the plaza de toros.

Corey related the details of his career in an interview with this writer. His professional debut was on October 9, 1966, in *Plaza Lu Aurora*, a small, but politically-important, Mexico City ring, in which success can translate to many more oppor-

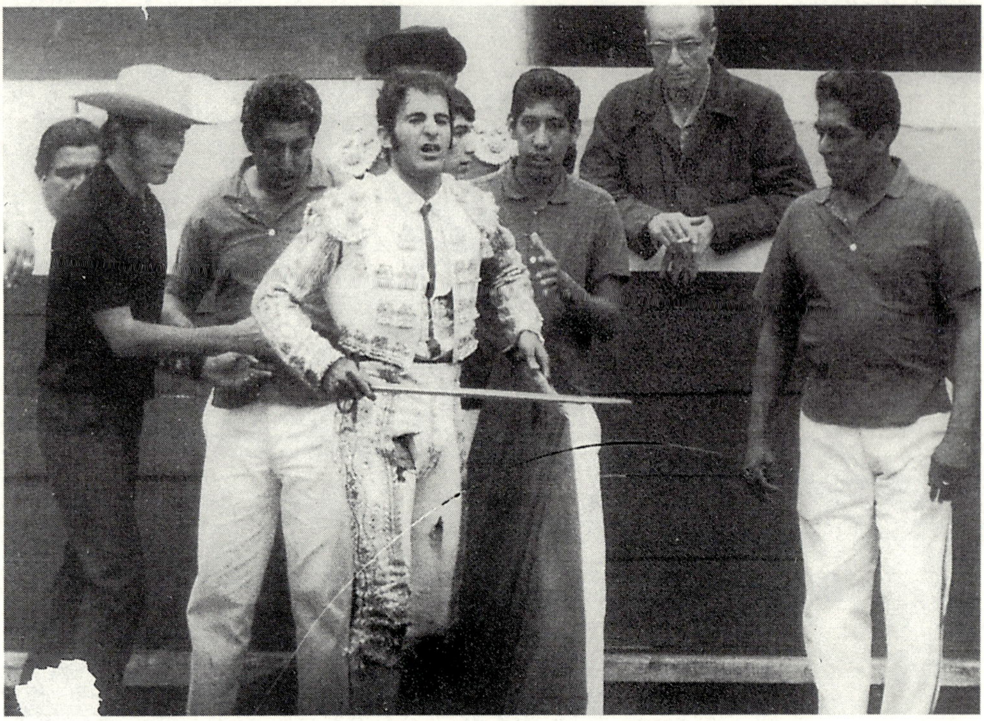

Grimacing, with the wound in his groin quite obvious, Corey insisted on killing his bull before retiring to the infirmary and the awaiting surgeons.

Corey performed six times in La Plaza Mexico in 1970. Here, prior to the paseillo, Cory poses with Mexican film star Cantinflas (center) and matador Adrian Romero (left).

Corey opened his first Plaza México performance with an exciting, kneeling *larga ambiada.*

tunities. Corey won the first ear of his career and heard his first addictive accolades. The enthusiastic fans carried him upon their shoulders.

But, when the anticipated flood of contracts didn't materialize, Corey decided to resort to an extreme method of attracting the public's attention. In *Plaza El Toreo de Cuatro Caminos*, just outside the federal district of Mexico City, on an afternoon that featured Mexico's *número uno* matador, Manolo Martínez, Corey became an *espontáneo*, a spectator who jumps into the arena and attempts to get off a few passes, knowing full well that the price for his illegal quest of glory is usually a beating, followed by a jail cell.

Espontáneos disrupt the formal flow of the corrida. And, as their inexperience so frequently results in their being caught, gored, or even killed, they teach bad habits to the bull. The danger to the matador is dramatically increased when he must face any animal that has roughed-up an espontáneo. Therefore, it is a very serious offense.

But, if an *espontáneo* is lucky enough and good enough, he might just capture the enthusiasm of the crowd. Richard Corey was lucky and good enough. After four tremendous right-handed muleta passes, he was manhandled out of the arena and into the *callejón* (alleyway, surrounding the red fence), where the police began to severely beat him. The crowd protested, as did Manolo Martínez, causing a furor that convinced the plaza judge to pardon the impertinent but courageous Yankee scofflaw.

Corey didn't get another real contract until May 7, 1967, in Tampico, where he failed to register a triumph. Months later, on October 7, he returned to La Aurora, where he won a turn of the ring. His career got into a higher gear in June of 1968, when he was contracted to perform in Monterrey, the cradle of Mexican bullfighting. He cut two ears and was returned the following Sunday to cut two more ears. People began to take notice.

The following Sunday, June 16, Corey

refresca
en grande
CARMONA

Opposite: Walking the paseillo into the world's largest bullring, La Plaza México, Mexico City, is like carrying the world on your shoulders. (Carmona photograph.) ***Above:*** Corey set his eyes on Spain; here he debuts in Sevilla's Plaza de la Maestranza.

Corey worked honestly and bravely in La Plaza México. Here he performs a chest pass.

performed in Guadalajara, and although nobody cut ears, he was granted a *vuelta* (turn of the ring) and left on the shoulders of the fans. Two weeks later, it was another novillada in Monterrey and another vuelta. The following weekend, he cut an ear in Saltillo. Two weeks later, he won an ear in Monterrey.

On July 25, in Veracruz, Corey received still another ear. He also suffered his first goring. A minor one, for sure. But, in the world of bullfighting, it is said that the brave blood flows first. How would the injury affect Corey? The Virginian apparently had plenty of brave blood in reserve. He performed three times in September, winning a pair of ears and Monterrey's Silver Sword trophy. He also suffered another goring, this time a grave one, in the right side of the groin. But, he refused to leave the ring until he had killed his bull.

In December, he performed three more times, registering a big success in Guadalajara, where he won two ears and that city's version of the Silver Sword trophy. In all, in 1967–68, Corey fought in 13 novilladas, killed 24 novillos, won 11 ears, and suffered two gorings.

His total for 1969, he related, was eight novilladas, 19 novillos, and five ears. He also suffered a depressing failure in Monterrey, where one of his two animals was returned to the corrals, alive, after Corey had exceeded the time limit for killing it.

In 1970, the Yankee worked in 18 novilladas, winning 14 ears, one tail, and the "Cristo Negro" trophy of Aguascalientes. He also suffered three more injuries. The first, in Juárez, resulted in a small goring over his left eye and a fracture of his forehead. The third, in Plaza

Corey's outrageous courage shocked the Sevilla crowd. Said John Fulton, "I had never before seen a man appear to be doing his best to commit suicide." (Photograph by Beret.)

Mexico, was in his right armpit. He fought six times, that year, in Plaza Mexico.

But, in order to attain any degree of international acceptance, toreros must perform in Spain. So, with 90 Mexican novillos, 33 ears, and one tail to his credit, Corey went to Spain, where he lived in Sevilla and performed in pueblos and small cities, usually for very little money, sometimes just for expenses. His incredible courage thrilled the Spanish fans. Billed as a Mexican, he performed in nine novilladas and won 13 ears.

But, for taurine unsophisticates who see only a few bullfights per year, working in the small towns is one thing. Working in front of knowledgeable aficionados in the major cities is quite another, much more formidable challenge. As he was managed by Canorea, the empresario of Sevilla's magnificent Plaza de la Maestranza, Corey was contracted to perform in that prestigious bullring. Remarkably, in spite of a hard tossing, he won the only ear of the day.

"I had never before seen a man appear to be doing his best to commit suicide. He seemed to have a death wish," observed Sevilla resident Matador John Fulton.

Perhaps a bit too impressed by his own press clippings, he admitted, on October 10, 1971, Corey received his alternativa, in Guadalajara (Spain), and won his first ear as a full matador.

But, Corey had moved up to the big leagues, where the competition in the rings, as well as in obtaining contracts to perform in them, is intense. Opportunities to torear as a matador dried up. So, he renounced the alternativa and returned to the status of novillero. In an interview, in Madrid, with taurine writer Muriel Feiner,

A fine chest pass by Corey.

Corey admitted that taking the alternativa had been a mistake.[1]

"I knew I wasn't ready, but I really didn't have much choice. All I wanted to do was torear," he told Feiner.

In 1972, concentrating mostly on small towns, Corey fought in 10 Spanish novilladas, winning 21 ears and three tails. In 1973, he fought in 11 novilladas, winning 22 ears and six tails. His fame spread. And, on October 12, he was presented in Madrid's Plaza de Las Ventas, the home of Spain's toughest, most hard-to-please crowds. Although he titillated the fans with his seemingly casual courage, it was not a successful day. He also suffered another goring. The critics, who by that time had discovered Corey's true nationality, ate him alive.

In the 1974 season, he recalled, Corey worked 11 afternoons, winning 24 ears and two tails. He again took the alternativa, August 4, in Cabra, a small town near Córdoba. His sponsor was South American Matador Curro Girón, while well-known Spaniard José Fuentes was the witness. Even considering that it was a pueblo, in which trophies are much easier to win, it was a sensational day for all of the matadors. Ten ears and two tails were cut, of which four ears were awarded to Corey.

Next came other pueblos. In Torremolinos, Corey's overtly courageous interpretation of the taurine arts was enthusi-

[1]*Newsletter of the Los Aficionados de Los Angeles club, June 1972.*

Opposite, top: **In spite of his succeed-at-all-costs determination, Corey could still perform in the classic manner, as in this elegant** ***Verónica. Opposite, bottom:*** **Running the hand long, Corey triumphed in Sevilla. (Photographs by Arjona.)**

Corey climaxed his first performance with this perfectly-executed sword placement. (Photograph by Arjona.)

astically received. He performed on seven consecutive afternoons there and cut ears every time. In all, from August through November of 1974, Corey was awarded 24 ears and two tails. On two occasions, he left the ring upon the shoulders of the fans.

But, for some reason, in the season of 1975, Corey began to lose his enthusiasm for bullfighting. He worked only five corridas and won only three ears. On the bright side, he suffered only one goring.

"I was contracted for Barcelona, and it was a 'make-or-break' opportunity," he said.

Barcelona doesn't have great taurine importance to serious Spanish aficionados, but it's still a major city and a triumph there can lead to more contracts. However, the bulls were bad, the crowd was impatient, and Corey was tired and uninspired. He was 33 years old. He had made money but was far from wealthy. And, he had a body full of scars.

"I was tired of putting my ass on the line," he admitted. "I needed to take a break, get away from it, for a while."

And so he took a hiatus from the bullrings, and it became a permanent one. He never again wore the suit of lights.

Today, Richard Corey is a family man. He lives in Charleston, where he has a wife and three kids. He's involved in a variety of businesses, including produce distribution, a chain of taxis, and a delivery service.

And, thus, the curtain fell on that which was one of North America's greatest hopes to give birth to a man of fame and fortune in the exotic world of bullfighting. Had he continued, who knows what he might have achieved? But, just as easily, he could have been killed.

Gusanos are known to become tired.

Eventually, however, they reawaken and hungrily drag their hosts back into the plazas de toros. But, Richard Corey's worm of *afición* remains in a state of suspended animation, ensconced among his many trophies, newspaper clippings, and other memorabilia that testify to the glories of his other life, an almost dreamlike existence of horns, brave bulls, crowds, critics, empresarios, sunshine, rain and wind, a world of delicious triumphs, haunting failures, blood, pain, and disillusion.

Was Richard Corey a great artist, or merely a torero whose incredible courage carried him just so far, but not quite far enough?

That is a question that history will have to decide.

CHAPTER 8

The Ballad of El Texano

From the time that Fred Renk married Barbara, her son, David, was raised within a taurine environment. Bullfight posters and photos adorned the walls of the Renk's Alamo, Texas, home. It seemed that there was always a matador or a novillero sleeping on the couch.

Fred had been a novillero, so perhaps, subconsciously, he hoped to inspire in David dreams of glory in the ring. Perhaps, by infecting him with the desire, then watching the boy's talents develop, Fred could vicariously share David's success.

"Capper [Fred's nickname] and I had known each other only three weeks, before we got married. He was a water softener salesman, and as any successful salesman, about 50 percent bologna," Barbara recalled. "He showed me the press clippings about his bullfights, and he told me all about them, too. But, I just accepted it all, without really believing it," she added.

Unquestioning acceptance seemed to be the philosophy of Barbara Renk. She was capable of demonstrating a red hot temper, but rarely did so. And, in spite of her diabetes, dwindling eyesight, weekly kidney dialysis, and intense pain, she seemed to have a big smile permanently etched upon her face. She never complained.

Born with club feet, David had always been a shy kid who was embarrassed by his gimpy limbs and the leg braces and special shoes that he had to wear. Certainly, his inability to compete well in sports imparted a deep psychological scar and an intense desire to find his own limelight. Kids find it easy to be cruel to those who don't fit in.

So, whether it was Fred's influence and David's intense desire to please him, or whether it was a natural result of growing up around bullfighting, or a combination of both things, the *gusano* of passion that lives in the belly of every torero took up early residence in David. He was too young to realize what a demanding tenant it could be. He was a little over two years of age when he announced, "When I grow up, I'm going to be a matador."

"At first, I thought it was cute," said Barbara. "David's playing with *capotes* and *muletas* was like other kids playing with toy guns. I didn't feel threatened by it. Even when he started fighting tiny animals, in special festivals, I went along with it because it was giving him the self confidence that he had always lacked," Barbara recalled.

"By the time the reality hit me that he would become a professional bullfighter, and that there was a very good chance that, one day, a bull would gore him, or even kill him, it was too late. I couldn't do anything about it."

"David loved to watch sports, but he didn't show any interest in competing in them until he was about eight or nine years old," Fred Renk related. "It was about a year before the first operation, on both feet. We were living in the lower Rio Grande Valley and he had a chance to play Little League Baseball. He watched basketball and football, but baseball was his first love. He trained and worked so hard. And, in batting practice, he was one of the best hitters. Well, we were there when he got his first at-bat in a real game. And, he really hit that sucker! A good, solid wallop to left field. For anybody else, it would have been a double or a triple, but David was thrown out, at first base.

"It didn't discourage him, though. And, after a while, the other kids stopped making fun of him. They realized that David was giving 110 percent, but his legs were responding at about 20 percent. He got in three or four games that season. And, he was out there, training and working out, all the time."

David was always a good kid, a typical Texas country boy who was respectful of his elders and shy around girls. He and his brother, "Binker," were responsible for plenty of chores on the ranch, including caring for about 300 rabbits. Also typical of any kid growing up on a ranch, David loved hunting. He killed his first deer when he was 10.

"I bathed his face with the blood. He had to wear it 24 hours, you know, just like the Indians used to do with their kids," Fred said. "I guess it seems sort of enigmatic, because he kills bulls for a living. But, the fact is that David always loved animals. And, he's responsible about them too. He knows how to dress a deer, age the meat, and even make venison sausage. Texas is that way; everybody's a hunter."

But, although he was typical in so many ways, David had something that none of the other kids had: the desire to fight bulls.

"He was about two-and-a-half, the first time that he went with us to Don Arturo García's ranch of fighting bulls, near Reynosa, Mexico," Fred reflected. "We were watching a group of brave toros in the field. Naturally, we kept a respectable distance. All of a sudden, we realized that David wasn't standing with us. Then, we saw him. He was carrying a muleta and walking toward the bulls. He yelled, challenging them to attack him.

"One of the bulls examined David, as if deciding on which horn he was going to spear him. The kid just stood there, profiling proudly and renewing his challenge. Luckily, one of the ranch hands was able to grab him, before the bull could charge, but Don Arturo was really impressed with David's nerve."

Indeed, a few years later, García allowed David his first opportunity to face a young animal of brave blood.

Toro Bravo is an anomaly, a quirk of nature, only a distant cousin of the domestic beef animal. Its bloodline has been protected for centuries, on ranches such as that of Don Arturo García. And, as is the case in so many other members of the animal kingdom, purebred Toro Bravo

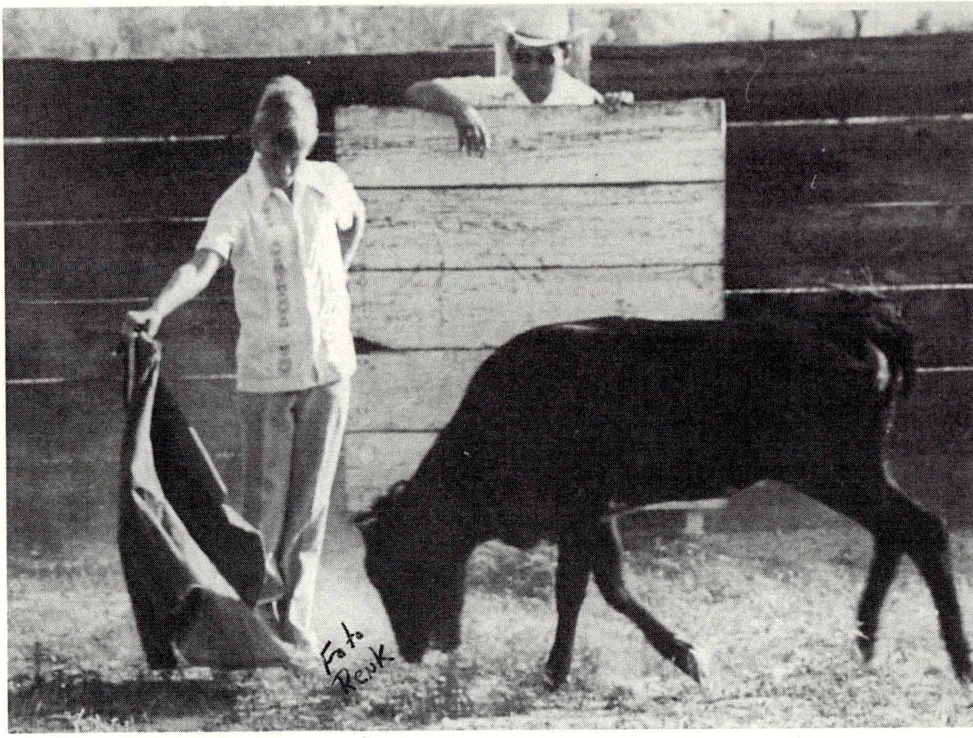

David began participating in the tientas at Don Arturo García's ranch.

inherits its strength and size from its father, but its killer instinct from its mother, the *vaca*.[1]

During its life of four or five years, Toro Bravo's exposure to man on foot is only minimal. But, the vacas, at one or two years of age, are tested for bravery, in *tientas,* which are held annually at every brave bull ranch. Each ranch may test a hundred or more vacas over a span of several days. Those invited to participate in the tientas include active and retired matadors, novilleros, amateur toreros, and other invited guests.

To the guests and the participants, the tientas[2] are festive occasions, with plenty of drinking, eating, and music. But, to the *ganadero*, the bull breeder, it's a serious event. Vacas that pass their tests are reserved for breeding. Those that show anything less than bravery are assigned starring roles in barbecues.

The Renks had always attended the tientas at Don Arturo's ranch. Fred would help test the vacas, while Barbara, David, and Binker watched. But, after the incident in the field, David was determined to participate. In one tienta, Don Arturo first made certain that the cow being tested was a good one, that its attack was straight and honest, and that its horns weren't big enough to do too much damage. Then, he invited David to take a turn.

"It was both meaningful and comical," Fred related. "David threw back his head and grandly cited the cow. He thought he was Tyrone Power in *Blood and Sand*. The vaca weighed about 200, per-

[1] *Frontain, Richard,* How to Enjoy a Bullfight, *pp. 6–7, Hooper Press, Phoenix, Arizona, 1966.*
[2] *Fraser, Allan,* The Bull, *pp. 100–101, Osprey Publishing, England, 1959.*

haps 250 pounds. She spotted David and made a beeline at him. I had to hand it to the kid; he stood his ground. But, the vaca hit him, tossed him into the air, then pranced all over his body. Naturally, we ran to his rescue, as quickly as we could. But, David jumped right back to his feet, picked up the cape, and cited the vaca, again. Again, she knocked him down, and again he got back up. It happened about six times.

"But, finally, he actually got off a couple decent passes. Then, he turned his back and looked at us as if we were a crowd of 50,000 in La Plaza México. He was so darned proud. And, so were we. So were we."

Thereafter, David spent every free moment miming the disciplines of bullfighting. He participated in tientas at Don Arturo's ranch and was hitting the ground a lot less frequently. He began to show some genuine talent, in spite of his physical limitations.

But, at eight years of age, he had to take a recess from fighting vacas in order to endure a series of surgeries on his feet and ankles. He spent long months in a wheelchair, his legs encased in plaster casts. Fred then related the afternoon in which he took David to see a family friend, Matador Pepe Luis Vásquez, perform.

The anemic-looking kid sat in his wheelchair in the front row of Plaza Monumental de Juárez. Pepe Luis Vásquez decided to dedicate a bull to him, which is a great honor. As the matador raised his black *montera* (embroidered, black silk headpiece) in the formal dedication ceremony, he said, "You can accomplish anything that you want; you can be whatever you want to be."

Traditionally, the recipient of a *brindis* (dedication) responds with a simple, "Gracias, Matador." Instead, David asked, "Even a torero? Could I be a matador?"

Momentarily surprised by the question, but wishing to be gracious, Pepe smiled and said, "Yes, even a matador, if you want it badly enough."

Naturally, Pepe was merely humoring David, helping him play a childhood fantasy. He had no way of knowing that, 10 years later, on Easter Sunday of 1981, in that same Juárez plaza de toros, David Renk would become the seventh, and the youngest, Yankee in history to become a matador. His manager and mentor would be Pepe Luis Vásquez.

After that afternoon in Juárez, all of David's waking moments became dedicated to preparing himself for a life in which only one out of 500 aspiring kids will be successful. By the time that he was 13, David was ready for his public debut. He and a Mexican kid, Hector Escobedo, were presented as added attractions during a festival bullfight in Reynosa's Plaza Santa Fe, which was owned by Don Arturo García. The youngsters fought, but did not kill, a pair of 300-pound, brave-blooded calves.

After that, there was no stifling David's enthusiasm. He trained, constantly, and fought Don Arturo's vacas at every opportunity. He received help and inspiration from Diego O'Bolger, the American matador from Tucson. David related some advice that Diego had given him:

"David, bullfighting is like opening the bowels of the earth and letting the devil out into the ring to kill you. More than once in your life, you will no doubt feel the horn, but the sanctuary that you have is that there isn't one man in 1,000 who has the guts to face this horned Iberian creature that they call the fighting bull. But, once you've heard the roar of the crowd, and your sword has found its mark, there is no power on earth that can pull you away from the spectacle. The bulls become all there is in life, and they demand satisfaction, Sunday after Sunday. It leaves you very lonely."

Left to right: **David Renk, John Fulton, and Fred Renk, in Plaza Las Florecitas.**

David's first formal appearance in which he actually killed a young bull was in the tiny Tepositlán plaza, near Mexico City, where, although he suffered a hard tossing, he won his first ear.

He became part of a group of aspiring youngsters called *Los Niños de Monterrey*. On Nov. 20, of 1977, Los Niños were presented in Reynosa, where — as in his premiere presentation in Plaza Santa Fe — the animals were not killed. And, again, he impressed the crowds with a brand of natural ability, desire, and courage that overcame his gimpy legs.

Somehow, facing the horns, David didn't seem quite so frail. His smile lightened the entire plaza. His courage was incredible. And, although his handicap was obvious, his knees incredibly weak and his legs like toothpicks, it was also apparent that here was a young man who possessed a very deep, very special talent.

Barbara Renk's diabetes became worse. To be closer to proper medical facilities, the Renk family bought a 20-acre ranch in Magnolia, near Houston. Fred planned to, one day, breed fighting bulls on "Rancho El Texano." David registered at Cypress–North Houston High School. To make up for the time already lost, he attended summer school, in addition to the regular spring and fall semesters.

"The teachers helped him," Fred reflected. "He carried his books and we made him study and do his makeup work. Except for the bullfighting, he was just a normal teenager. But, he had a somewhat schizophrenic lifestyle. I had created a Jekyll and Hyde."

David fought four times in 1977,

Then-novillero Diego O'Bolger and David, in Plaza Santa Fe, Reynosa.

including his first opportunity in the traditional *traje de luces* (suit of lights). He worked as the *sobresaliente* (understudy), in a formal novillada, featuring aspiring kids and three-year-old bulls. David was allowed to do a series of cape lances with a rather large *novillo*.

"I could feel the ground tremble, as the animal charged by," David later related. "I was terrified, but it was a delicious kind of fear."

Throughout all of this, Barbara Renk admitted being terrified for her son, but she realized that it would have been useless to complain.

"It's either help him now, or he'll run away when he's sixteen or seventeen and do it anyway," she said, with a sad grin. "But, before, it was a game; now, it's for real, and it scares me to death."

On January 1, 1978, David and Los Niños were again contracted to perform in Reynosa, but this time as the main attraction. They would wear suits of lights. The animals would be much larger, and would be killed. The afternoon would provide a benchmark in David's life.

People magazine covered the fight. A nine-page story would be published. Associated Press photos were printed all over the world.

On the way to the plaza, Barbara broke down in tears.

"This is really happening, isn't it?" she asked.

David had grown to love the cheers of the crowd. Just the fact that this so very skinny, so obviously vulnerable, kid would stand up to anything with horns was reason enough to support him. And, there

David made his debut in Reynosa. Here he's being assisted by novillero Alfredo Martínez.

would be plenty of his school companions rooting for him during that New Year's Day performance.

Also, as the media had discovered David, he had begun to enjoy seeing his photo published in magazines and newspapers. Celebrity had its impact on his personality. His previously shy demeanor evolved into a bit of cockiness. But, a heavy dose of humility awaited him in the plaza. Triumph was denied. His cape and muleta work were applauded, but his sword failed him. Another novillero had to kill David's bull. The Texan was disgraced.

"I was really scared," he admitted. "And, not being able to kill, well that really blew me out of the saddle. I didn't know what I was doing; I just wanted it to be over."

David began to mope around the house. His school grades fell. The failure in Reynosa was eating at him. He spoke of quitting school.

Fred and Barbara knew that their own moment of truth had arrived. Either they would have to convince David that the fun and games were over and it was time to concentrate on more important things, such as school, or else they would have to allow him a full shot at either success or failure as a bullfighter. They chose the latter route.

"It was still raining outside when the folks came to me and woke me up. They had been up, all night, talking, and I could tell that mother had been crying. She said, 'We need to ask you a question. Is this what you really want to do?' Well, I was still half asleep, but I said, 'Of course, I do.'

"No other answer was possible. I very much wanted to make the old man proud of me. Bullfighting was his life, the only thing that made him happy. He wanted so much for me to fight, I couldn't disappoint him. It wasn't until much later in my career that I really began to enjoy fighting for myself," David admitted.

But, Fred Renk doesn't do anything halfway. If David were to pursue bullfighting as a profession, nothing less than total dedication would suffice. He contacted Pepe Luis Vásquez.

Pepe had never been a great star, but he had a solid following. He was from the old, traditional school of bullfighting which was based on solid technical knowledge and concentration on the most difficult and dangerous part of the fight: the kill. Aficionados didn't go to see Pepe do great things with the cape or muleta; they went to see him kill. He was one of the finest swordsmen in Mexican bullfight history.

After some encouragement, Pepe agreed to manage David, to teach him the techniques of bullfighting and to direct his career. But, little could be accomplished while David lived in Texas and Pepe in Mexico City. Vásquez insisted that the boy be with him, to devote all of his waking hours to thinking, talking and living the bulls. So, a hiatus was called on David's formal education. Fred and Barbara sent him to Mexico City, where he lived with the family of novillero Paco Olivera. Every day, David trained with Pepe. He also spent plenty of time on bull breeding ranches, fighting anything that came out of the chute.

But, Barbara Renk had attached a condition to her permission to allow her son to go to Mexico. He had until August to prove that the training had had positive results, or he would have to return to the United States to resume the life of an ordinary teenager.

On Easter Sunday of 1978, Pepe's tutelage was put to the test. David and Paco Olivera were contracted to fight *mano a mano* in Reynosa's Plaza Santa Fe. Each would face two bulls.

In the 18 months since his debut, David had grown five inches taller, to just a fraction under six feet, but he weighed only 115 pounds. The form-fitting suit of lights only accentuated his skin-and-bones physique.

The scene in the motel suite that Easter Sunday was a somber one. A makeshift altar had been set up on the dresser. Three candles cast flickering shadows upon various religious icons, including, of course, the Virgen de la Macarena, the patron saint of bullfighters.

As Pepe assisted David into his suit of lights, a newspaper photographer took pictures. Friends stood around, nervously. Barbara was in another room, watching television and chain smoking, trying not to think about the approaching hour of the bullfight.

David did well with the cape to his first bull. But, while working with the muleta, he was caught and pummeled, while the capacity crowd looked on in horror. But, he wasn't injured. It took two sword thrusts to dispatch the bull, but the plaza judge, nevertheless, awarded two generous ears. David refused the trophies, feeling that he hadn't really deserved them. It was obvious that Pepe Luis Vásquez had taught David more than mere technique. Some of the retired matador's dignity and pride were now reflected in the psyche of David Renk.

At the end of the afternoon, David had been limited to honorary turns of the ring, but a great change was noted in his work and in his attitude. Pepe Luis had planted the seeds of professionalism. But, there was a great deal more to learn before David could truly be considered an aspiring matador.

At first using the nickname "El Fenómeno," David adopted Reynosa's Plaza Santa Fe as his home plaza.

Pepe taught me how to kill bulls, and I was having success. He began to use me as an example for his son, Pepe Jr., whose nickname is "Pato," because he walks like a duck. When Pato and I fought together, Pepe would tell him, "Watch the way that David kills. Why can't you do it like that?"

Then, Pepe started teaching me other things. There was an awful lot that I needed to learn, but I didn't really realize it, at that time. Things were going well; I was cutting ears. I started thinking I was pretty hot stuff. Pepe wanted me to change things that had been working for me. But, why should I change? He forced me to train, really hard, six, seven, sometimes eight hours a day. He was drilling the stuff into my head, forcing it into me, making me do it over and over again, and I didn't like working that hard. I was just a punk kid, and I had had it easy. I had never been hungry, and maybe that was a bad thing; maybe I needed some hunger, some humility. I remember thinking, "I don't need this jazz. I know how to do a *derechazo* [right handed muleta pass]; I know how to do a *Verónica* [the most basic, yet most dangerous, cape lance]." But, I didn't. I didn't know anything; I just *thought* that I did.

I never rebelled, though. I hated all the hard work, but I put up with it. And finally, things began to sink in. He taught me how to make a correct Verónica, how to link a series, gaining ground with each cape lance, working the animal to the center of the ring, then doing the *remate* [climaxing lance].

David was quiet, long seconds. He took a sip of brandy, then sat back and expelled air, before continuing.

"He taught me terrains [the geometry of bullfighting] and distances and things that only a torero of his knowledge and experience could know. I took it all in. Maybe I acted kind of cocky and smart alecky about it, but I took it in. And, finally, it began to have impact. I used what he taught. I took bits and pieces of him and began putting them into myself. It began to work. Instead of cutting one ear in an afternoon, I began cutting two."

David was admitted to the Mexican Novilleros' Union in 1978 and performed throughout the provinces, some of which were genuinely rustic. In Jonuta, he fought in a makeshift bullring that was constructed for the first bullfight ever held in that Tabascan jungle pueblo. The heat and humidity were overwhelming, and there were no medical facilities within 100 miles.

Dad came to Mexico and we got to Villahermosa with Pepe Luis Vásquez, Longinos Mendoza, and myself. There were two other guys on the card, but I'd never heard of them. They'd probably never heard of me, either. Guys who fight bulls in the jungle aren't likely to be very famous.

We rented a car, and with Pepe acting as navigator, we went about 40 or 50 miles, over dirt roads, with iguanas running all over the place. Three times, we had to cross rivers by hand-pulled ferries. And, there were piranhas in the water. Finally, we found the town, which was celebrating its annual fair. The bullring was only half built and the fight was the next day. They were nailing these little, perfectly straight tree trunks to the wall. Something resembling grandstands were built. But, there wasn't a hotel in the entire town.

Dad and I had to sleep in the car. Pepe slept in a hammock, hanging from the bullring rafters. And, you know, it was terribly hot and humid, and the mosquitoes were even bigger than the ones down home. But, nothing bothered Pepe. I don't think he got one mosquito bite, and he never even sweat! The only place where we could bathe was in the river. So, they'd send these kids out, 20 or 30 yards, to keep us safe from the piranhas. I guess they must have known what they were doing, 'cause none of the kids got hurt.

Well, the next day comes the fight, and I was supposed to work in third place. It had already been raining about an hour when it was my turn. As I began, I heard a tremendous commotion behind me. Somehow, the fourth bull had gotten into the ring. So, there

The Renks traveled to Jonuta, in the Tabascan jungle. To David's left, on the other side of the fence, with his elbow on the gate, is Pepe Luis Vásquez.

> I was, offering my muleta to one bull, while another was behind me, looking for trouble. I just got behind the fence.
>
> They worked like crazy to get one of the bulls out of the ring, and wouldn't you know it, they got mine. So, the fourth novillero came in and fought, and after he was done, they let my bull back in, and I finished my fight. I cut an ear, but all I really thought about was getting out of there. It was so hot and humid, there was actually steam coming off my *zapatillas* [slippers].

Fred Renk had other recollections of the afternoon.

"These were Indians, most of whom had never seen real civilization. To them, David seemed like a god. He was so tall and blond. And, when it was his turn to fight, and the rain just suddenly stopped, it reinforced that illusion. This crazy ground fog came into the plaza. You could see David and his bull from only the knees up. It was freaky, like something out of *Twilight Zone*. I could hear the Indians, chanting, as David fought. They thought it was some kind of religious sign. I knew we'd have to get the hell out of there, right after the fight, or else they'd want to keep him."

After that weird adventure came other opportunities and triumphs in the Mexican interiors for the kid from Texas. To accommodate his career, the Renks had moved to McAllen, just across the border from Reynosa.

David's reappearance in Plaza Santa

Fe was marred by rain and high winds. He tried hard, but was unable to achieve the triumph that he so desperately sought. He returned for another performance in Reynosa, February 5, performed and killed well, and won an ear. Then, on Easter Sunday, *mano a mano* with Paco Olivera, David killed two bulls and was awarded an ear from each.

On Sunday, September 3, David again fought in Plaza Santa Fe, alternating with rapidly-rising Mexican newcomers Juan Jaime Montoya, Pedro Escamilla, and Pepe Luis Vásquez, Jr. Each faced a young bull of Don Arturo García's ranch, in competition for a bronze trophy. David, who had adopted the sobriquet of "El Texano,"[3] performed grandly, killed with a great sword thrust, and cut the only ear of the day. The bronze trophy was his. The plaza band played "The Eyes of Texas."

Meanwhile, David was gaining national celebrity. He was featured in a full color page in the *Chicago Sun*, and there was a spread on him in *Argosy Magazine*.

In all, David made five appearances, facing six bulls and cutting five ears in Reynosa, in 1978. Convinced that David was on his way to great success, Fred sold his water softener company and invested all of his time and money in his stepson's career.

Mexican novilleros are a sorry lot. In most cases, not only are they paid nothing for risking their lives in the rings, they must finance all of their expenses. That involves buying their own bulls, as well as paying all of their expenses, including their subalterns and the necessary bribes to the notoriously corrupt taurine press.

El Texano opened the Reynosa season, January 7, in a *mano a mano* with Jaime Montoya. No ears were awarded in the afternoon, but David worked well and took a turn of the ring. He reappeared in Plaza Santa Fe, February 11, in a *mano a mano* with Paco Olivera, killing each of his bulls with one thrust, winning a pair of ears from his first and a singular appendage from his second. Olivera was awarded one ear. Even John Fulton, the famed matador from Philadelphia, was present to witness the novillada.

David was offered a chance to appear in Mexico City's "La Aurora" plaza, where success can result in a debut in the world's largest bullring, La Plaza México. So, on Fathers' Day of 1979, David was presented in La Aurora. He dedicated his bull to Fred. At the end, although there was heavy petition from the crowd, the plaza judge would not grant an ear. David settled for a turn of the ring. The reviews in the Mexico City newspapers were complimentary, but reserved. El Texano still had a long, hard road ahead of him before he would be accepted by the Mexican aficionados in the capital.

David accepted a contract to reappear in La Aurora. This time, he triumphed, winning an ear. That success set up other contracts in Zacatecas, Tepoxotlán, and Acapulco.

In all, David's 1979 campaign resulted in 14 ears, one tail, and three *triunfador* trophies. David was on a roll. But, success has a nasty habit of turning on those who take it for granted.

It was Sunday, September 9, once again in Plaza Santa Fe. David, perhaps thinking himself immortal, arrogantly made a technical error, and paid for it. Violating the geometric precepts that make bullfighting possible, he was caught and tossed into the air. He landed, unconscious, bleeding from the head. After reviving, and in spite of being terribly beaten up, he staggered back to the bull and completed the performance, winning

[3]*Technically, the word for Texan is "Tejano," but Fred and David preferred "Texano."*

Clutching a pair of ears, El Texano takes a triumphant turn of the ring.

a pair of ears, before being rushed to McAllen General Hospital.

"All I remember is that when I raised the sword, I saw two heads and four horns. I just aimed between them," said David.

Luckily, he had suffered only a concussion, but it got him thinking about the violent possibilities that befall those who even momentarily ignore the technicalities of bullfighting. And, he wondered about the validity of his progress. He began to have doubts about himself.

> Dad had made it all possible. It was like he cleared the path through the forest. The newspapers were giving me great reviews, and I wondered how many of them I really deserved and how many were the result of my dad's money. Every time I cut an ear, I wondered if it was because of me or the dollar. But, what could I do? I couldn't change the old man, and even if I could, I don't know if I would have. His support had gotten me where I was; without it, I might never have done anything. Things were really going well, but it was like a fresh, fall green snow always covered everything.
>
> "DAVID RENK, TRIUNFADOR!" There it was, in black and white. But, other guys on the same card had cut ears, too, and their names weren't headlined in the reviews. But, that's the way things were. I'd cut an ear and everybody traveling with me was happy. I'd cut two ears, and they were even happier. But, down deep inside, I was troubled.
>
> The only time I really felt like I had earned what I got was when I fought in

Barbara, David, and Fred Renk. (Photograph by Antillón.)

> Nuevo Laredo. The ring had been open about a year, and nobody had cut an ear. Curro Rivera and Eloy Cavazos [big name Mexican matadors] had fought there, and not even they had cut ears. I cut the first ears in the history of the ring, and I was confident that they were authentic.
>
> The judge was tough. Boy, was he tough! When I fought in Reynosa, it was almost like it was already determined that I'd cut ears, so they didn't mean anything to me. But, those ears in Nuevo Laredo were really important.

David's career was skyrocketing. But, a crisis was looming. Fred had already sunk nearly $100,000 into David's career, and he wasn't a wealthy man. He had sold his business, home and land in Alamo, Texas, and invested all of it in the torero.

David was still comparatively inexperienced. It would have been preferable for him to remain a novillero for another two or three years, but such was not financially feasible. Barbara's worsening health contributed to the family's financial troubles. So, Fred and David began looking for an opportunity for the alternativa.

David inaugurated the Plaza Santa Fe season on January 28, 1980, cutting an ear from one of the two bulls that he faced. The following week, he traveled to Zitacuaro, Michoacán, to perform in a *mano a mano* with Pepe Luis Vásquez, Jr. Although one of his bulls caught him and raked a horn across his ribs, David recovered well and cut two ears. In late April, David fought three novilladas in just one week.

On April 27, he made his debut in Monterrey, the veritable cradle of some of the Aztec nation's greatest toreros, the home of such renowned matadors as Rodolfo Gaona, Manolo Martínez, and

El Texano made a technical error, and paid for it. He suffered only a concussion.

Eloy Cavazos. David was the first Yankee to perform there in more than a decade.

After dedicating his toro to the Eloy Cavazos bullfight club, David performed extremely well, impressed the crowd, and cut an ear.

In mid–May, he returned to Monterrey, where he was once again caught and pummeled, but El Texano recovered, then deftly and smoothly took over the crowd and triumphed in grand style. The sword placement to his last bull was, perhaps, the greatest of his career. The bull stood only a few seconds, then collapsed, dead, upon the sand. An ear was awarded.

The press loved him, and the people loved him. Two hours after the fight, he was still signing autographs, outside the plaza.

David told reporters, "I've got my school books under one arm and my capes and swords under the other. I have to keep doing the make-up work, or I won't pass. I've managed to maintain a decent grade average, though. College is the next step and after a hard Mexican campaign, followed by a trip to Spain, I'll enroll in the University of Mexico."

Another date in Juárez; a third in Monterrey, where he was proclaimed the top novillero of the season; more actions in Reynosa; a debut in Acapulco—David was performing and triumphing throughout the republic. His confidence and his abilities grew in proportion to his experience. Although not all of El Texano's afternoons were triumphant, he still managed to surprise tough crowds that hadn't believed it possible for a non–Latin to demonstrate such classical style. However, as his talents grew, so did the resentment over his heritage. Some crowds, especially those in Mexico City, were downright hostile.

The tutoring by Pepe Luis Vásquez resulted in a greater depth to David's work. He was more poised and confident.

In his third performance in Mexico City's *Florecitas* bullring, he faced a huge Tequisquiapan bull. After a good performance that attracted music and cheers, he made a spectacular sword placement that dropped the big animal and won an ear for David. But, one particular critic, Pérez Cutberto, "Topa Bocas" of the *Ovaciones* newspaper,[4] remained unimpressed.

"He doesn't know how to handle the cape, muleta, or sword. He doesn't know how to fight and is totally lacking in class.

[4]*Cutberto, Pérez,* Ovaciones, *July 11, 1980.*

Elegant and erect, in the classical style, David performs a fine *derechazo*. Watching him carefully from behind the barrera is Don Arturo García.

He should consider a different occupation," the critic wrote.

"That fight in La Florecita demonstrated the truth, that it would take plenty for the Mexico City crowds to accept a gringo in the ring," Fred admitted.

"I was feeling great about everything," David reminisced. "Finally, I felt professional, and I was enjoying fighting. I needed it. I needed my fix, out there in front of the bull. Before, I had fought for Dad; then, I did it for Pepe Luis Vásquez; but during the summer of 1980, I began doing it for myself. The gusano dominated my thoughts, until I would wake up at night, sweating, thinking, and anxious to fight. It really sank its teeth into me.

"But, I also knew that I wasn't ready for the alternativa. I didn't deserve it. I didn't have enough experience. But, I had to face financial reality. I guess that's why they call it the 'alternative.' In my case, due to the problem of money, the alternative to not receiving the alternativa was to quit bullfighting."

David closed the 1980 season with a resounding triumph in Plaza Santa Fe. It was billed as a *mano a mano* with Rodolfo Morales, "El Chiquilín," but Morales failed to show up. So, David killed all four bulls, cutting one ear from his first, one from the third, and both ears from the last of the day.

In all, in 1980, he performed in 21 novilladas, cutting 35 ears and two tails. It was a very good year. But, money was becoming ever more scarce. Some decisions had to be made. David had come a long way, but in the world of bullfighting, he had hardly just begun.

Then, it was 1981. David would soon be 18 years old. He stood six foot, three inches and weighed 140 pounds. He was no longer the gawky little kid whose cuteness would excuse his inexperience; now he was a gawky-looking adult, who was expected to demonstrate technical and artistic talent.

So, somewhat reluctantly, on behalf of the Renks, this writer telephoned bullring owner Major López Hurtado and asked him to allow David to take his alternativa in Juárez. The author was rather hoping that he would deny the request, but he responded, "Which date does he want?" The die was cast. There was no turning back. David would be jumping from a top rung of one ladder to the bottom rung of another.

The alternativa was set for Easter Sunday, April 19, in Major López Hurtado's Plaza Monumental de Juárez. Working toward that big day, David fought as many novilladas as possible.

As usual, he opened the Reynosa season, March 1. It was David's birthday, and he provided a triumphant gift for the crowd. It would be his biggest triumph in Plaza Santa Fe. David's performance, as reviewed by this reporter, was as follows:

> Renk received his bull with six superb Verónicas, then went to the center of the ring to offer three grand Chicuelinas and the climaxing *rebolera*. His work with the red muleta, in the third act, began with statuesque high passes, followed by two, behind-the-back "pendulum" passes. He worked on both sides, inspiring enthusiastic applause, olés and music. One full sword climaxed the performance and resulted in the granting of ears and tail to Renk.

It was a great triumph. But, ahead lay Juárez and still another test of David's courage and determination.

On Saturday evening, at Del Camino Motel in El Paso, a lavish reception was held for David. Members of *Barrera Taurina*, the aficionados club from El Paso, showed up in force, as did other Texas friends, including Jim Kirby, "Silver" Contreras, Paco Olivera, Don Arturo García, Harry and Mary Conner, Dick and Mona Frontain, and Barnaby Conrad, Jr., who would cover the alternativa for *Sports Illustrated*. Friends and fans from as far away as Chicago and New York were on hand. Telegrams, wishing good luck, were received from the White House and from the governor of Texas.

Barbara Renk remained her calm, quiet self, while Binker Renk was running around selling color "El Texano" posters to raise money for a new suit of lights.

And then it was Sunday. Fred, David, Pepe Luis Vásquez, and this reporter went to the *sorteo* to draw lots for the bulls of the Armillita Hermanos ranch. For his alternativa bull, David drew #84, "Pepete," a well-built *berrendo* (black and white). But, his second toro, #91, was the biggest of the lot and had the most menacing horns.

Later, David was checked into his room at the Fiesta Real in Juárez to rest before the corrida. Pepe Luis began to sharpen swords and arrange equipment. All too quickly, the hour arrived. Everybody piled into the white van. On the outside was painted: "DAVID RENK, EL TEXANO." Below that, temporarily covered with newspaper and masking tape was the title "Matador de Toros."

On previous occasions, David had joked and horsed around on the way to the plaza. Not this time. The importance of the afternoon lay heavily upon his shoulders. His entire career was on the line.

Bullfighting is steeped in history and

filled with ritual. Normally, the matadors perform according to seniority, measured from the dates of their alternativas. The most senior matador fights the first and fourth bull; the next senior works the second and fifth; and the least senior is responsible for the third and sixth. But, during an alternativa afternoon, the torero receiving the doctorate faces the first and last bulls. With the first bull, the sponsoring matador, the witness matador, and the graduating novillero meet on the sand. The sponsor loans his muleta and sword to the graduate and wishes him well. Then, all three toreros embrace. Later, the three again meet and the new matador returns the sword and muleta to the sponsoring matador.

"Even though I didn't feel ready for the alternativa, I had to project professionalism. I had to make myself *feel* professional. There was a big lump in my throat. It wasn't fear of the bulls; I knew that they would be honest with me. The bull is honest. He'll never lie to me. If he's got *sentido* (cunning, wisdom), he'll show it to me. If he favors one horn, it'll be obvious. The real fear is of failure. I had to make myself be professional, so the people would feel it. I was determined to do well, and convince Major Hurtado that he hadn't made a mistake by allowing me the alternativa in his plaza."

The *paseillo* (parade of the toreros into the ring) was over in seconds. Then, the alternativa bull came blasting from the chute. When David offered the cape, the animal charged in an erratic fashion. He was unable to encourage any attack that would allow him to do artistic lances. It was a devil bull, totally lacking in nobility, but very dangerous.

Then came the alternativa ceremony, with Fermín Espinosa Armillita as the sponsor, and his brother, Miguelito Armillita (Chico), as the witness. The Armillitas are a family dynasty of matadors. Their father, the late Fermín Espinosa, was one of the greatest toreros in Mexican history. An interesting footnote is that he was never gored.

After saluting the plaza judge, thus receiving permission to enter the third act, David called Fred into the ring and dedicated Pepete to him. "This one's for you, Dad. We're on our way. Thanks, Pop," he said.

With the red muleta, David worked hard, obtaining several very good, but singular, passes. The bull searched for flesh and wouldn't allow El Texano to link the passes in series. Disappointed, David buried the sword and was granted a turn of the ring. But, it hadn't been a triumphant debut. At times, David's spindly legs refused to respond, making him seem graceless and timid. The crowd wasn't pleased; his friends were concerned.

The next four bulls passed quickly. The Armillita brothers both showed good work, but only two ears were cut, both by the charismatic Miguelito.

Suddenly, the wind began to inspire sand and pieces of paper to dance. Clouds cast ominous shadows over the arena. The last bull of the afternoon plunged into the ring. Without allowing his *peones* (assistants) to test the animal, David ran out to greet it. He seemed so determined, I thought he might take a bite out of the toro. Six fabulous, exceptionally low and slow Verónicas ignited thunderous *olés* and music. The climaxing Media Verónica was perfect. David turned his back and strode away from the bull. The applause was deafening.

El Texano dedicated to the crowd, then initiated the third act with *estatuarios*, the so-called "pass of death," in which the torero remains as motionless as a statue, allowing only his arms and wrists to lead the thundering toro past his chest. The bull's charge was clean and honest, and

The alternativa ceremony. *Left to right:* Miguel Armillita (Chico), Fermín Espinosa Armillita, and El Texano.

David was inspired. Running the hand long, he offered a series of six great *derechazos*, finishing with the chest pass. After acknowledging the crowd's accolades, he returned to give four more sets of derechazos, each series with five or six passes and the climaxing chest pass. The bull seemed to get better and David was becoming even more enthusiastic.

Switching the muleta to his left hand, he again ran the lure long, showing great control and clean, classical art. There were numerous series of *naturales*, each crowned with the chest pass. Then, he knelt in front of the animal and stared, arrogantly, into its face, a bit of showmanship fluff, demonstrating domination over the bull.

"*Manoletinas!*" Pepe Luis ordered. David snapped into position and gave several statuesque Manoletinas. He glared at the crowd, not even looking at the bull, as it passed mere fractions of inches from his body.

"*Mátelo!*" (Kill it!) Pepe ordered.

David worked the bull into position and lined up the hooves, so that the shoulder blades would be open to receive the sword. Raising the blade in his right hand, while offering the muleta in his left, he sighted and crossed over the horns, burying half the steel. Almost immediately, the bull coughed and collapsed. The stands filled with white handkerchiefs. The plaza judge measured the petition, then granted an ear, but denied the crowd's strong demand for the second appendage.

Clutching the hairy trophy as if it were made of gold, David toured the plaza. The fans bathed him in flowers and wineskins.

Later, outside the ring, the aficionados mobbed David. He spent nearly 40 minutes signing autographs and posing for photos. Even after the entourage was inside the van, it was difficult to leave the plaza, so enthusiastic were the people. The paper and tape that had covered "Matador de Toros" was removed from the side of the vehicle.

But, a very big question remained in my mind. Could David make it? He had the talent, the courage, and the dedication. He had an excellent teacher. He had the alternativa. If he could stay away from serious injury, if he could get the right bulls, if he could get contracts in the right plazas, if he could impress the tough crowds in the interiors...

Although as a matador David was paid for his labors, such was a mixed blessing, for there are many fine Mexican matadors who drive taxis in order to live between opportunities. The politics of bullfighting are depressing.

El Texano didn't get another contract until July 5, when he performed in a *mano a mano* with a third Armillita brother, Manolo Espinosa, in Piedras Negras.

It was an excellent afternoon for both matadors. Armillita cut one ear from his first bull. His second bull was extraordinary, and, following a grand performance, was granted the life-sparing *indulto*, an honor reserved for only the bravest, most noble bulls, animals that are assigned to sire other brave toros. To Armillita went symbolic trophies of ears, tail, and hoof.

The Mexican aficionados had come out of curiosity, but they stayed to cheer the Texan, as he surprised them with a pair of performances that won ears and tail from his first bull and a single ear from his second.

"That was a wonderful afternoon. The bulls were fantastic and I felt good. I hadn't cut many tails, but I was confident that I deserved that one," David said.

But, in spite of the triumph, contracts remained elusive. El Texano fought in a couple of American-style bloodless fights in Houston, San Antonio, and Dodge City, but the Mexican empresarios weren't turning cartwheels to hire him to fight in their plazas.

Major López Hurtado, on the other hand, had compassion for young, Yankee matadors. He had given opportunities to John Fulton, Diego O'Bolger, and Robert Ryan. He had allowed David the alternativa in his Juárez bullring, and now he would give him a chance in his other ring, Plaza Monumental de Tijuana, the world's second largest plaza de toros.

The date was set for August 30, but the competition would be tough. Two of Mexico's really big name matadors, Mariano Ramos and Curro Rivera, with 34 years of experience between them, headlined the card.

Luck wasn't with David, who admitted to being nervous about competing with such big stars. He tried, but the most that he could garner was a turn of the ring. Compared to toreros of the expertise of Ramos and Rivera, David's greenness was obvious.

Manuél Lourdes Camino, Rivera's manager, asked this writer, during the afternoon, "Do you know the biggest difference between David and Curro?" Then, he answered his own question. "Fifteen more years of experience."

But, later in the year, David returned to Tijuana to give a free performance

"*Manoletinas*!" Pepe ordered, and David snapped into position, performing the pass while staring at the crowd.

Receiving his first accolades as a full matador de toros, David acknowledges the cheers of the crowd.

during the annual convention of the National Association of Taurine Clubs, USA. A large Santoyo bull, armed with needle-sharp horns, allowed El Texano a pair of ears, but also caught him and knocked him unconscious. Honorary plaza judge of the day, retired Matador Eliseo "El Charro" Gómez, observed, "How did El Texano get 10 years of experience in only one year as a matador?"

On February 28, 1982, David fought for the first time as a full matador in Plaza

David offered series after series of excellent left- and right-handed passes.

Santa Fe. Following David's 10-page spread in *Sports Illustrated* and appearances on such television shows as *Good Morning, America*, and *Real People*, a large crowd turned out for the event, which resulted in a tumultuous triumph for Renk. It was just one more step toward Mexico City, home of the world's largest bullring and the most hard-to-please aficionados.

David performed in many of the comparatively antiseptic "bloodless bullfights" in the United States, where the animals couldn't be harmed. But there were no rules against the bulls harming the men. It's a strange system of priorities.

He was contracted to perform in San Antonio's Astro Arena before a large crowd and the cameras of the *That's Incredible* television program. David stole the show.

Thereafter, he guested with Don Rickles and David Brenner on *The Tom Snyder Show*, in New York City. A movie option resulted.

News of the skinny Texan, who had abandoned his wheelchair in favor of the sword, reached Spain. Don Alvaro Domecq, one of the most powerful and influential bullfight figures in Spain, extended an invitation to David to participate in the tientas at the famed Domecq ranch, near Seville. It would be El Texano's first encounter with animals of Iberian blood.

"Man, I was scared," David remembered. "I was just a green matador, and I was going to the cradle of bullfighting, where the bulls are huge and the crowds are tough. I mean, these were real *taurinos*, and I was just a skinny cowboy from Texas."

In addition to making their famous brandies and wines, the Domecq family raises fine horses and magnificent fighting bulls. Many Domecq males have been *rejoneadores*, performing from horseback, in the Portuguese style.

"I and Charlie Scanlon, a fine aficionado from Houston who had spent a lot of time in Spain, headed for Sevilla. I was excited, but terrified. They received me very well, and Don Alvaro Domecq sort of took me under his wing. He took me to the fair in Sevilla. Just being with him was a privilege and an honor."

David was allowed to participate in the tientas of the Domecq fighting cows, but it was a far different experience than those animals that he had faced at Don Arturo's ranch. He took turns, working 12 mature cows, during a three-day period.

"I had fought bulls that were smaller than those vacas. They were huge, and their horns had really sharp points. I just swallowed a couple times, took a deep breath, and went out and did the best that I could."

But, aside from fighting, David was a normal teenager. He was in Spain, and he wanted to have some fun, see some flamenco, and get away from the watchful eye of Don Alvaro. He mentioned this to Curro Romero and Rafael de Paula, two of Spain's top matadors, who were also participating in the tientas. They told David to sneak out of the house that night, and they would take him into Seville to see a flamenco show.

"Well, that was pretty cool, but it turned out that nothing escapes Don Alvaro. He knew exactly what was going on. In any case, Curro, Rafael, and I went to a *Taberna Andaluz* [flamenco theater]. The show wasn't scheduled to begin until one o'clock in the morning, so we arrived early, to get good seats. Up on the stage, sitting on a chair, was an old woman who looked like a *bruja* [witch]. She sagged all over. Her arms sagged, her legs sagged, her face sagged. I wondered how long she had been dead.

"But, then, a guitarist struck a flamenco chord, and she stood up. All of a sudden, everything started coming back into place. Her face and body formed. The sagging flesh turned into healthy flesh. She was proud and beautiful. She might have been 60 or 65 years old, but she looked like a 20-year-old girl, and I immediately fell in love with her."

At about daybreak, with no sleep, and having consumed large quantities of fine Domecq sherry, Romero and de Paula took David back to the ranch. But, the door was locked, so David just hung around, outside. A few minutes later, a window opened and a smiling Don Alvaro leaned out.

"Good morning, David. Are you ready?"

El Texano's first ear as a matador.

Man, I hadn't slept a minute. I had done a lot of drinking, too. The last thing in my mind was fighting more cows. But, I couldn't very well tell Don Alvaro that I would rather sleep a few hours. The next thing I knew, we were at the *tentadero* [tienta ring]. And, you know, to the breeder, the tientas are very serious. Protocol is important, too. You don't go into the ring until the *ganadero* invites you to do so. Well, the gate opened and the first big cow ran into the arena. Almost immediately, I heard Don Alvaro's booming voice: "Renk!"

Wow! Before, I had been allowed to give a few passes, only after three or four other guys had worked each cow. This would be the first time, that I'd be the first to fight. And, all of those matadors and other important *taurinos* were watching. I just *had* to do well. I knocked myself out with that vaca. I gave everything I had. And, Don Alvaro kept shouting instructions. "On the left! On the right! Move it over there! Move it back over here!"

By the time that he yelled *"Puerta!"* [Door!], ordering the vaca out of the tiny arena, I was exhausted. I just leaned against the barrera and tried to get my breath. Then, the next cow came in. And, Don Alvaro shouted, "Renk!" Oh, no! This cow was for me, too! Well, somehow I found the strength and fought it. By the time she was taken out, I was really tired.

"Renk!" shouted Don Alvaro when the third cow came in. Oh, God! I don't know where I got the energy. I felt like a wet dishcloth, but I did it.

David's debut in Plaza Monumental de Tijuana wasn't a good one for him. But he had moments of brilliance, such as in this low, slow *Verónica*.

> The fourth cow charged into the arena. "Renk!" boomed Don Alvaro's voice. Suddenly, I knew what was up. These people were trying to get me killed! They'd send me home in a box! I was so thankful when the fifth animal came in, and Don Alvaro didn't shout "Renk!" I could have kissed him.

Later, Domecq told David and Scanlon that he was genuinely impressed with El Texano's abilities and that a Spanish campaign might be possible. But, David would first have to confirm his alternativa in Mexico City.

It was a happy and confident David Renk who returned to Texas.

Although opportunities continued to be elusive, his triumphs were many. David was contracted to reappear in Piedras Negras, the scene of his earlier triumph with Manolo Armillita. For his second corrida there, he would compete *mano a mano* with Pepe Luis Vásquez, Jr., who had also recently received his alternativa.

CBS's *What's Up, America?* TV cameras were present, adding to the tremendous national interest that was building for the skinny Texas youth. Still another big day was in store. Vásquez, for once, outdid El Texano, cutting ears and tail to David's two ears.

More corridas followed. On September 5, in Reynosa, David cut the only ear of the afternoon. He triumphed in Monterrey and in three corridas in Nuevo Laredo. He returned to Juárez, winning

During a free performance in Tijuana, following a series of passes, David interjected a bit of showmanship fluff by kneeling in front of the bull and staring into its face.

still another ear, in competition with the new *matadora* Raquel Martinez.

But triumphant afternoons in the provinces do not carry much weight in Mexico City. The press began to ask when David would perform his art in the capital. "Soon," Fred Renk responded. "Soon."

David fought 10 corridas in 1982. No matador can make a living with so few performances, but it was a beginning. And his successes were impressive.

Date	*Place*	*Bulls*	*Results*
Feb. 28	Reynosa	2 Golondrinas	3 ears
May 13	Piedras Negras	2 Golondrinas	3 ears/1 tail
June 7	Piedras Negras	2 Golondrinas	2 ears
Sept. 2	Tijuana	1 Santoyo	2 ears
Sept. 5	Reynosa	2 La Ronda	1 ear
Sept. 12	Monterrey	1 La Ronda	vuelta
Oct. 16	Juárez	2 Golondrinas	1 ear
Oct. 23	Nuevo Laredo	2 Milagro	2 ears
Nov. 7	Nuevo Laredo	2 La Playa	2 vueltas
Nov. 14	Nuevo Laredo	1 Milagro	bronze trophy

From February through mid–November, David faced 17 bulls, winning 14 ears, one tail, and a bronze trophy.

Through the close of 1982, David kept busy. When he wasn't fighting in formal corridas, he was at the ranches, facing anything that the breeders were willing to throw at him. David was so excited, he would have fought an elephant, were one available.

He had become a folk hero to handicapped kids. David spoke to groups of crippled youngsters, wherever he traveled. To inaugurate the 1983 season, February 6, in Reynosa, David performed in a charity corrida, with the profits going to handicapped children. He and Pepe Luis Vásquez, Jr., would face a quartet of bulls from the Golondrinas ranch.

Plans for the affair attracted the ire of the Humane Society, but it didn't stifle the attendance at the plaza de toros. It was a complete sellout. The only other matador in history to have accomplished such in Reynosa was the famed Spaniard, El Cordobés. Neither did it stifle the enthusiasm of the matadors, each of whom won ears and tail.

David's awards were symbolic and historic. His second bull of the afternoon was granted the indulto and left the ring alive. It was the first indulto in 30 years for the Golondrinas ranch and the first ever for any Yankee matador in Mexico. David performed an estimated 150 passes with the bull. At the end of the afternoon, the enthusiastic fans carried El Texano upon their shoulders from the bullring all the way to his hotel, nearly a mile away.

Two weeks later, alternating with three other matadors, El Texano cut the only ears of the day. He was immediately signed to repeat, the following Sunday, when he successfully faced a bull that weighed nearly 600 kilos.

Shortly thereafter, the David Renk Scholarship Foundation was established to assist handicapped children in attending college. Barbara Renk reflected on those happy days.

"Listen. That's all I could really do. All those years ... they were rough ... and, today, I sometimes wonder if I was really there, if I had really lived, or if I was only a detached something, like a string of chiles hanging on a hook, only expected to be there.

"You see, I'm a woman, and bullfighting is a man's world. I sew rips and tears in capes and outfits; I offer comfort or congratulations, but I'm not supposed to actively participate, or even to offer my opinions. It's kind of empty. The world of

Left to right: **Don Alvaro Domecq, David, and aficionado Charles Patrick Scanlon, at the Domecq ranch, in southern Spain.**

bullfighting is very chauvinistic, but I had to put up with it, because that was my son out there!

"Reflecting on it now, it's an eerie feeling. So much has happened, so many years have passed, so much joy and so much sadness. And, everything is still up in the air," El Texano's mother mused.

In spite of having to occupy a backseat in David's career, Barbara was a pillar of strength, lending support or condolences as needed.

In 1983, David performed in Monterrey, Nuevo Laredo, Juárez, Reynosa, and other rings of the provinces, receiving excellent press reviews. But Mexico City remained skeptical. Although his photograph adorned the cover of the respected taurine journal, *El Redondel*, the aficionados of the capital wouldn't take El Texano seriously until he confirmed his alternativa in La Plaza México. And that was seemingly an impossible task, one steeped in complicated politics.

At that time, two major ruptures in relationships would dramatically affect El Texano's psyche and progress. First, because of the Renk's financial problems, and the desire of Pepe Luis Vásquez to dedicate more of his time to his own son's career, it was decided to sever the manager-matador relationship. Then came a dispute with Don Arturo Garcia. The ganadero/empresario planned only a limited 1983 season, exclusively of novilladas, while his competitor, Don Jorge Cuesta, empresario of Plaza Monumental de Reynosa, planned a full season of corridas and offered contracts to El Texano. Fred accepted the contracts, thus severing relations with Garcia. It was a decision that he would come to regret.

Meanwhile, the press media of both countries bannerlined the successes of the long, tall Texan's efforts in the bullrings, and of his work on behalf of crippled children. Requests for interviews poured in from throughout the nation. David was confident and busy. He appeared on several more national television programs. Fred kept him insulated from the politics of the Mexican bullfight world.

Perhaps it was his overwhelming celebrity status; or it was a case of his looking beyond toward Mexico City; more likely, it was the absence of Pepe Luis Vásquez. Whichever theory is the most accurate, in June 1983, David received his first serious goring. Fred related the event.

"It happened in Matamoros. It was a complete surprise. David was doing well and seemed to really be enjoying himself. Then, the bull picked him up, tossed him into the air, and caught him on the way down. The horn drove into his left leg and ripped upward. David bled like crazy. I feared that a major artery had been ruptured. But he got up and killed the bull. There was no infirmary, so we helped him hobble to the ambulance, where Red Cross attendants taped him up. I asked him, 'Are you going to fight your second bull?' He answered, 'You're damned right I am!'

"So, when they opened the gate and David limped back into the plaza, the place came unglued. Blood seeped through the bandages. The stands were packed, and everybody came to their feet and applauded. He triumphed with the animal, winning an ear. Then, we took him to the hospital, where surgeons operated on the wound."

El Texano couldn't allow the injury to cost him any time off. He spent hours in a therapy bath, and more hours exercising, willing the torn muscle to heal and respond. The annual benefit corrida for crippled children, in Reynosa, was scheduled for the following Sunday. He had to be there. It took an injection of cortisone, but he made it. And, he cut an ear.

At that time, the author had been making plans for David's freshman tour of Spain. A year earlier, this writer had returned to the country that had given birth to my own love of bullfighting and re-established the contacts that could make David's tour possible. Opportunities in Spain are hard to find, and the crowds are extremely knowledgeable and critical. Overt bravado won't impress the Spanish aficionados; it takes honest, hard-nosed bullfighting.

Not only are the Spanish crowds tougher than those of Mexico, so are the

David became a hero to physically-challenged people. He set up an annual charity corrida in Reynosa, and he established a college scholarship fund for the handicapped. (Photograph by Antillón.)

bulls. In addition to being larger and older, the bulls of Spanish blood are far less naïve than are those of Mexico. When a torero makes a mistake with a Spanish bull, it usually results in a goring. Where the Mexican *Fiesta Brava* is a happy, festive event, the Spanish *Fiesta Nacional* is a deadly serious performing art.

This reporter's long-time friend, retired Spanish Matador Fermin Murillo, viewing photos of El Texano, remarked, "He's too tall and skinny. He doesn't look like a torero." And, he was right.

Nevertheless, Murillo agreed to open some important doors for David, if he would first confirm his alternativa in La Plaza Mexico. Murillo advised me to take David to Andalucia, Spain's southern cradle of bullfighting, and have him participate in the tientas of the famous ranches of that area.

"Then, get him in a few corridas in the small towns, where he probably won't be paid more than his actual expenses," Murillo advised. "When you feel confident that he can handle Spanish bulls, let me know. I'll arrange for a closed-door test, in Madrid. The only people present will be important empresarios, breeders, managers, and taurine journalists. That test will determine if El Texano has a future as a matador in Spain."

The timing was perfect. Finally, David's fame became too great for Mexico City to ignore. A call came, offering El Texano the opportunity to confirm his alternativa. To that point, three other Yankees had performed in La Plaza México, but only as novilleros: Robert Ryan, of Inglewood (Calif.), Diego O'Bolger, of Tucson (Ariz.), and Richard Corey, of Charleston (W. Va.). Another gringo

Posters in both Spanish and English were printed for David's alternativa confirmation performance in Mexico City.

novillero, Walter de La Brosse, was presented in the *El Toreo de Cuatro Caminos* plaza, just outside the Mexico City Federal District.

Harper B. Lee and Sidney Franklin had fought as matadors in Mexico City's old *La Condesa* ring. But, with the technical exception of Jesus Córdoba — who was born in Kansas, but later became a Mexican citizen — until October 2, 1983, no Yankee Matador de Toros had confirmed his alternativa in La Plaza México.

However, the opportunity to be the first would also inspire a controversy that confused and saddened El Texano. Many U.S. aficionados believed that the honor of being the first Yankee matador to confirm in La Plaza Mexico should have been extended to toreros of greater experience, principally John Fulton, Diego O'Bolger, Robert Ryan, and Richard Corey.

There was validity in that opinion. John Fulton, for example, had taken his alternativa in Spain and was the first and only Yankee to confirm in Madrid. In fact, he had been actively seeking the Plaza México confirmation, and such had been promised to him. But, for whatever reasons, the promise never bore fruit. John was victimized by the Machiavellian politics of the bullfight world.

Robert Ryan, who had fought and triumphed as a novillero in La Plaza México, and as a matador in both Spain and Mexico, likewise had a legitimate claim to the Mexico City confirmation. The confirmation had been offered to him, the year after his alternativa, but he didn't consider himself to be ready for it. And by 1983 he had retired.

O'Bolger, who had been fighting twice as long as El Texano, and had proven himself to be a thoroughly capable matador, should definitely have been afforded a confirmation opportunity. But he, like Fulton, was shut out. Fulton, Ryan, O'Bolger, and Corey had professional seniority over Renk. Such were realities, and David said so, in every interview in Mexico City.

"What was I supposed to do, turn down the confirmation as a statement of support for Fulton, O'Bolger, Ryan, and Corey? I respect all of them, I admire them, and I sympathize with them. But, I didn't invent the politics of bullfighting. If the situation were reversed, I very much doubt that any of them would refuse the opportunity," David reflected.

Then came the weeks of waiting and wondering. Every newspaper and radio and television station in the city conducted interviews with El Texano, to be published or aired when the date of the confirmation was announced.

"They wouldn't give me a firm date. For six weeks, I hung out in Mexico City. Every Monday morning, I picked up the newspapers to see what the following Sunday's cartel was, to see if it was my turn. By about the fourth week, I began getting burned out by the anticipation of it. I'd rather be told that I'm fighting in two hours. That's better than weeks of waiting and wondering. That took a lot out of me. Still, I dreamed about the fight. I pictured myself being carried out on shoulders through the main gate, all the way to the street. When I finally saw the published card, announcing 'David Renk, who will confirm the alternativa,' it was almost anti-climactic. I had already exhausted so much energy, waiting and dreaming."

The hype began. Newspapers published the interviews that they had conducted, weeks earlier. But, such only served to add fuel to the resentment of the Mexico City aficionados against the gringo torero who would dare to think himself worthy of performing in La Plaza Mexico.

Mexico City bullfight fans pride themselves on being *muy exigente* (very demanding) and are notoriously hostile toward any torero who doesn't please them. Especially if he happens to be non–Latin. But, later, those aficionados proved themselves unworthy of their reputation.

David was stuck in a three-way squeeze between his own desire to succeed, the expectations of his supporters, and some aficionados from either side of the border who could not transcend their own prejudices long enough to give him an even break. His mental attitude was less than positive. His own doubts haunted him.

And, why not? Who wouldn't be intimidated? La Plaza México is, to Mexican

In the long days and weeks leading up to his confirmation performance, David trained in La Plaza México, the world's largest bullring.

toreros, as The Met or Carnegie Hall are to musicians or dancers. Additional history would be recorded in the fact that the afternoon would see eight bulls, presented for four matadors. Such had occurred only one other time in Plaza México history.

The bulls for the afternoon were from the Manuel de Haro ranch. They were huge, mature, and possessed of menacing horns. All were *cárdenos* (grays) and weighed from 458 to 512 kilos. For the ceremony of the alternativa confirmation, the sponsoring matador would be Rafaelillo Gil. Matadors David Liceaga and José Lorenzo Garza would be the witnesses.

The days prior to the event were hectic, filled with visits by aficionados, matadors, and news media.

"Thinking back on it, now, it would have been better had I gone to a hotel on the other side of the city and hidden out, by myself. But, these were my friends and supporters who had come from Texas and other parts of the United States. I appreciated their coming; I wanted to be cordial and respectful, but it was exhausting."

On Saturday evening, a banquet was held, ostensibly for David, but in reality for his many friends who had shown up to see his presentation in La Plaza México.

Then, suddenly, it was Sunday morning. In a maelstrom of activity, the *sorteo* was held. Four hours later, the corrida would be celebrated.

Famed taurine author Barnaby Conrad wrote in *Clarín* magazine:

> He came out of the elevator and into the lobby of the hotel in Mexico City, tall, gangly, looking like a young, blond version of Jimmy Stewart.
>
> Except that the young man was dressed in a flamboyant costume that Jimmy Stewart wouldn't be caught dead in: a $3,000 suit of lights ... cerulean blue silk with sparkling gold spangles. ...
>
> An old bullfighter lurched out of the bar and headed for the young man. Actually, the bullfighter wasn't old, he was just ex, and there is nothing more ex than an ex-matador.
>
> His eyes were like two *huevos rancheros* (fried eggs in red Mexican salsa) and his breath, as they say, could have started the windmill in an old Dutch painting.
>
> "David," he said hoarsely, "you are going to make history today. May God be with you."
>
> David was aware of this burden. Even the President of the United States, never unmindful of a newsworthy event, had telephoned David, the day before, wishing him luck. ...
>
> David said nothing during the interminable ride to the bullring. The rest of us seemed to be babbling, out of nervousness.
>
> We said to David the perfunctory things people say at the last moment to a matador, and then we headed down a long tunnel to our seats in the second row. The plaza was not filled entirely, but it was estimated there were some 28,000 people there, double what most bullfight arenas hold. ...
>
> Near me, I saw the fine American matador with the improbable name of Diego O'Bolger, and he made his way through the jammed aisles to say hello.
>
> "Did you see David's second bull?" I asked. "Big. Really big."
>
> Diego shrugged amiably. "Who cares about the weight? Nobody's asking him to pick it up and carry it on his back."
>
> An old, bullfighting gallows-type joke. If he was jealous of David's success in landing this big chance — something O'Bolger has coveted for 10 years— he did a gentlemanly job of concealing it. Perhaps, a triumph for one American would help others.
>
> My seat was directly behind David's mother, Barbara. David's father was in the alleyway, talking to a reporter. Fred looked calm, very calm. But, Barbara tried three times to light her cigarette. Not only was her hand trembling, but her whole arm and shoulder were shaking. Her younger son, John (Binker), finally held her wrist to get the job done.
>
> A bugle sounded exactly at 4 p.m.— a bullfight is still the only function that starts on time in Mexico. Then, the band blared out the traditional *Cielo Andalúz*...

At the sorteo, El Texano examined the bulls in the corrals.

David's confirmation bull would be #13, the 460-kilo "Cuentagotas." His second bull, at 512 kilos, was "Noventón," the largest of the group.

It's difficult to describe the feeling of standing in the *puerta de cuadrillas* (matadors' entrance gate), looking up at the towering grandstands of La Plaza México. The plaza's very size is impressive; filled with people, it's intimidating. For the torero making his debut, it must be like carrying the world upon his shoulders. The responsibility is intense.

As the trumpets sounded, a thunderous *OLE!* greeted the beginning of the *paseillo*. David and the other toreros wished each other good luck, then began their solemn march into the world's largest bullfight arena.

As in his alternativa ceremony, David would face the first and last bulls.

Brief minutes later, the *toril* gates opened, granting admission to Cuentagotas. After a few testing passes by his *peones*, David stepped out, to offer his cape. His Verónicas were nervous, lacking rhythm. The public remained silent, waiting. After three pics, the act was changed and the banderilleros quickly placed their barbed sticks. Again, the trumpets sounded. All four matadors met in the ring. Rafaelillo offered his muleta and sword to David. Then, all exchanged embraces.

After making the mandatory salute to the plaza judge and thereby receiving permission to enter the third act, El Texano went to the center of the arena, where on one knee, he dedicated the performance to his grandfather, Fred's dad, who had died only a few weeks earlier.

Then, he unfolded the muleta and challenged the animal, which charged from a great distance. However, it quickly became obvious that the bull was terribly far-sighted. In close quarters, it was practically blind and attacked seemingly by

Fred Renk put his hand in the hat and pulled out the numbers of the two bulls that David would face later in the afternoon in La Plaza México.

Braille. Such presents an extremely dangerous situation, which is particularly acute at the point of the kill. To kill a bull, it must be able to see the muleta. Otherwise, it attacks merely by sound.

David worked hard, trying to perform with the deadly animal. Each charge began well, but, as the toro would arrive, its faulty vision resulted in an erratic, uncontrollable attack. David was forced into a defensive posture, which emphasized the weakness of his legs, making him appear

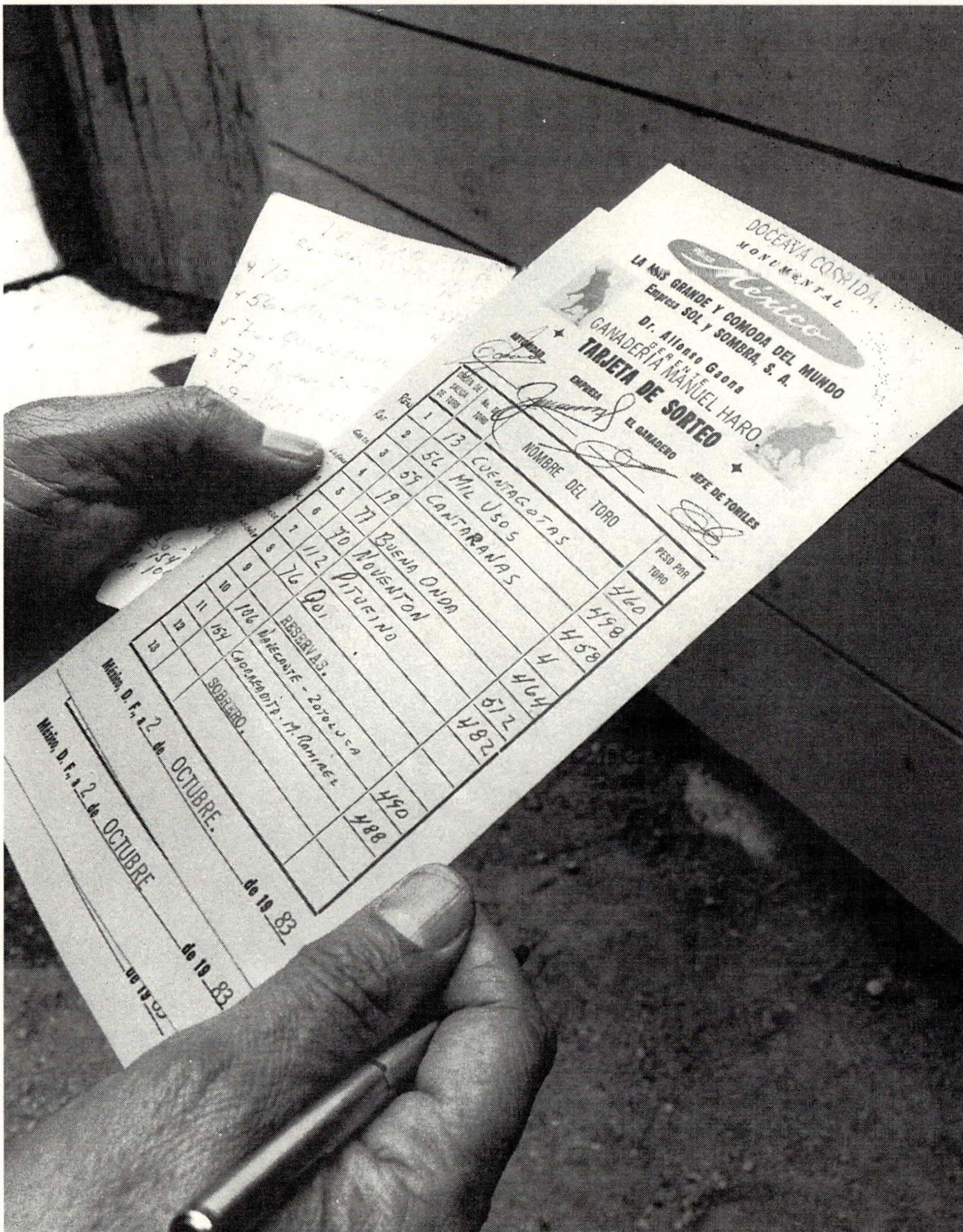

The official sorteo card told the story. David had drawn Cuentagotas and Noventón.

clumsy. The crowd became abusive. It was amazing that an audience of such renowned aficionados could be so oblivious to the impossibility of trying to fight a nearly blind bull.

Nothing could be accomplished. David lined up to kill. But, in order to be within the animal's field of vision, he had to stand at least four feet farther away than he normally would, thus throwing off his timing. Every time that he tried to set himself to place the sword, the bull charged,

David would face the 450-kilo Cuentagotas and the 512-kilo Noventón, photographed at the Manuel Haro ranch a couple of weeks earlier.

Marching in the paseillo in La Plaza México.

blindly, forcing David to abort the entry. Finally, after several attempts, he placed the blade, but it didn't penetrate deeply enough. Neither did two more entries.

He got his *descabello,* a shorter sword with a heavy tip, designed to sever the bull's spinal cord at the base of the skull, bringing instant death. But, each time that he raised the instrument, the bull would attack, forcing David to take defensive action.

According to the rigid rules of bullfighting, upon entering the third act, the matador has 20 minutes to kill the bull. If not, an *aviso* (warning) is sounded by a trumpet from the judge's box, granting a leeway of two more minutes. At the end of that time, if the bull still isn't dead, a second aviso sounds, granting still another minute. But, if the bull still isn't dead upon the sounding of the third aviso, it is removed, alive, from the arena.

David was doing his best, but the bull refused to cooperate. The first aviso was heard. The horn seemed to mock the torero's efforts. David attempted another sword, but discovered only bone. The second aviso sounded. El Texano began to get rattled. When the third and final aviso reverberated over the sand, David, with head down, turned and walked back across the arena. The bull was returned to the corrals, where it was shot. For the first time in his young career, David heard the crowd soundly boo him.

The situation was made worse for Renk by the fact that the next bull, for Rafaelillo, turned out to be the only decent animal of the day. With it, Rafaelillo was able to register a triumph, winning an ear

What thoughts run through the head of a matador waiting for his first bull?

and taking the afternoon's only turn of the ring.

The balance of the afternoon lacked anything resembling triumph. The bulls were terrible. There were some death-defying placements of banderillas by Liceaga and Rafaelillo, and some strong efforts by Garza, who suffered a slight goring in the buttocks, but there was nothing else of note. There were no ears, no turns of the ring, and no bows from the center of the arena. Garza and Liceaga both

The alternativa confirmation ceremony in La Plaza México.

received bulls that, as those corresponding to El Texano, suffered severe sight deficiencies. Neither was able to garner more than polite applause.

When Noventón entered the ring, it drew a gasp from the crowd. A huge creature, with head held high and horns that seemed to tickle the clouds, it was an imposing and frightening sight. Without waiting for his peones to test the animal, David ran to greet the toro with a series of Verónicas, climaxed with a Media Verónica that left Noventón in the center of the ring and rocked the big plaza with

Cuentagotas left the ring alive, to be shot later in the corrals.

a thunderous ovation. The crowd, ever fickle, had become inspired by El Texano.

Noventón proved strong against the picadores, offering hope that a triumph was within reach. But, those hopes were quickly dashed in the third act, when it became apparent that Noventón, as all but one of its brothers, should have carried a white cane.

Nevertheless, determined to redeem himself, David inspired strong *olés* and music for several series of excellent right-handed muleta passes. Under the circumstances, they were deadly. Just as it seemed that El Texano might have something going, the bull lost its strength, becoming defensive and unpredictable. The balance of David's performance was limited to technical, nonaesthetic, horn-to-horn work that inspired sarcastic *olés* from a crowd that should have known that this was the correct and proper way to handle a bull such as Noventón.

Two sword attempts hit bone. Then, apparently deciding that it was either kill or be killed, David threw himself over the horns and drove the sword to the handle. The bull's right horn caught him in the left arm pit, but luckily did not penetrate. The animal collapsed, dead.

For this, at least, David heard strong applause and took a bow in the center of the ring. Hoping to redeem himself, David attempted to purchase a gift bull, but was told that none was available.

"I was so ready to fight. If I had had better bulls ... if ... for whatever reasons, certain things happened. I don't know if it was the pressure of the plaza, or whatever, I just knew that I had done very poorly," David reflected.

In retrospect, although El Texano failed to realize his desired triumph in La Plaza México, he nevertheless conducted himself with dignity and honor. And, with Noventón, he had triumphed over both Garza and Liceaga. Nevertheless, some of the critics were very hard on the matador from Texas. Mexico's most powerful critic, Pepe Alameda, hadn't seen the corrida. He wasn't even in the city, and the event hadn't been telecast. Yet, his assessment of David was devastating.

But, at least one reviewer, *El Redondel*'s editor-publisher Alberto Bitar, one of the few whose words could not be purchased with bribes, wrote:

> David's first bull could not see up close. Nothing was possible. With his feet together (second bull), he worked high passes, then later offered low passes with an animal that wasn't very much, but to which the youngster gave some good passes that were applauded....
>
> The de Haro bull was stupid, faulty in vision and short in charge, but the North American showed *aguante* (held his ground), in spite of the bad luck that he suffered in the sorteo.... Unjustifiably, one sector of the crowd verbally abused him. But, in actuality, if there was anything to criticize, it was the bulls, not the torero.[5]

Although David's presentation hadn't been a grand success, neither was it a total failure. He had received applause and an official salute, something that neither Garza

[5]*Bitar, Alberto,* El Redondel, *Mexico City, Oct. 3, 1983.*

Opposite and above: **In the center of the arena, El Texano performed several outstanding series of left- and right-handed passes, inspiring applause and olés from the crowd.**

or Liceaga had been able to achieve. And, he had accomplished that which no other Yankee matador had been able: he had confirmed his alternativa in La Plaza México.

The next day, in the De Carlo Hotel, a group of South American promoters visited the Renks, offering contracts to El Texano. But, Fred turned them down, saying, "It's time to go home and rest, a while. Come on, son. Deer season opens, in a couple weeks. Let's hit the bush and let the world go by, until next year."

In retrospect, things could have been a lot worse, and in fact, had been so for numerous other famed matadors. Nevertheless, it was a sad contingent of Texans that left Mexico City the next day. The Renks returned to their ranch, and David entered a period of disillusionment and self-doubt. Fred was broke. Investment and loan sources had dried up. And Barbara Renk's diabetes was worsening.

Never having been involved in the business side of bullfighting, David didn't know how to promote himself. And, his failure to register a clear triumph in La Plaza Mexico seemed to have sapped his energy, enthusiasm, and confidence.

The Renks opened a restaurant, *El Matador*, in the little town of Tomball, Texas. With posters, mounted bulls' heads, photos, and taurine memorabilia covering the walls, the place was practically a shrine to bullfighting, and particularly to El Texano, who basked in its glory. He began emulating the role of a playboy, forsaking training for fast lane living. He and Fred fought about that, and finally there was a rupture in their partnership.

"I said I would finance you to your alternativa. I went beyond that to your Mexico City confirmation. You're no longer a little kid; you're a man. Your career is now up to you. Floundering around in self-pity won't accomplish anything. Go to Mexico, where you belong; get yourself a manager," Fred said.

Those plans were put on hold when word reached the author that David was out of training and was drinking heavily. He was fighting only in Reynosa and in bloodless bullfights in Texas, Kansas, and other cities where his celebrity was enough to attract crowds. And, he was bombing, badly. Knowledgeable aficionados reported that he seemed to have lost his desire. His gusano was hibernating. He didn't even train.

In an effort to reinspire him, Fred began offering bullfights on his "Rancho El Texano," in Magnolia. He also began breeding fighting bulls. For a while, David was somewhat enthusiastic. Novilleros began showing up, and he trained with them. But, his spark of enthusiasm had evaporated.

"I think he was just angry at me. He had lost his leader, his PR man who had handled all of his problems. And, I suppose that I, too, had lost my confidence in him," Fred reflected.

A temporary period of decadence is not unusual in any torero's career. Following a long, hard campaign, the man sometimes just gets tired of the hassle, the constant travel, and the need to prove himself, day after day, week after week. He needs a respite. This writer had to determine if there was any hope for a continuing career for El Texano, or if all was lost.

The author arranged a contract for him to work a bloodless fight, in the northern California town of Gilroy, which isn't exactly a booming metropolis. Its only real claim to fame is garlic. Restaurants even feature garlic ice cream and garlic wine.

Contrary to popular belief, bullfighting in most of the United States is not illegal. But, the killing of bulls, or the shedding of their blood in the ring, is strictly forbidden. Theoretically, the men know the chances they're taking, while the bulls have never read the script or formed a union. From Las Vegas to Detroit, Philadelphia, San Francisco, and in many other American venues—especially in California—bloodless bullfights have become quite popular.

Heavy Velcro padding or pieces of cork are attached to the bulls' shoulders, to receive the banderillas. And, the kills are simulated. But, there are no picadores. Thus, the bulls' incredible strength is never tempered; they still carry their heads and horns high. Because of the supreme danger of facing mature, un-pic'ed bulls, the animals used in American bloodless bullfights, although of fighting stock, are younger and smaller than those presented in authentic corridas de toros. But, the mature fighting bull has killed its share of trees and spent plenty of time sparring with its brothers. Such an animal is horned fury, whose aggressiveness must not be depleted, but must be tempered and directed, something that can be accomplished only by the picador.

California has a sizable Portuguese community to which bloodless bullfighting is common to its heritage and culture. In several parts of the state, the Portuguese breed and raise bulls of brave blood. California law permits bloodless bullfights, if they are held in conjunction with religious observances. Therefore, on practically any Saint's Day, the Portuguese community promotes bloodless corridas. Dozens of such functions are held annually.

It was this forum which greeted the toreros of the day in Gilroy. David alternated with Matadora Raquel Martinez and journeyman Portuguese Matador Armando Soares. The portable plaza had no infirmary or team of skilled surgeons standing by. The crowd was large and noisy, and the weather was warm and clear. There was a distinctive aroma of garlic in the air. In the interests of religious authenticity, the afternoon was inaugurated by a priest, who conducted a benediction. It seemed slightly incongruous.

The bullfighting offered was pure border-style bologna, plenty of excitement, but very little artistry. And David was terrible. Obviously out of training, his timing was off. He was inept and awkward.

Then, he made a grave technical error which could easily have had fatal results. He was caught, tossed, thrown to the ground, picked up by the collar, and finally knocked unconscious. When he revived, this writer was shaking him by the shoulders and yelling, "You stupid ass! You know better than that! Do you want to die in this miserable little town?"

The only bright spot of the trip occurred the next morning. While having breakfast in a local truck stop, we were approached by a scruffy, bearded, exceptionally mean-looking biker weighing at least 300 pounds. David and I looked at each other with expressions that conveyed concern. Neither of us was the least bit interested in being beaten up in a coffee shop in the garlic capital of the nation.

"Ain't you the guy who fought bulls, here, yesterday?" the biker growled.

"Yessir," stammered David.

"Well, I'm glad to meet you. You make me feel proud to be an American."

The huge, potbellied biker just wanted David's autograph. I thought my pants would never dry.

David had impregnated a groupie, and, a few months later, in typical Texas Gentleman fashion, he married her. It couldn't have happened at a worse time. The last thing that a struggling, young matador needs is the added burden of a wife and child. For toreros, that type of perk is reserved for later, after they have captured a position of respect on the taurine ladder of matadors. David got married, and before long, was a daddy. It was obvious to me that his career in the ring had ended, not in noisy triumph, but in silent defeat. Both of us knew that the Spanish tour was canceled. If I had any doubts about that fact, they were erased, a few months later, in Pasadena, Texas.

While Pasadena, California, has the Rose Bowl, Pasadena, Texas, had Gilley's. Although it has since burned down, Gilley's was the blue jeans, boots, cowboy hats, country music and "good old boys" capital of the world. It was larger than the average circus, and a lot noisier. Gilley's was so big, it had an indoor rodeo arena. It was a great venue for rodeos, but a lousy one for bullfights.

Fred Renk, who set up the fight in Gilley's, hired the author to narrate the action, which featured El Texano, novillero Dennis Borba (who would, two years later, receive his alternativa), Rejoneador Mario Cuello and Armando Soares, the Portuguese matador with whom David had fought, in Gilroy.

By comparison, in terms of sophistication, the bullfights at Gilley's made Gilroy seem like Madrid. The good old boys seemed to consider bullfighting to be a bit sissy. "I ain't gonna spend good beer money to buy a ticket to watch characters in pink socks fool around with steers," was a typical comment. Others were even less complimentary.

But the depressing environment of Gilley's was nothing compared to the sad performance of El Texano. He acted as if he had mercury in his slippers. His bulls were good, but he couldn't keep his feet still. He looked not only bad but sloppy and lacking in confidence. It was almost as if he had flopped on purpose.

After making a technical error, David was caught by the bull and tossed into the air.

David's depression was manifested in the ring. But, Fred's was equally as deep, and made even more complicated by Barbara's worsening health and Fred's own guilt for having neglected her, in favor of David's career. It seemed to be an insoluble problem — all of that time, work, and money, only to result in failure.

Before returning to California, this reporter told Fred, "Leave him alone. Get no contracts for him. Do nothing. If he's going to continue his career, he'll have to first find himself. In time, he'll either come back strong, or he'll give it up, entirely. You can do nothing more for him."

More than a year passed, during which time, the writer put El Texano out of his mind. I declined to obtain any contracts for him. I couldn't bear to see him fighting as he had in Gilley's. I sent him a letter, taking him to task for wasting a potentially great career. I asked him, "Do you really want to be remembered as the greatest American matador in Reynosa history?"

Several months later, David was contracted to fight in another bloodless action, in the Astrodome. He would perform with Mexican stars Rafaelillo Gil, the great David Silveti, and Armillita Chico, plus North Americans Diego O'Bolger and Raquel Martinez. For the first time, David's infant son would see his father perform.

Something seemed to click with David. He used his long arms to run the muleta in many series of slow, close passes. He was rewarded with a strong ovation and a turn of the plaza, and David Silveti ran to the center of the ring to embrace El Texano and to offer congratulations.

While David lay helpless upon the sand, the bull stuck its right horn into the matador's collar and again lifted him into the air.

A week later, David telephoned me to say that he had returned to his training and was determined to make a comeback. The author invited him to California, where we could discuss it in person. During the visit, this reporter taped an interview with him.

What happened to you, after Mexico City?

I thought I was going in there and either come out with ears or be carried out on a stretcher. It didn't happen that way. I didn't come out with ears, but I did it. I was confirmed. It was over with. I was sick and tired of the politics, I was so drained of it, I didn't care what the next step was. I was the only American that had confirmed there, but I knew that it should have been John, Diego, Robert, or Corey. I couldn't help it; that's the way things sometimes happen. I flopped. I did my best, and that was all I could do.

Afterward, you went into a gray funk. Not for just a period of weeks or months, but for nearly two years. You were playing the part of the great retired figura, *in Texas. You discovered girls and booze; you were emulating a playboy. What happened? What were you thinking of?*

I was just full of it. I was tired of it. I had a lot of feelings I had to drink away, and just plain forget about everything. I just had to be me. Not El Texano. Just David Renk. I did a lot of things that I hadn't done in my life. I had to get a new meaning, to do something else and not have to worry about getting up in the morning and going out to

In Gilroy, David performed with Raquel Martinez and Armando Soares. At the left is Ciego Múñoz, Raquel's manager.

train. Even in those fights in Dodge City, I didn't train, even once. I couldn't get out of the lull. I was in such a low state, it didn't matter. I didn't give a damn.

In the fights that you got, you bombed.

I bombed. Totally. I bombed in Gilroy, twice in Dodge City, twice more in Gilley's. I didn't want to bomb, but I just couldn't get myself back in the groove to be ready for those fights. It wasn't me. I wasn't myself. I wasn't the torero that I should have been.

Was it the failure to triumph in La Plaza Mexico?

It was the pressure, the release of the pressure. When I walked out of Mexico City, I knew that I had done very poorly. I was ready to fight. And, if I had had a good group of bulls ... but I was glazed over with the fact that I was there. The plaza was heavy on my shoulders. After that, I got home, it was over with, man. I got through it. I had so much pressure relieved, I let loose, I had to get away and not have to think about it, not having to think that I have to fight in two weeks. I started working in the restaurant, I'd stay out, all night, I wouldn't get to bed till dawn, and get up at nine o'clock in the morning to go to work. I had always had that burden on my shoulders of I've got to be ready for my next fight, 'cause I've got to please the old man, and I've got to cut ears, so I can get another fight, so I can please the old man, again. It was over. I got to that point. I confirmed. He got me there. He paid the money. And, I guess that was what really blew it all out of the saddle. Then, I flopped and disappointed him. I disappointed you. I disappointed everybody.

At that point, your father told you, "I'll finance your career to the confirmation, and after that, you're on your own." And, the fact that he was out of money afterward, how did you feel about that?

It's kind of cold, but he did what he wanted to do. He wanted to get me there, and I felt I did my part by being there, all the way through to that point, and I was the one out there with the bulls, but I hadn't earned being there. He got me there, I didn't get me there. The next time I step into that ring, it'll be a different story. You don't respect the things that people give you. You have to earn them. I have to earn my own respect, to prove to myself that I deserve to be in the ring.

After the Gilley's fiasco, I sent you a pretty vicious letter. I asked you if you really wanted to be remembered as the best North American matador in Reynosa history. How did you accept that?

At first, it was hard. But, I like those who tell it like it is. I guess that when you sent me that letter, we were supposed to go to Spain, but, I wasn't ready for that. You've always told me exactly what you thought. You've always told me what a bear does in the woods. And, I looked down on myself, 'cause I couldn't give you the same respect, the same honesty.

So, what has happened? All of a sudden, you've decided that you want to do it, again. And, according to the reports that I've heard, and what David Silveti told me about your last fight in Houston, you went out and fought with a brand of dedication that hadn't been seen in you since you were a novillero. What happened?

I don't know. I'm married. Got a little baby, somebody to carry on for me. Now, I'm ready to go out there and do it, because now I hunger for it. The gusano is still there. The gusano never dies. He may have gone to sleep for a while, for a very long winter, but he never died, and now he's waking up and starting to eat away.

Are you ready, at this point, to pay the price that it's going to take to make it as a professional, full time torero?

I feel that now, if I could have five fights in a row, in five weeks or less, or even ten weeks, I would fight like nobody has ever seen. I know that.

Are you ready to accept the fact that you're liable to fail?

No.

David was ready for a comeback. But, still another tragedy would challenge him. His mother's diabetes became critical. The doctors said that without a kidney transplant, she couldn't make it. Realizing that with only one kidney it would be too dangerous to continue his bullfighting career, David checked into the hospital anyway to donate one of his kidneys. His mother's life was of far greater importance.

But, her surgeons wouldn't allow the operation. Her heart was too weak; she could not survive it. It was decided to perform a quadruple bypass on her. Then, six months later, if she had regained enough strength, they would do the kidney transplant. They performed the bypass surgery. But, Barbara's health did not improve. She lay, expressionless and wordless, staring straight ahead, in her hospital bed.

A few weeks later, David accepted an opportunity to fight in Matamoros, where he registered an impressive triumph, winning two ears.

In the meantime, Barbara's condition worsened. She had suffered so much, for so long. That wonderful smile of hers disappeared. She had obviously lost her will to live. In mid–March of 1989, at 44 years of age, she died.

A few days after the funeral, David traveled to Matamoros to perform in a *mano a mano* with a rising Mexican star, Roberto Miguel. At David's request, the afternoon was dedicated to Barbara Renk.

The bulls were large and old, and as luck would have it, the picadores' horses didn't show up. The two matadors were afforded the opportunity to bail out.

"I can't speak for Miguel, but I want to fight. And, if he doesn't want to, I'll kill all four bulls, even without pics," El Texano said. Afforded no other choice, Miguel also agreed to perform.

The experience David had fighting un-pic'ed bulls in the bloodless bullfights would turn out to be a great asset. As he had in Mexico City, when he honored his deceased grandfather, David — wearing a black ribbon of mourning on his left arm — initiated the afternoon by going to the center of the arena, kneeling, and dedicating to his mother.

Who knows what inspired him? What kind of magic suddenly became apparent in the work of David Renk? Not even he could answer. In any case, the crowd was treated to a serendipity. A new dimension of excellence was obvious in the repertoire of El Texano.

Always a good technician and possessed of great courage, in this action David demonstrated a new depth of art that most aficionados had not realized was within him. His muleta passes were accomplished with great rhythm and tempo, more slowly than ever before. His entire presence in the ring was punctuated by an enormous gentleness that translated to grand art. These were big, strong, unpic'ed bulls, and David handled them as if he were training with calves on Don Arturo's ranch. He killed each with one sword placement, winning an ear from each, while Miguel was able to garner only applause.

The news of the exceptionally dangerous triumph made practically every Mexican newspaper. David Renk was back on top of it. And now free of thoughts of retiring, but determined to be successful as a tribute to his mother's memory, he was more enthusiastic than ever. But, the Mexican empresarios refused to be convinced. For the next several years, David worked as frequently as possible, but there were no opportunities in the big, important plazas.

It was then that David realized another moment of truth. March 21, 1999: The bull of brave blood exploded from the gates of fear. The black-eyed bovine eyed its adversary, as if thinking, "What does this skinny Yankee think that he's doing, here? Have I spent four years, waiting for this day, only to be confronted by a spangled mosquito?

The 6' 4", 136-pound Texan in the tightly-fitting gold and silk suit of lights threw back his head and challenged the killer bull. "Aha, toro! Aha!" he shouted. The animal attacked, viciously, its anxious horns shining in the sun. Slowly, the young man, who a moment before had seemed so gawky and frail, enveloped the deadly creature into his cape and lead it through a serenely graceful Verónica.

"Aha!" he yelled, again. "Aha, toro! Venga!" (Come!)

And, at the end of the afternoon, while the plaza band played *Las Golondrinas*, the traditional song of farewell, Fred and David Renk walked to the center of the ring, where Fred removed the pigtail from the back of David's head. Father and stepson took a turn of the ring, together, both of them weeping. Then, David took one last vuelta, by himself, as the crowd showered him in flowers and wine skins.

It had been David's *despedida*, his final performance in the suit of lights. And, his friends and family could only wonder, if the empresarios had allowed David to compete on a level playing field with others of his profession, if they had granted him the opportunities that he so desperately wanted and so very much deserved, if they had allowed him a chance to redeem himself in La Plaza México… It seems that the world of bullfighting is filled with ifs.

CHAPTER 9

The American Matador with a Portuguese Heritage

Dennis Borba, ready for action.

The forcados are a Portuguese tradition. After the rejoneador(a) has finished his/her work, the forcados line up, single file, and challenge the animal. The first in line encourages the bull to attack him, then leaps upon its head; the remaining forcados then jump atop the first one, and wrestle the toro to a standstill. The forcados take turns being the first in line. *Note:* The horns of the bulls assigned to rejoneadors are legally shaved (blunted), to help protect the horses.

As in the case of David Renk, Dennis Borba was raised within a taurine environment. But, Borba's upbringing was within California's sizable Portuguese community. His grandfather bred fighting bulls in the Azores. And, his parents own the first fighting bull ranch in the United States. The animals of brave blood that they breed in Northern California are used in Mexican bullfights and in the bloodless affairs that are popular in the United States. Borba's herds have been well received by aficio-

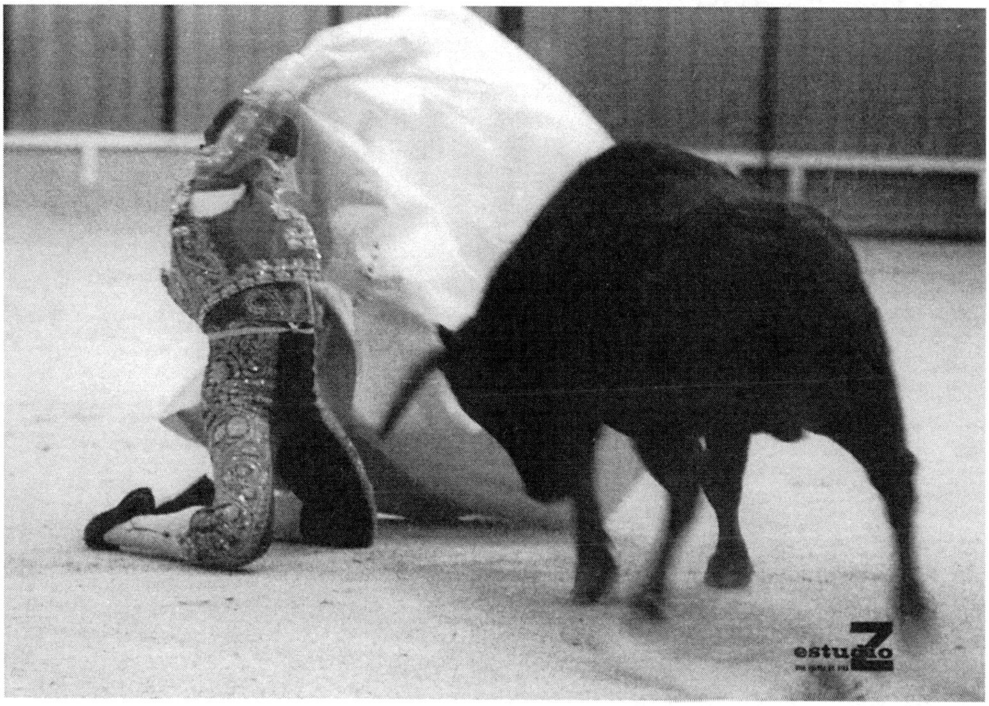

Borba, performing a *farol de rodillas* with a novillo in Villa Fraca de Xira, Portugal.

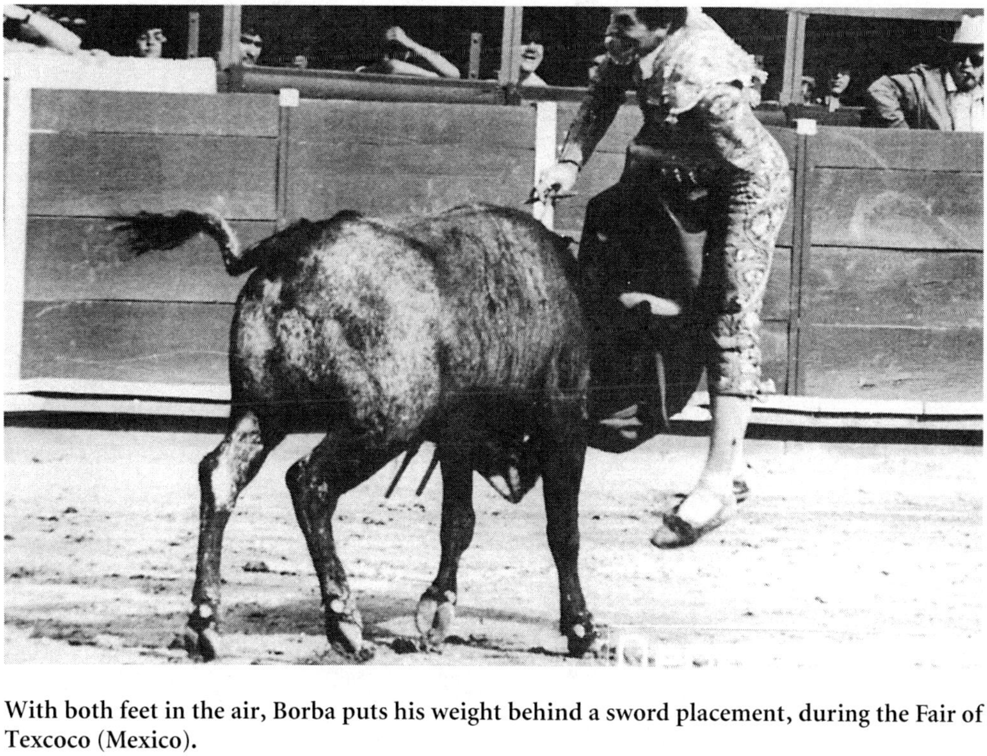

With both feet in the air, Borba puts his weight behind a sword placement, during the Fair of Texcoco (Mexico).

As a matador, Borba triumphed in Lima, Peru, winning an ear.

Dennis Borba (center) became a full matador on March 27, 1986, receiving his alternativa in Mazatlán, Sinaloa, Mexico. His sponsor was Manolo Arruza (right), while the witness was Jesús Jiménez, "Chicuelín." Borba won the only ear of the afternoon.

nados, toreros, and empresarios in Mexico. Two Borba animals have received the life-sparing *indulto* in Mexican bullfights.

Dennis' brother, Frank, Jr., was an amateur torero. Frank and his brothers were *forcados*, courageous, young Portuguese men who perform with rejoneadors. In Portugal, the bulls are not killed, but those presented to rejoneadors sport horns that are legally shaved (cut back an inch or so to make them less dangerous).

So, when the rejoneador(a) has completed his/her performance, enter the forcados, who line up, single file, to receive the animal's charge. The first man in line throws himself upon the bull's head. While the bull responds by attempting to shake loose the forcado, the other men jump on the first forcado and attempt to wrestle the toro to a standstill.

Although forcados are steeped in history, their work is, nevertheless—at least outside the Portuguese community—a rather esoteric discipline, one that often results in serious, sometimes fatal, injuries. And many traditional aficionados, including this author, consider that what the forcados do, although obviously dangerous, is rather demeaning to the bull.

When he was only nine years of age, Borba's family took him to Portugal, where he saw bullfights in Lisbon. The family also traveled to the Azores, where Dennis was exposed to his family's heritage, and the boy became enchanted by the Portuguese culture and history.

Likewise, as has been the case with so many other Californians who have been bitten by the gusano of afición, Borba enjoyed watching Tijuana bullfights on television. When he reached the age of 16, Dennis announced that he didn't want to follow in his brothers' footsteps as a forcado; he wanted to become a matador. He trained in the tientas at his parents' ranch, and he performed in bloodless bullfights in California. His first public appearance was in October of 1978, when he alternated with the ageless Portuguese matador Armando Soares.

In 1978, with his parents' blessings, and intent on learning the taurine arts, he went to live in Mexico, where he performed in novilladas throughout the republic. He also performed in Portugal and the Azores. On March 27, 1986, he received his alternativa in Mazatlán, Mexico, facing bulls of Santa Rosa de Lima. His sponsor was Mexican Matador Manolo Arruza, while the witness was Jesús Jiménez, "Chicuelín." Dennis cut the afternoon's only ear.

Since then, Borba has performed in many corridas de toros in Mexico, South America, Spain, Portugal, Panama, and frequently in California. He has also performed in, or acted as technical director for, television commercials for such companies as GTE, the Chevrolet S-10 pickup truck, and Blue Cross/Blue Shield.

Although he has faced literally hundreds of bulls, just like other Yankees, Borba has found it difficult to obtain many opportunities to perform as a full matador in Mexico and Spain. He dreams of confirming his alternativa in La Plaza México.

Dennis Borba is a complete professional who has proved his mettle throughout the bullfight world. Now married to Luciana, a former Brazilian model, he's a family man, and he plans to enrich his children with the culture of bullfighting. He and Luciana manage the family's ranch of brave bulls.

Will his dreams be fulfilled? That's a question that only the fates—not to mention the politics of bullfighting—can determine.

Chapter 10

Tracy Viser: The Newest American Matador

Viser opens a performance with a kneeling cape lance. (Photograph by Guillermo Escobar.)

Viser, doing a fine *Verónica.* (Photograph by Guillermo Escobar.)

For some young men, being born into the family of a successful matador represents an obligation of his birthright to carry on the family name, by facing bulls for a living. But, most Yankee toreros weren't born to bullfighting; it was born to them.

In almost every case, some event, perhaps a film, a book, or a movie, enamored them to adopt the taurine life for themselves. Sometimes, such kids have launched their careers by accident, perhaps as a lark, something that would separate them from the madding crowd and which would, eventually, cast them within the dramatic role of those who answer the esoteric and unforgiving call of the Fiesta of the Bulls.

Harper B. Lee had never dreamed of becoming a torero until somebody convinced him that it was something that he could do. Neither did Sidney Franklin, who, attempting to escape a brutish father, found himself emersed within the taurine profession.

John Fulton was looking forward to a life as a fine artist and illustrator. But, the film *Blood and Sand* inspired him to seek membership in the world's most difficult, dangerous, and exclusive fraternity. It was a similar case for Robert Ryan. Both Fulton and Ryan saw something magic in the taurine life, something that they could serve, and which, in turn, would serve them in their roles as creative artists. Both were proven to be correct.

After seeing their first bullfight, Diego O'Bolger and Richard Corey saw something that they could do, would do, *had* to do, in spite of the danger, and in spite of the overwhelming odds against their realizing success. It was the same case with Raquel Martinez. David Renk and Dennis Borba were the lone exceptions; they were raised within taurine environments.

Indeed, many young men and women who, although not making it to matadorship, were nevertheless inspired and vital-

In Saltillo, Mexico, Viser runs the hand long in a dominating *derechazo*. (Photograph by Guillermo Escobar.)

ized by the tantalizing illusion of romance and fleeting glory that only the world of sand, bulls, danger, and cheering crowds could provide. The gusano bit them, hard, and they could not ignore its tempting illusion, even when they realized that the seeking of enduring triumph would be a fruitless gesture, that genuine success would never be closer than just barely out of their reach.

Still, they had to give it a chance. Anything less than total commitment would result in love that would never be afforded a chance to be requited. As Alfred Lord Tennyson wrote, "'Tis better to have loved and lost, than never to have loved at all."

Tracy Viser still lives for his dreams. He still has faith that, eventually, the bullfight world will come to recognize that he deserves an opportunity either to prove himself or die trying.

He was a student at Conroe High School, in Houston, when the gusano first began nibbling at his psyche. As are Fulton and Ryan, Tracy is a fine artist. He didn't anticipate, though, that the first genuine test of his artistic talents would be with bulls, rather than canvas.

While in his high school library, researching bullfight photos for an art project, Viser came across John Fulton's outstanding book, *Bullfighting*. For Viser, it was an epiphany. It had never crossed his mind that an American, especially an artist, could become a professional torero.

He wrote to Fulton, at his art studio in Sevilla, asking for assistance in becoming a torero. John wrote back, warning Tracy of the costs in blood and toil that are

In Torreón, Mexico, Viser triumphed by offering excellent *derechazos*, such as the one pictured. (Photograph by Guillermo Escobar.)

the dues that must be paid for pursuing the taurine life. He suggested that Tracy read Luis Spota's *The Wounds of Hunger*, a novel that depicts the hardships of young, struggling toreros. If anything could dissuade Viser, that fine work should accomplish the job.

Undaunted, Viser again wrote to Fulton, pleading for assistance. A few weeks later, the matador from Philadelphia telephoned him from Dallas, where Fulton was exhibiting his art. He and Viser met, and John invited the teenager to visit him that coming summer in Spain. Viser accepted the invitation, saved his money and went to Spain, where he trained with Fulton and received his first experience with the horns, during tientas at bull ranches.

After returning to Texas, Viser—firmly committed to the notion of making bullfighting his career—made friends with another aspiring Yankee novillero, Kirk Farrell. The two trained together at every opportunity.

He also met Rudy Martinez, an ex-novillero with whom he performed in several taurine festivals in northern Mexico. Then, in 1978, Viser debuted in his first novillada, and in so doing, discovered the inflexible underbelly of bullfighting: the omnipresent politics, the bribes to bullfight critics, the corruption, and the financial costs that are demanded of toreros who seek opportunities.

He moved to Mexico City, where for two years he trained with Diego O'Bolger and lived a very Spartan lifestyle. He fought in ten novilladas and numerous festivals, including some in very seedy Mexican pueblos. He even performed in the Nuevo Laredo prison. His accommodations were not in a hotel, but a jail cell. On another occasion, he was contracted to fight in the Mexican drug country of

An excellent chest pass crowns a set of *muletazos*. (Photograph by Guillermo Escobar.)

Michoacán, where the crowd came fully armed with pistols, machine guns, and M-16s.

But, his artistic successes in the ring didn't translate to financial triumph. He wasn't earning enough money to make a decent living. He simply lacked the resources to continue his career. Disappointed and disillusioned, he impulsively quit bullfighting and joined the army, where he became a paratrooper in the 82nd Airborne Division and participated in the invasion of Grenada. Perhaps, he hoped that the military experience would kill his gusano.

After being discharged from the army, Viser decided to put bullfighting out of his mind and heart, settle down and really get his head on straight, to dedicate himself to a more rational vocation. He registered for college as an art major. But, after only one day on campus, he realized that bullfighting was so deeply etched into his mind that he would never be content until he gave it another try. He returned his books to the college store and once again headed for Mexico.

From 1984 through 1986, he fought wherever he could find an opportunity. In 1986, he performed in 14 novilladas, mostly in small towns and tourist venues, for very little money. Nevertheless, feeling confident and ready to make his mark in Spain, he returned to the Iberian Peninsula. But, after a full year, he had found opportunities in only two novilladas and a couple of festivals. He began to understand the type of discrimination that had held back John Fulton for so many years.

So Tracy returned to Texas where he and Kirk Farrell, assisted by a group of Houston lawyers, formed Fiesta Brava, Inc., which sponsored bloodless bullfights in such cities as Dallas and Houston; Phoenix, Arizona; Birmingham, Alabama; and Santa Fe, New Mexico. But the powers in control of Mexican bullfights aren't much impressed by those toreros who work in bloodless bullfights in the United States. They simply wouldn't allow Viser to receive his professional doctorate in the Aztec nation.

Still, he wouldn't give up. It took several years, but Tracy's dedication finally paid off. With 91 novilladas to his credit, Viser became a matador de toros. The alternativa took place on July 20, 1997, in Plaza de Toros La Morena, in San Joaquín, Venezuela.

Today, Tracy and his wife, Tammy, and their child live in Houston. Tracy has graduated from college and owns a vending machine business. He trains every day and is anxious to once again ply his talents in Mexico. Whistling past the cemetery, he predicts a bright future, ignoring the realities of a deck that, because of his Yankee heritage, is stacked against him.

Section III

The Women Bullfighters

Introduction

The bullfight world is one with some treacherous prejudices, not the least of which is male chauvinism. Women are patiently tolerated, as long as they sit in the stands and unobtrusively observe the action on the sand, covering their eyes, of course, at the proper times. But, those women who are impudent enough to actually attempt to invade the male-dominated Fiesta of the Bulls as performers, rather than mere shrinking violet spectators, have usually been considered nothing more than frivolities, not to be taken seriously.

"Oh, she isn't bad, for a woman," is the typical comment.

In only very few instances has any woman been considered talented and courageous enough to actually compete with men. Yet, hidden among the dusty pages of bullfight history are several references to toreras. Taurine journalist/author/photographer/college professor Dick Frontain, of Tucson, Arizona, discovered some fascinating stories which are related here.

The first reference to a torera was made in 1654, in Spain, but few details are available.

In Mexico, in about 1700, there was a black woman *charra* (Mexican cowgirl), who fought and killed from horseback. And, of course, art fans are familiar with the Goya etching of *La Pajulera*, performing with a toro, in the Zaragoza (Spain) arena.

In the 18th century, a nun, Doña María de Gaucín, left the convent and spent several successful seasons as a torera. A similar event was recorded at about the same time, involving a Peruvian nun.

In the 19th century, an attractive torera, Teresa Bolsí, dressed in a somewhat short, frilly dress, fought and killed a large, well-armed novillo. Her exploit was recorded by Gustave Doré, one of Europe's most celebrated illustrators.

In 1900, ill health forced Spanish Matador Antonio Escobar to retire in Mexico. Thereafter, his family was supported by his wife, *La Fragosa*, who fought frequently and well, killing hundreds of bulls over a period of 12 years.

Certainly, the most diverting epic was that of Augustín Rodríguez, a Spanish torero of limited talents. Using the name "La Reverte," and outfitted in drag, with stuffing in his chest, he appeared in scores of Spanish arenas. Between 1898 and 1908, La Reverte was very successful. When women were banned from Spanish plazas de toros, La Reverte revealed his true gender. But, as a male bullfighter, he was a total flop.

The first lady bullfighter to perform in Tijuana was Paula Soto, who appeared on January 8, 1905. On September 17 of that same year, five young women were presented in Tijuana. The lead from *The Union* (San Diego), the next day, read: "One young girl was tossed over a bull's head, another knocked down and trampled upon ... was the casualty record in the Tia Juana [sic] bullring, yesterday afternoon."

On the following Sunday, the same women put on a better show. One of the ladies, Ramona Segovia, did a stunt that had been common, earlier in the 20th century. She stood on a pedestal, three feet high, in the center of the arena, her back to the gate from which the bull entered. The bull rushed into the ring and stopped some 10 yards from the pedestal, and eyed it, curiously. Then, all of a sudden, the bull charged directly at the girl, but she never moved, and the bull stopped short, just before it would have reached her. He was then enticed away by the men, and Señorita Ramona scampered away.[1]

Such was known as the *Don Tancredo*, named for Tancredo López, a Spanish bullfighter who introduced it in his native Valencia, in 1899, after watching a Mexican experiment with it, in Havana the previous year. López' wife, Maria, attempting it in Madrid, was gravely wounded, and Orizabeño was killed while trying it.

Until the laws were again changed, the title of Matadora de Toros simply did not exist. The highest level attainable by toreras on foot was that of *novillera*. Several women of various nationalities, including North American, have been successful *rejoneadoras*, performing exclusively on horseback, in the Portuguese style. Unlike male performers in Spain, rejoneadoras were not allowed to dismount.

On May 30, 1968, for the first time, the doctorate of matadorship was granted to a female. As chronicled by *Clarín* magazine,[2] in the Plaza de Comalcalco, Morenita del Quindio, who was known as the "Empress of the Rings," received the alternativa from her sponsoring matador, José Ramón Tirado, while Matador Marco Gómez, her husband, was the witness. The bull of her doctorate weighed 490 kilos. Following her first performance as a matadora, she was awarded both ears and the tail. According to reports, she performed a suicidal faena to her second bull, cutting still another ear.

Born Bertha Trujillo, in Armenia, Colombia, Morenita attended corridas from the time of her childhood. As a teenager, she saw then-novillero Marco Gómez, "El Colombiano," and was captivated by his feats. They fell in love and, eventually, were married. The husband-wife team performed throughout the rings of the taurine countries of the Americas. Morenita received several gorings, one of which resulted in the rupturing of her femoral artery. On four occasions, she faced six bulls on the same day.

Since then, several women, including one Yankee, have — in spite of the prejudices against them — proven their mettle in plazas de toros throughout the bullfight world. The following are their stories.

[1]Clarín, *Vol. 7, No. 3, September 1971.*
[2]Clarín, *page 3, Vol. 4, No. 3, summer 1968.*

CHAPTER 11

The Blonde Goddess

Conchita Cintrón, in 1945.

Back in the days of Spanish yore, one of the most popular pursuits was riding to the countryside, to hunt feral bulls in their natural habitats, then to play them from horseback.[1]

Oh, they had grand times, those cavalier sons of royalty and their humble manservants. When a horse was toppled, serfs, waving blankets, lured away the bull from the fallen equine and its highborn rider. Once in a while, a serf would be killed while protecting his prince. But, so what? They were only serfs.

Unfortunately, royal blood was a rather precious commodity, and as so much of it was being spilled in pursuit of the bull-baiting sport, the king sought help from the Vatican. So, on November 20, 1567, Pope Pius V issued a papal edict,[2] excommunicating any Christian princes who should permit bullfights in their countries, and, incidentally, excommunicating anybody who might thereafter be killed by a bull.

[1]*Macnab, Angus,* Fighting Bulls, *p. 55, Harcourt, Brace and Company, New York, 1959.*
[2]*Carrie, Douglas B.,* Bulls, Bullfighting & Spanish Identities, *pp. 109–114, University of Arizona Press, 1962.*

Conchita was the beauty who tamed the beast.

popular attraction in all countries in which bullfights are held, although modern historians refer to rejoneo as the "Portuguese" style of bullfighting, for that style is the most popular among the aficionados of Portugal. And, it is not unusual for women to perform from horseback.

Easily the most famous of all *toreras* was the half–Yankee Conchita Cintrón. Dubbed "The Blonde Goddess," she practiced the timeless art of rejoneo—challenging, performing with, and killing bulls from horseback. But, she was equally as talented fighting on foot.

She was always a tough, feisty, outspoken lady, who was never afraid to voice her opinions. When, years after her retirement, the author asked her how she felt about toreras, she told me, "If women insist on fighting bulls, they should at least have the decency to do it from horseback."

Such a harsh proclamation stifled the enthusiasm of the royal progeny. But, the serfs weren't members of royalty, so they commercialized the sport, capturing wild bulls and transporting them to towns and pueblos, where they would build rustic rings in which they would play the animals. Such gave birth to the ancient art of rejoneo, horseback bullfighters.[3] To this day, it is still a very

She said it, but there is substantial doubt that she really meant it. For it was her own violation of the early Spanish laws against women toreando on foot that ignited one of the biggest controversies in Spanish bullfight history and brought her career to a premature close.

Wrote Orson Welles, in the introduction to Conchita's book, *Memoirs of a Bullfighter:*

[3] *Fraser, Allan,* The Bull, *pp. 101–111, Osprey Publishing, Ltd., Berkshire, England, 1961.*

> Conchita Cintrón ... is a very great rarity, indeed. Her record stands as a rebuke to every man of us who has ever maintained that a woman must lose something of her femininity if she seeks to compete with men. Conchita competed. Nobody was ever more perfectly feminine, and she triumphed, absolutely, in the most flamboyantly masculine of all professions.

Conchita's mother was a socially-prominent North American, while her father, Francisco Cintrón Ramos, was a Puerto Rican of Spanish heritage.[4] He was only the second Puerto Rican admitted to West Point, from which he graduated in 1918.

Conchita, born in Antofagasta, Chile, and raised within a privileged lifestyle, spent most of her early childhood in Lima, Peru, home of the *Plaza de Acho*, the world's oldest bullring. For her seventh birthday, her parents gave her a horse, thus initiating an odyssey that would result in Conchita becoming a beloved, international heroine.

Conchita's Spanish manager was renowned matador Nicanor Villalta.

At 11, she received her first formal lesson in equitation from retired Portuguese Rejoneador Ruy de Camará,[5] who, detecting natural talent in the young girl, became her Pygmalion. He taught his young protégée the disciplines of the art of horseback bullfighting and later managed her career. Although at first repulsed by the blood and brutality of the bullring, Conchita studied rejoneo as a natural part of her equitation training. At only 12 years of age, she made her first formal appearance in a bullring. But, it was all in fun. At least in the beginning.

In 1936, Ruy de Camará arranged for Conchita to perform a series of riding and rejoneo exhibitions in Portugal, where the bulls are not killed in the ring but are afforded the ignoble death of the slaughterhouse. But, just in case she might some day be called upon to kill a bull from the ground, Conchita learned to use the muleta and sword of the traditional matador. Prior to that time, for Conchita, the bull was only a tool used to demonstrate the agility and grace of the rejoneador's magnificent horses. But, performing on the animal's own level, she began to appreciate the beauty and nobility of Toro Bravo. And, her gusano of *afición*, which had been incubating in her psyche, was born into full-blown passion to make bullfighting her career.

So, after receiving the reluctant

[4]*Reamis, Huldine,* Cavaliers of Portugal, *pp. 67–68, Bantam, New York, 1966.*
[5]*Cintrón, Conchita,* Memoirs of a Bullfighter, *p. 16, Holt, Rinehart and Winston, New York, Chicago, San Francisco, 1958.*

blessings of her father, Conchita and Ruy de Camará went to Mexico for her professional debut—fighting both on horseback and on the ground—in Mexico City's *El Toreo* plaza.[6] She was only 15 years old. Although she was awarded no ears, she did well enough to get the aficionados talking about her. She was contracted to repeat the following Sunday and registered a triumph, winning an ear. The taurine journal *El Redondel* reviewed her work: "She was more a phenomenon in the truest sense of the word than all of the Belmontes that have been or are to come. Don't you think it extraordinary that this little girl of 15, who looked as if she were made of porcelain, not only fought like an angel, but was an expert horsewoman and a first-class rejoneadora?"

Astride her magnificent horses, Conchita projected great beauty and femininity.

The debut in Mexico City paved the way for a long, successful tour of the Aztec nation, one that was marred only by a pair of tragic afternoons. In one, a young novillero, Juan Gallo, was gored to death. A few weeks later, Conchita was on the card in Juárez, when Mexican Matador Alberto Balderas was killed. On still another occasion, in Portugal, shortly after the famous Manolete had been killed by a bull, Conchita was fighting on a card with Carnicerito of Mexico. Gravely wounded, Carnicerito looked at the torera and said, "Conchita, he has killed me." He was right.

In Torrecillas, Conchita's horse was hit and she suffered her first goring. As her assistants carried her to the infirmary, she regained consciousness, struggled out of their arms, and returned to rejonear and killed her bull. Later, she carried two ears,

[6] *Cintrón, Lola Verrill,* Goddess of the Bullring, *pp. 174–191, Frederick Muller, Limited, London, England, 1960.*

Opposite: **Outside her hotel in Mexico City, Conchita prepares to be transported to the plaza de toros.**

With the bull's horns only inches from her horse, Conchita Cintrón places a rejón in perfect position.

as she walked, unassisted, to the infirmary and the awaiting surgeons.

In her book, *Memoirs of a Bullfighter*, Conchita brilliantly summarized the feelings of a bullfighter, just before entering the ring.

> In the high-vaulted tunnel of the patio of the *cuadrillas* (where the toreros assemble, just before marching into the arena), isolated from the rest of the world, the agonizing transition from ordinary human being into torero begins. Not in the arena, but here in the patio, is where pain and fear exist. ... Here, where there is neither sunshine or sand, the bulls are not ordinary bulls, but fantasy beasts, which one moment charge as no other bull has charged, and the next moment turn into beasts, with no fighting form, at all.[7]

Conchita totally dominated Mexico. Then, Ecuador, Peru, Colombia and Venezuela were captured by her charms and abilities. Following her first big triumph in Bogotá, she was treated like a visiting head of state. She and her entourage were received by the Colombian president. Crowds mobbed her on the streets. Her hotel room resembled a florist's shop.

For her second performance in Bogotá, the military had to be called out to control the crowds. A music fan, complaining that a great, touring violinist had played to a nearly-empty auditorium, asked why such a huge throng had preferred watching Conchita to listening to the musician.[8]

"Because, you see, no violinist has ever been killed by his violin,"[9] Ruy de Camará told him.

[7]*Cintrón, Conchita,* Memoirs of a Bullfighter, *p. 172, Holt, Rinehart & Winston, New York, 1958.*
[8]*Cintrón, Lola Verrill,* Goddess of the Bullring, *p. 176, Frederick Muller, Limited, London, England, 1960.*
[9]*Cintrón, Lola Verrill,* Goddess of the Bullring, *p. 177, Frederick Muller, Limited, London, England, 1960.*

Conchita Cintrón was also talented with the muleta, although she wasn't allowed to perform on the ground in Spain. Here, in spite of a dangerous high wind that blows her muleta, she prepares to offer a *derechazo* to a huge bull.

Thereafter, Conchita offered a free performance to all of the children of Bogotá. Thirty thousand kids filled the stands. Conchita was brilliant, winning ears and tail.

Then, it was off to Spain, where, for the first time, Conchita saw Manolete. She, as every other torero who had ever seen *El Monstruo* (The Monster, Manolete's nickname) perform, was deeply affected by his quiet, statuesque style.

"I was surprised by the extreme seriousness of this torero, his grave austerity ... was totally different from anything I had seen, before. ... Erect and aloof, he let the bull pass and return as if he were unaware of its presence. ... Feet firmly planted in the sand, Manolete waited for the bull, for death, with what seemed like a sense of inevitability," she wrote in *Memoirs of a Bullfighter*.

But, contrasting her joy over seeing Manolete was her anger over the Spanish law prohibiting women from fighting on foot. It was even difficult, at first, to find opportunities for her to perform from horseback. The Spanish and Portuguese rejoneadors weren't anxious to work on cards with Conchita Cintrón. So, Ruy arranged for a corrida in Lisbon, in which Conchita performed, alone. She overwhelmed the crowd.

But, looming in the distance were the ultra-critical aficionados of the world's most beautiful bullring, Plaza de la Maestranza, in Sevilla, the heart and soul of Andalucía. In addition to being the cradle of Spanish bullfighting, Andalucía is horse country. Some of the finest horses in the world are bred in and around Sevilla, the most Spanish of all Spanish cities.

Following weeks of negotiations, Ruy de Camará and Conchita's Spanish manager, Matador Nicanor Villalta,[10] arranged

[10]*Cintrón, Conchita,* Memoirs of a Bullfighter, *p. 189, Holt, Rinehart & Winston, New York, 1958.*

Conchita Cintrón being interviewed by the author in Tijuana. (Photograph by William Bible.)

for the torera's debut in the Maestranza, where she would be allowed to place rejones and banderillas from horseback, then allow a *sobresaliente* (novillero understudy) to kill with a sword. As her presentation in Sevilla was so very important, she reluctantly agreed. Although she had a successful day, she felt that, as she hadn't killed her bull, her performance was incomplete.

However, de Camará and Villalta soon opened a tiny crack in the government's resolve. Conchita would be allowed to perform on foot, but only in informal, charity festivals, without pay. In spite of such restrictions, Conchita began registering tumultuous triumphs in the charity events, winning ears, tails, and even hooves. Spanish officialdom became concerned, fearing that public opinion might become too strong to ignore, so Conchita was thereafter forbidden to perform on foot.

Her horsemanship was spectacular and her abilities as a rejoneadora were as good as any of her profession, male or female. But, she still yearned to work on the ground, to show the Spanish aficionados that a woman could be capable with muleta and sword.[11]

Finally, that yearning became too intense for Conchita to ignore. In 1949, in Jaén, Spain, after she had accomplished a masterful performance from horseback, the public began to vociferously shout for the plaza judge to allow her to complete the performance, on foot. The petition was

[11]*Cintrón, Lola Verrill,* Goddess of the Bullring, *Frederick Muller, Limited, London, England, 1960.*

denied. Conchita rode her horse out of the arena, removed her spurs, and grabbed the muleta and sword from the young novillero who had been preparing to kill the bull. *Olés* echoed throughout the plaza, as Conchita performed series after series of muleta passes. The bull was brave and noble — too much so, she felt, to die. So, at the moment of the kill, Conchita profiled, then allowed the sword to fall to the sand. She dived over the horns, killing, symbolically.

As the cheers enveloped her, she strode from the arena, and the novillero re-entered to kill the toro. There was heavy petition for the ears, but the plaza judge refused to grant them. Nevertheless, the ears and tail were cut from the dead bull in spite of the judge, although Conchita didn't "officially" receive them. She did take several turns of the ring, accepting the enthusiastic cheers of the public. Naturally, she was arrested, but the crowd screamed for the judge, who was also the governor of Jaén, to pardon her. Finally, facing a possible riot, he granted the request and Conchita was released from custody.[12]

It was the last time that Conchita Cintrón would ever face a bull for the public.

Today, Conchita Cintrón, as ramrod erect and as beautiful as ever, and still possessed of a razor-sharp tongue, is a citizen of the world, although Peru claims her as its own. When she's not in Peru or Portugal, she lives in Guadalajara, Mexico. She is married, has six children, and maintains her interest in La Fiesta, which must lament the opportunity that it missed seeing one of history's finest, most honorable figures perform as only she was able.

Conchita Cintrón, the regal First Lady of Bullfighting.

Thanks are gratefully extended to Wayne G. Pearce, of Felton, California, whose computer skills were responsible for most of the photographs used in this chapter.

[12]*Cintrón, Conchita,* Memoirs of a Bullfighter, *pp. 264–266, Holt, Rinehart and Winston, New York, Chicago, San Francisco, 1958.*

CHAPTER 12

Patty McCormick: The Torera from Missouri

Although Conchita Cintrón was the most internationally-celebrated torera, and on numerous occasions demonstrated that she was quite capable of performing on the ground, she achieved her greatest celebrity as a rejoneadora.

Patricia McCormick, on the other hand, worked exclusively on the ground, and knowledgeable aficionados insist that she was superior to many of her male counterparts. Although it will never be known just how good she could have become, the fact remains that she was, some claim, the foremost female bullfighter. She was truly dedicated to her profession, performing in the Spanish *Rondeño* style, and refusing any consideration for being a woman.

Many other toreras have treated their gender as handicaps. They faced only smaller, less dangerous bulls, whose horn tips were shaved. But, Patty insisted on being treated as any other young, upcoming novillero, and frequently fought full-size, thousand-pound bulls.

Still, hers was a venture that had no chance for a happy ending. In the '50s and '60s, although she fought throughout Mexico and Venezuela, she had virtually no future. The title of *Matadora de Toros* simply did not exist. In Spain, as Conchita Cintrón had learned, it was illegal for a woman to perform, except from horseback. Had Patty McCormick come along 30 years later, she most certainly would have received the alternativa, and would probably have had an excellent chance to become a genuine star among all toreros, not just women.

She was born November 18, 1929, in St. Louis, Missouri, a venue that isn't exactly known as the birthplace of famous toreros. Like the outstanding Matador Jesús Córdoba, who performed as a Mexican and later became a Mexican

Patricia McCormick, torera! (Photograph by Philippe Halsman, New York.)

citizen,[1] Patricia McCormick spent much of her early childhood in Kansas, specifically Arkansas City, only 12 miles from Winfield, the birthplace of Córdoba.

While Córdoba was establishing his own reputation in the bullrings of the world, Patty was blossoming into a beautiful young woman, one who was recognized by the Mexican Matadors' union as a top-ranked novillera. McCormick and

[1]*Bitar, Alberto A., ed.* El Redondel. *2a Epoca, Año 1, No. 9, Editorial La Tauromaquía, Mexico, 1950.*

McCormick offers an excellent *Verónica* to her bull.

Córdoba met for the first time while performing together in a novillada. They subsequently became very good friends.

The daughter of Mr. and Mrs. E.B. McCormick, Patty was a typical little pigtailed girl who was constantly collecting menageries of stray dogs and cats. She was a genuine softy when it came to animals, certainly not the type who, bullfight antagonists might assume, would be expected to pursue a career in which the killing of animals is part of the job description. In fact, the love of animals is essential to taurine afición.

Patty's parents were born in Indiana. Her father, a graduate of Purdue University, was a civil engineer. Their plans for Patty cast her in the role of a refined, sophisticated, educated, young woman who would marry well and live happily ever after. The possibility that she would run off to Mexico to become a bullfighter was a remote, outrageous, and totally incredible notion.

As a child, Patty accompanied her parents on a vacation trip to Mexico City, where she saw her first bullfight. And, as has been the common denominator of so many other Americans— ordinary aficionados, as well as those who became toreros— she immediately fell in love with the pageantry of the plaza de toros. She announced that she would become a bullfighter. Her parents sloughed off the idea as merely the overactive imagination of a young girl.

In 1943, when Patricia was only 13, the McCormick family moved to West Texas, where her father became chief engineer for a major refinery. Patty enrolled at the University of Texas, in Austin, where she majored in music. She later changed her major to art and studied sculpting under Spanish sculptor Urbici Soler. But, although her parents had no suspicion of her extracurricular taurine activities, she began bullfight training under the tutelage of Alejandro del Hierro, who would later become her manager.

Fighting in Acapulco, Patricia performs on the right-hand side.

Here, McCormick performs a very difficult discipline, the ***Arrucina***, which was invented by Carlos Arruza.

McCormick takes a stance of triumph, after having placed the sword.

In August of 1951, in Juárez, she faced a bull for the first time, as the *sobresaliente*. She was allowed to do a set of cape lances, and was strongly applauded. But, when her parents read the newspaper accounts of her participation, they went ballistic. They pulled her out of college, although she lacked only 16 units for her degree. But rather than stifling her enthusiasm, their admonitions added fuel to her gusano. She ran away to pursue her real calling: risking her life in the bullrings.

As any other who pursues the bulls as a profession, she spent many months training on the ranches and preparing herself for her ring debut, which took place on January 20, 1952, in Juárez. That performance established her as a professional Yankee woman bullfighter.

By December of that year, sponsored by Mexican matadors Alfonso Ramírez, "El Calesero," and Luis Castro, "El Soldado," she was accepted as the only woman member of the union, and was granted the rank of Matadora de Novillos/Toros, a novillera, a previously nonexistent title.

For males, the title of novillero is a prelude to the alternativa and the official graduation to Matador de Toros. But not for Patty. It was simply unheard of, not to mention illegal, for a woman to receive the Doctorate of Matadorship. Nevertheless, as a novillera, she was expected to perform according to the same stringent standards and regulations as those imposed on males.

During the following ten years, Patty fought more than 600 bulls, thrilling the crowds with her courage, and impressing critics and knowledgeable aficionados with her artistry and technical abilities.

Likewise, as any other of her profession, she suffered her share of gorings. During her career, she was gored six times. One *cornada*, in 1954, brought her to the brink of death. The horn penetrated her vagina and continued up, into the intestines. It was such a severe wound, she received the Last Rites. She would, thereafter, be unable to bear children.

She recalled every moment of that tragic afternoon.

> It happened in Ciudad Acuña, in a *mano a mano* with Manolo Marqués, who was getting ready to receive the alternativa. He was a wonderful torero, very talented. Because he was being touted as a future great, it would have been very good for me to have a big afternoon.
>
> It was a hot, sticky day. I had kind of an omen, a very oppressive feeling. The bulls were six-year-olds, and when toros get that old, they also become erratic, unpredictable, and much more dangerous. They lose their naiveté. My first bull had a good charge and I was able to register a total triumph. I cut ears and tail. But, my second bull was awful, a nightmare creature, the kind that every matador hopes to never receive. It had a short, vicious attack. Half way through the pass, it would stop and search for flesh. It acted as if it had read the "Encyclopedia of Bullfighting," in three languages. My manager told me to kill it, quickly, without even thinking of attempting to accomplish anything artistic with it.
>
> But, I was young and overconfident. I had had a big triumph with my first bull, and I wanted to repeat. But, while attempting a chest pass, I miscalculated the distance. The bull caught me and carried me around the ring. I was impaled on the horn. I opened my mouth to scream, but I couldn't. When they finally got me off the horn, I wanted to return to my bull. It's kind of a thing with toreros. Although severely wounded, they always want to complete the performance. But, I couldn't.
>
> I remember being carried to the ambulance. At the hospital, there was

> one very rough, tough American nurse, who obviously did not approve of female bullfighters. She said, "Well, young lady, maybe this will teach you a lesson. For certain, it will be the last time that you'll ever fight bulls."

"There is nothing more that we can do for her," the surgeons said. They told her parents to take her home, to die. But, six months later, Patty McCormick returned to the rings.

Ten years after beginning her career, and having very little, other than scars, to show for it, Patricia decided to take a hiatus from bullfighting and to go on the lecture circuit. She never returned to bullfighting.

How good was she?

Said Mexico's great Carlos Arruza, one of the most famous toreros in history and the prime rival to Manolete in the 1940s, "She fights larger bulls than does any other woman, and ... she kills well. Her defect is that she is a woman."

Respected Mexican bullfight critic Rafael Solana told me, "She was the most courageous woman who I had ever seen."

Writer-aficionado Dick Frontain observed, "I have seen all of the contemporary toreras, and Patricia was easily the best of them."

In fact, all who saw her were impressed with her courage and artistry. But, their plaudits were always modified with "for a woman."

Today, Patty McCormick lives a quiet life in picturesque Pebble Beach, California. Her autobiography, *Lady Bullfighter*, covering the first 2½ years of her career, was published in 1954 by Henry Holt of New York.

She writes, sculpts, paints with water colors, and reflects upon a career that was doomed from the beginning. She realizes that being a woman and a North American represented two strikes against her before she even stood at the plate.

But, nevertheless, she did it. She went up against a foe that was more deadly than any bull, and a national obsession that doesn't easily recognize the abilities or courage of female bullfighters, especially Yankee ones. She left her mark on La Fiesta Brava. And, she has no regrets.

Chapter 13

The Amazing Taurine Odyssey of Harriet Elizabeth Dingeldein

Bette Ford offering a long *derechazo*. (Photograph by Olivar.)

Bette was a hit in Mexico City. Here she does a chest pass. (Photograph by Mayo.)

The story is almost a cliché. A beautiful girl from a small town is discovered as an actress and enters the glamorous world of stage, screen, and television. But, the odyssey of Harriet Elizabeth Dingeldein has a rather different twist.

She was born in 1937, in McKeesport, Pennsylvania, and raised by her father and an older brother. At 20, she was already making a name for herself on Broadway. But, she took a five-year hiatus from acting, in order to perform on

Bette performs an *estatuario*, also known as the pass of death. (Photograph by Canales.)

a far more dangerous stage: the plaza de toros.

Her afición was born in Bogotá, where she was doing a New York modeling assignment. There, she met Spanish Matador Luis Miguel Dominguín (one of the subjects of Ernest Hemingway's *The Dangerous Summer*), who introduced her to bullfighting.

After returning to New York City, Ms. Dingeldein married David Ford and became known as Bette Ford. The marriage lasted only nine months, perhaps because, although her acting career was going very well, as a regular on the *Jackie Gleason Show* and other live television programs of the early '50s, Ms. Ford's mind wasn't on acting and modeling, but on that bullfight that she had seen in Colombia.

"It was such a Hemingway time," she recalled.

So, the 5' 4", 100-pound brunette left a role in a Broadway play to go to Mexico City, where she entered bullfight training under the direction of Samuel Solís, Antonio Rangel, and Alfredo Aguilar. With Don Juan Bilbao as her manager, Bette Ford performed in a number of novilladas in the Mexican provinces.[1]

With only 13 months of experience, she was presented in La Plaza México and won two ears. Thereafter, in addition to several more appearances in that presti-

[1]*Bitar, Alberto A., ed.* El Redondel. *2a Epoca, Año 2, No. 25, Editorial La Tauromaquía, Mexico, 1959.*

With excellent form, Ford places a sword, in La Plaza México. (Photograph by Mayo.)

gious plaza de toros, she performed in all of the major bullrings in the Aztec nation. In her third year, she was listed among the 10 best matadors and novilleros who had fought in the Mexican capital that season.

"I cried when I killed my first bull. I don't think I could kill a man or an animal that couldn't kill me. I don't believe in hunting, because the animals are defenseless, but in the arena, that bull could kill *me*."

She estimates that she killed 400 bulls in her brief career. In the Philippines, a bullring was built in her honor. She was given motorcades, had meetings with President Magsaysay, and was awarded that nation's Citation for Bravery. There was talk of her being appointed American ambassador to the Philippines.

Her injuries were few, but painful: a broken lower back, both shoulders dislocated, and a goring in her left hand.

Bette Ford attributes her success in bullfighting to having maintained her femininity, and by not attempting to compete with male toreros.

"Bullfighting is a man's profession, but I was never in competition with men. I was more concerned with the bulls. To me, bullfighting was best described by Hemingway, who called it 'grace, under pressure.'"

She, as had her counterpart Patricia McCormick, wore the *traje corto* (festival outfit) rather than the formal *traje de luces*, which is traditionally a man's outfit.

She performed in a Warner Bros. film, *Beauty and the Bull*, which was

In the Philippines, Bette captured the hearts of the crowd and the country. She was given motorcades, had meetings with President Magsaysay, and was awarded that nation's Citation for Bravery. (Photograph by Constantine Mengason.)

nominated for an Oscar as Best Documentary. In 1958, MGM Studios brought her to Los Angeles to meet with screenwriters to do a movie of her life. It was then that she met John Meston, the creator of *Gunsmoke*. Ten days later, they were married.

"I promised myself that if I ever married, I would quit bullfighting. It would be too much to ask a husband to watch his wife, fighting bulls."

So, Bette Ford Meston bid adiós to the blood and sand of the bullring and initiated her career in films. And, she registered equally as many triumphs in acting as she had in the plazas de toros.

"As in acting, concentration is the ultimate key to bullfighting. I *acted* brave, and soon even convinced myself. And my fans. And, thank God, the bulls."

Among her many films were *Sudden Impact* and *Honky Tonk Man*, which starred and were directed by Clint Eastwood. Her television career continued to be highly successful, with roles on *Jack's Place, The Wonder Years, The Commish, SIBS, Fresh Prince, Dragnet, Hunter, Benson, Cheers, Divorce Court, St. Elsewhere, Falcon Crest, Rockford Files, L.A. Law*, and many others.

Particularly outstanding were her two appearances on *Cheers*, which brought her consideration for an Emmy, and her critically-acclaimed role on *L.A. Law*, in which she played "Rusty," an ex-porno queen, Douglas Brackman's older lover

Bette Ford is a popular star of stage and film.

and the mother of Brackman's sleazy stepbrother.

She has also enjoyed a stellar career on stage, doing *Virginia Woolf, Pal Joey, Lovers and Other Strangers, Angels Fall,* and numerous others.

But, her working mostly in New York while her husband was living in Hollywood was not a formula for a perfect relationship. Nevertheless, Ford's and Meston's marriage lasted nearly ten years. In 1974, she began playing house with real estate agent Scott Wolkoff, and nearly twenty years later, their relationship was still going strong. The couple lives in the upscale Southern California city of Toluca Lake.

From small town to New York City, to Bogotá, back to New York City, from there to Mexico City, then to Hollywood, back to New York, then back to Hollywood, with many exotic stops along the way, Bette Ford, aka Harriet Elizabeth Dingeldein, is a lady who knows where she has been and where she is going.

And, she has had a hell of a lot of fun on her journey. But, one can only imagine what she, and several other toreras, might have accomplished had women been allowed to receive the alternativa.

CHAPTER 14

Raquel Martinez: The Mexican-American Matadora

Young American sees first bullfight in Tijuana, Baja California, and decides to become a torero. It has become an almost commonplace story. Robert Ryan, Richard Corey, Rocky Moody, Jeff Ramsey, and who knows how many others all saw their first bullfights in Tijuana and became instantly addicted. And, they had something else in common. They were males.

Raquel Martinez could hardly be mistaken for a man. The attractive, very feminine, 5' 4", hazel-eyed blonde also saw her first bullfight in Tijuana, in 1969. And, as her male counterparts, she fell in love with La Fiesta Brava. But, where others have suffered discrimination because of their nationality, Raquel was given short shrift because of her gender.

A United States resident by choice, Raquel was born in Tijuana, Baja California. When she was three years of age, the Martinez family moved across the border to San Diego. Upon graduating from high school, Raquel became a flight attendant for a small Baja California airline. But, after a particularly harrowing flight through a hurricane, she resigned and returned home, by train.

In 1968, Raquel was working as an electronics technician for Honeywell, Inc., when some friends convinced her to see a bullfight. It was rather ironic that she saw the same corrida — featuring Spanish matador El Cordobés— that had inspired Richard Corey to become a matador. A new gusano of bullfight passion was born.

She began as an aficionada práctica (amateur), competing with other part time toreros/as in festivals presented in rather humble rings and witnessed by comparatively small crowds. The more frequently that she performed as an amateur, the hungrier her gusano became. Although she married in 1972, and two years later became a mother, she was determined to

Petite and pretty, Raquel doesn't look like somebody who would fight bulls for a living. Here she poses with famed author/photographer/professor Richard Frontain. (Photograph by Maria Frontain.) ***Below:*** Raquel performs a nice ***Verónica*** to a huge bull.

In Aguascalientes, Raquel fought a bull that weighed over 600 kilos and had horns like cathedrals. (Photograph by Saucedo.)

pursue her dream of becoming a professional torera.

Not thrilled by the thought of his wife going to Mexico to fight bulls, but convinced that it was something that she had to do, that she would never be content until she had given it her best shot, Bill Robinson, public relations director for the San Diego Police Department, reluctantly gave her his blessings. He had to be content with seeing Raquel and their young son, Scott Jacob, only three or four times a year, when they made visits to San Diego.

In one respect, Raquel came along in a more difficult time frame than had Patricia McCormick and Bette Ford. In the '50s, when Patty and Bette were popular, there were plenty of opportunities for those who had something unique to offer. Being a Yankee and a woman was a most unusual combination. But, due mostly to the retirement of El Cordobés, the biggest taurine attraction in history, the '80s were a down period in Mexican bullfighting. Far fewer novilladas were being presented. Costs had dramatically soared. Bulls were much more expensive, and top-seeded matadors were earning big money, leaving fewer profits for empresarios to invest in novilladas.

Two other realities played important roles. Toreras were no longer the novelties that they had once been. And, extremist North American antibullfight groups were becoming ever more vociferous and were succeeding in intimidating the print and electronic news media by threatening to promote boycotts against advertisers. Publishers and editors, choosing income over standing up for their First Amendment rights, feared reprisals for carrying

The matadora gives a right-handed chest pass.

anything about bullfighting. Such is still true today.

Raquel found a well-connected manager, taurine journalist and ex-torero "Ciego" (blind) Múñoz, who gained his sobriquet because of his Coke bottle–thick eyeglasses. With Ciego handling her publicity and business affairs, and Ciego's daughter helping to care for five-year-old Scott, Raquel fought in tiny villages and pueblos, where good doctors and medical facilities were practically nonexistent. Her successes in such places as Nochitlán, Pachuca, and Autlán eventually led to appearances in Mérida, Guadalajara, and Acapulco.

In 1979, Raquel performed in 40 novilladas. She worked 45 times in 1980. She had triumphs, and she had failures. In Guadalajara, she had such problems attempting to kill a bull, she inspired a near-riot; the police had to escort her from the ring.

While toiling in the minor leagues of bullfighting, she went through "shoot-outs, robberies, and I was even threatened, once, by the Guatemalan army," she recalls.

During a tour of Costa Rica, "The women, there, were parading in the streets, banging pots and pans, and cheering, in my support. It was like I was their hero, like I was giving them a purpose in life," she reflected.

She had only 14 novilladas in 1981, because on September 20 of that year she received her alternativa in Tijuana. She was the world's first official Matadora de Toros, a title that had only recently come into being in Mexico, and would soon be adopted in Spain. Several years earlier, Mexican torera Morenita del Quindio had received the alternativa, but the title was not recognized.

Cristina Sánchez, whom the world's press media mistakenly proclaimed the

Martinez gives a ***pase de trinchera*** (trench pass) to a large, black bull.

world's first matadora, came along many years later. Morenita del Quidio and Raquel Martinez preceded Cristina by two or three decades.

Bullfighting's traditional prejudice against women in the ring hadn't played a big role in Raquel's life as a novillera. After all, aspirants on the way up are in no position to argue about who performs on cards with them; they just want to torear. If presenting a two-headed novillero translated to ticket sales, the empresarios would gladly contract him.

But, it's a far different case with matadors. And, perhaps fearing the possibility of being bested by a woman, very few top-ranked Mexican matadors were willing to appear on cards with any torera, unless, of course, she were on horseback.

In her first year as a matadora, performing in Mexico and South America, Raquel cut 29 ears and a tail. But, it seems that the greater her triumphs, the fewer were her opportunities to perform. The growth of her celebrity could not overcome the unwillingness of front line matadors to work on cards with her.

By 1993, Raquel was performing only a few Sundays per season. It became ever more obvious that she would probably never be allowed to confirm her alternativa, either in Mexico City or Madrid.

But, there was one hopeful matador-of-the-future who looked forward to fighting on cards with Raquel. Known as El Rubito (The Little Blond One) de San Diego, Scott Jacob had witnessed most of his mother's career. By the beginning of 1993, he had performed in a few novilladas and showed great promise. Nearly every weekend, Scott would take a bus from Mexico City to San Luis Potosí, where he trained with cows on Matador Curro Rivera's ranch. Raquel and Scott hoped to become history's first mother-and-son bullfight team. But, eventually, Scott lost his desire to make bullfighting a career.

Raquel never made it to genuine stardom; neither did she earn impressive amounts of money. But, even those aficionados who aren't supporters of toreras must admit that Raquel Martinez endured and overcame enormous obstacles in order to follow her dream.

Raquel Martinez wasn't a bad torera. She was filled with personality and charisma. And, she faced animals that might have caused a few males to reconsider their decisions to become toreros. And, unlike Cristina Sánchez, Raquel was willing to endure the male chauvinism that resulted in an early retirement for Sánchez.

"I did it all alone, in Mexico, almost starving half of the time, like the old stories of poor kids, achieving riches by risking their lives to become matadors," she reflected. "And, if I could turn back the clock, even knowing ahead of time that the male matadors would refuse to compete with me, I would still do it all over."

Chapter 15

Ana de Los Angeles

Honey Anne Haskins was born in Los Angeles, of aficionado parents. As members of Los Aficionados de Los Angeles, they frequently attended the corridas in Tijuana in the late '50s and early '60s. There were plenty of taurine books in the house, and her father shot Super 8 films of the corridas. He even purchased a capote, because the *quites* were his favorite part of the corridas.

Although her parents rarely took the children to the corridas, Honey Anne's afición grew, and by the time that she was a high school senior, she thirsted for increased knowledge of La Fiesta.

When her parents divorced in 1973, Honey Anne and her mother moved to Mexico City, where the young woman hoped to write a book on bullfight photography, but she soon learned that to do so would require that she actually have first hand knowledge in the arena. She began training with a couple of novilleros and searched for an opportunity to challenge the horns.

But, as she had neither money or connections, chances were few and far between. She began hitchhiking to Tlaxcala to attend the tientas. Other days, she participated in festivals and attended taurine classes in the Restaurante Chucho Arroyo, which has an attached bullring, in Mexico City. In 1974, she fought in a formal festival there alongside such notables as Luis Castro, "El Soldado"; Alfonso Ramirez, "El Calesero"; Alfredo Leal, and Jaime Rangel.

She finally got an opportunity to perform in a full novillada, in the Plaza La Tapatía in Mexico City, and although she was very green and was tossed several times, she managed to cut her first ear.

That year, she fought nine times in Mexico, including one afternoon in which she performed alongside Matadora de Toros "La Morenita del Quindio." Honey, fighting under the name of "Ana de Los Angeles," cut the only ear of the day. Acting as judge that afternoon was the great Armillita, who was very complimentary of

Ana de Los Angeles salutes the crowd.

Ana de Los Angeles fought nearly 100 times in Spain.

Ana's abilities, especially how she worked the novillo with Verónicas from the red fence to the center of the ring.

But, she quickly became jaded by the politics of Mexican bullfighting, which deny opportunities to all but the wealthy or well-connected. She didn't have the money to pay for bulls and the necessary publicity. She was denied membership to the novilleros' union.

However, on one of those rare occasions when she was able to perform in a tienta on the Manuel de Haro ranch, she was noticed by Spanish matador Antonio José Galan, who convinced her to go to Spain. The prohibition against torearas had recently been lifted on the Iberian Peninsula. In 1975, Ana de Los Angeles sold everything that she had, worked for a while in Los Angeles, and was finally able to save enough money to travel to Spain.

She arrived in June, with half of the season already completed. Nevertheless, she was contracted to perform in nine novilladas that summer. Unfortunately, while training that winter, she suffered a severely broken wrist, and was in a cast for six months. She wasn't able to perform again until the summer of 1976, where she again fought in ten novilladas.

"I found Spain to be very different from Mexico. I was treated with respect and was recognized as a professional. I joined the union and I earned money. Nobody ever asked me to pay for the privilege of performing," she related.

She fought nearly 100 times, including the season of 1977, when she earned 52 ears and eight tails in 25 novilladas. She even won the mayor's trophy for a performance in Jaén.

But, her initial success did not include

Ana de Los Angeles earned 52 ears and 8 tails in 1977.

the promise of the alternativa. She was told that she performed beautifully, but that women never go anywhere in the taurine world. Disillusioned, she returned to Los Angeles in 1980. She fought, sporadically, in Mexico in 1981 and 1982, but once again, she had to pay to be included on the cartels. She just didn't have the money to continue.

She returned to Spain in 1990 to give it another try. She found a benevolent *apoderado*, Ricardo de La Fuente, a well-connected former empresario of the Plaza de Toros in Cádiz. Things began looking up. But, two years later, de La Fuente suffered a fatal heart attack. Afterward, Honey Anne discovered that, for novilleros on their way up, Spain had become just as corrupt as Mexico and was demanding that toreros pay for their opportunities in the arena.

She was finally forced to give up entirely, and returned to Los Angeles, where she began working in film and video. At this writing, she was working on a feature film for Non-Linear Productions.

Honey Anne Haskins became just another statistic, one of the multitudes of otherwise talented toreros/toreras who were never afforded enough opportunities to succeed, unless they were willing to pay for the privilege.

Section IV

The Novilleros

American Toreros
Who Failed to Achieve
Matadorship but Nevertheless
Left Their Marks on Bullfighting

Chapter 16

Porter Tuck, "El Rúbio" de Boston

Those who aspire to be professional toreros should be certain of their decision at a very young age, usually nine or ten years of age. By the time that a boy is 15, he should be an active, aspiring novillero, performing wherever and whenever he can, and spending plenty of time on ranches, learning everything that he can. After many years of starvation, the youngster seeks his alternativa, his doctorate of matadorship. That's when the real work begins. Only one of 100 aspirants ever make it to their alternativas. And, only one of 50 matadors earns a decent living from the profession. Of course, those who are successful can quickly become millionaires. Just as easily, they can suffer severe, career-ending gorings, or they can be killed.

Perhaps one of the potentially best Yankee novilleros, and certainly one of the most tragic figures ever to enter a plaza de toros, was Porter Tuck, "El Rúbio (The Blond One) de Boston."

Tuck's sister, Toni Christian, remembers Porter as a laughing, skinny, restless kid, whose interests were varied and who invested great enthusiasm in everything that he attempted. Ms. Christian offered the following anecdote as an insight to her brother's psyche.

"He got a BB gun for his birthday. And, after getting bored with shooting at bottles filled with water, he took aim on a songbird that was sitting on the roof of the house. He hit that bird with the first shot. It fell, slowly, bouncing a couple of times. He picked up the bird, stared at it a minute, then made a grave for it, complete with a marker. He never again touched the BB gun."

Reading and writing were among his major interests, with particular emphasis on history journals. He also loved poetry and music. But, it was the arts that held the greatest fascination for Porter Tuck. He wanted to paint, but when he couldn't find canvas or board of the size that he needed, he painted a mural of General George C. Custer and Crazy Horse — on his bedroom wall.

For a while, he dabbled in magic. He sent away for magic tricks and secrets, and spent hours learning to accomplish them. He delighted audiences by breaking eggs into their hats, and multiplying little red balls, with only a flick of his wrist. Next, came fencing. In a secondhand store, he found an epée, with which he practiced lunges and parries. According to his sister, "His biggest problem was finding willing opponents."

Porter attended military school, but hated it. And, although he vowed that he would one day join the Foreign Legion, he ended up in the U.S. Army. He was an intense youth, who always seemed to be searching for his role in life. And, he seemed to find it, when, after completing his obligation in the military, he went to Mexico, where he saw his first bullfight. He identified with La Fiesta Brava's pageantry and the gallantry demonstrated by the toreros. That was the turning point in his life. From that time, forward, his passion was the bulls. He was consumed with the determination to become a matador. But, realizing that the only proper place in which he could learn was Spain, that's where he went.

It was 1953. On a hill, overlooking Alcalá de los Panaderos, near Sevilla, he lived and studied with "The Bullfighter from Brooklyn" Sidney Franklin. Day after day, month after month, he worked with capote and muleta, honing his talents and pushing his tall, slender body to its physical limits.

According to those who saw him perform, Porter had an innate sense of grace. His body flowed effortlessly into the very definition of elegance. In his hands, *La Verónica* became poetry in motion. When he began fighting on the ranches and in the small, dusty pueblos, the aficionados were amazed at his courage, his art, and his determination.

Porter's hero was the immortal Spanish Matador Juan Belmonte. Years later, an old man in boring retirement, raising bulls with which others could win applause, or be killed while trying, Belmonte shot himself to death. His own gusano had killed him.

Tuck's career paralleled that of any aspiring matador. As a novillero, he fought wherever and whenever opportunities presented themselves. Sometimes, he was paid only his actual expenses; other times, not even that much. In 1955, he got his first big break, a contract in Madrid's secondary plaza, Vista Alegre. And, in that outing, he first experienced the pain of a goring. Blood soaked his lavender and gold suit of lights.

"Now, I am one with the bull," he told his sister.

His fame began to grow. Empresarios offered more and more contracts, and the name of El Rúbio began to be spoken in the dusty taurine bars, where the old aficionados congregate to swap memories and lies. He was offered a contract in one of Spain's most important plazas de toros, that of Valencia. The date was Sept. 25, 1955.

He performed well with his first bull, winning an ear, no small achievement in a plaza as tough as Valencia. Few cities can boast of aficionados as knowledgeable and demanding as the *Valencianos*.

His second novillo of the Don Cesareo Sánchez ranch was an excellent animal, with great bravery and an honest charge, and El Rúbio was registering a resounding success with it. The music played, while the *olés* resonated throughout the plaza. Then, as it is so prone to do, fate raised its deceitful head, and the results were horrifying. The bull drove a horn into El Rúbio's stomach, chest and lungs.

El Rúbio never again wore the suit of lights. Numerous surgeries were performed, but the damage that the horn had inflicted was too severe. His career was finished, just as it was getting into high gear.

In 1965, Porter Tuck, 33, was discovered, propped up against a tree, in a New York City park. The life of one of America's brightest hopes for fame and glory in the world's most treacherous profession had ended in tragedy. Not by the horns of a bull, but, as with Juan Belmonte, by a bullet in the brain. A pistol lay nearby.

Chapter 17

The Tragedy of Rocky Moody

Anybody who ever saw Rocky Moody perform in the arena insisted that the young torero had everything necessary to become a very successful matador. He was good with the cape and muleta, and excellent with the sword. If anything, he was just a bit too courageous.

Rocky was born in Colfax, Iowa, in 1932, and led the life of a small, farm town, *Summer of '42*–type youth. But, as so many other young people who grow up in such a torpid country environment, he yearned to get out, to make his mark in a world that didn't involve crops or livestock. At 16, he took a trip to California, and purely out of curiosity, saw a bullfight in Tijuana. And, as has been the passion common to so many other Americans who became toreros, he was immediately and completely captured by the intensity, drama and the excitement of the bullring. This, he knew, was something that he could do. *Had* to do. *Would* do.

At 17, he joined the Navy. Stationed in San Diego, he began attending Tijuana bullfights on a regular basis. A few times, he even went AWOL in order to see a corrida. But he was never caught.

His passion for La Fiesta Brava grew deeper. And, on one particular Tijuana afternoon, it got the best of him. He jumped into the ring as an *espontáneo*, dropped to his knees, and got off some of the most heart-in-throat passes ever to be seen in that plaza de toros. The crowd went wild! Rocky's small taste of glory was delicious, but very brief. The police grabbed him and began to roughly haul him off to jail. But two of the matadors on the card, Mexicans Pepe Luis Vásquez and Rafael Rodríguez, interceded. Thereafter, they became his mentors.

After he got out of the Navy, Rocky invested all of his money in a used suit of lights, some rather shabby capes and muletas, and an old, rusty sword. He dedicated

Rocky Moody prepares to perform a *derechazo* during a novillada in Juárez. (Photograph by Fred Renk.)

Here, Rocky performs a ***Mondeñina***, which was invented by Spanish Matador Juan García Mondeño. (Photograph by Frank Renk.)

Rocky prepares to receive the bull. (Photograph by Fred Renk.)

full time to training and preparing for his new career, one to which he was convinced he had been born.

"He was one of the most courageous men who I've ever seen in the bullring," reflected Pepe Luis Vásquez. "He seemed driven by an intense passion. And, he had natural talent, too."

Rocky became an instant hit in Juárez. Whenever the Iowan's name was announced on a bullfight card, the stands became filled with aficionados from both sides of the border. He was on his way. Within only another few weeks, he would receive his alternativa. But, fate has a way of juxtaposing dreams and nightmares. Tragedy struck, in dramatic, permanent fashion.

On July 20, 1958, alternating with Raúl García and Jorge Rosas, Rocky was gored in the inside of the right leg. The blood erupted as if someone had turned on a hydrant, full blast. His femoral artery was ruptured. His assistants rushed the hemorrhaging torero to the infirmary, but the surgeons were afforded no choice. The damage to arteries and muscles was so extensive, they had to amputate Rocky's leg.

For months thereafter, Rocky trained constantly, strengthening his upper body. He was determined to return to bullfighting, in spite of the prosthesis that he hated so much. But, it was not to be. All of the courage, heart, and talent in the world are impotent if the man lacks physical faculties. He performed in a couple of festivals, doing comparatively well, but his lack of agility was the harsh traitor that betrayed him. Finally, the toreros' association, afraid for his life, would no longer allow him to perform.

He became a permanent fixture in the Bar Sevilla, an aficionados' hangout in

Juárez. But, eventually, he could no longer tolerate being limited to only the perimeters of the bullfight world. Watching others perform served only to intensify his own frustration. He had to get away. Far away. Some place where clarions don't sound, where bulls don't threaten, fans don't cheer, and gusanos don't bite.

Embittered, Rocky moved to Mercier, Tennessee, where he became a bail bondsman. He also owned a small liquor store and a 14-acre chicken farm. But, he discussed bullfighting only with old friends and toreros. Somewhat paranoid, he trusted very few people, outside of his longtime buddy, Fred Renk.

In September of 1990, Rocky Moody died, a solemn, defeated man who never ceased cursing the fates that had denied him a greater opportunity for bullring glory.

CHAPTER 18

The Brainy Walter de la Brosse

Walter de la Brosse is probably a genius. He was only 15 years old when he graduated from high school, and under 18 when he completed college. He was a national swimming champion and a contract player for 20th Century–Fox. Between acting parts, the blond, blue-eyed glamour kid worked as a lifeguard at the very exclusive Ambassador Hotel in Los Angeles.

Somewhat arrogant and cocky at the time, Walter was ensconced within the glitzy Hollywood movie scene. Among his friends were Brian Keith, Ricky Nelson, Stephanie Powers, and Peter Brown. Especially in the '60s and '70s, attending Tijuana bullfights was the "in" thing among members of the Hollywood *dolce vita* set. So, on most summer Sundays, Walter, flanked by glamorous, human icons of the film capital of the world, could be found in the stands of either of Tijuana's two plazas de toros.

He had it made. He might have become a big time movie star simply because of his connections with important film executives and artists, not the least of whom was John Wayne. So, why did he decide to give up his front row, shady side seat, in favor of getting down on the sand, to fight bulls? It just sort of *happened.*

"At first, when I began training with the capes and muletas with aspiring novillero Ruben Corrales, it wasn't with any thought of becoming a genuine bullfighter. It was good physical conditioning and I was an athlete. Besides, it helped me to better understand and appreciate the bullfights. Then, things began to snowball, and the next thing you know..."

Walter befriended Jaime Bravo, a popular matador of the blood-and-guts kamikaze style, who married a Southern California girl, Ann Robinson, and was on the "A" list of prominent people who were always invited to Hollywood social events.

Only a 16-year-old kid, Walter de la Brosse chose bullfighting over a potential career in the movies.

The blond novillero performs a *derechazo* during a novillada. (Photograph by Murguia.)

Walter tests his novillo's attack with a low pass on one knee. (Photograph by Estrada.)

"Jaime and I trained in Griffith Park, and he was a relentless teacher. Then, one day, he told me that there was an opportunity for me to fight as *sobresaliente* in a novillada in Durango, Mexico. I said, 'Sure, why not?' Hell, there was no graceful way that I could turn it down! In the fight, I was allowed to do a couple of lances with the cape. But, at the end of the afternoon, I was just glad to get out of the ring alive."

Walter de la Brosse performing in a festival in Tijuana.

Walter couldn't admit to Jaime Bravo just how terrifying the experience had been. And, a month later, the matador offered him another opportunity, as sobresaliente for himself and Mexican Rejoneador Gastón Santos, in Nuevo Laredo.

"I did better in that fight. And, the fans began calling me *güero* [light-haired one], a nickname that stuck," de la Brosse related.

Thereafter, Walter became caught up in a taurine whirlwind, and he began to enjoy the unique spotlight of the celebrity that always shines on those who face bulls. He had some triumphant performances in the Mexican provinces, as well as in a festival in Tijuana, in which two other aspirants, Robert Ryan and Jeff Ramsey, also performed. In the stands that day was La Plaza México empresario Dr. Alfonso Gaona, who later convinced Walter to get serious and attempt bullfighting as a career. Dr. Gaona had extended opportunities to several other Yankee toreros. He seemed to be searching for someone who could become a star in the ring, while at the same time being a powerful box office attraction.

Walter went to Mexico, where he began to register some excellent afternoons. He was showing signs of genuine talent and a successful future. Then came his debut in the important *El Toreo de Cuatro Caminos* ring, just outside the federal district of Mexico City. It was Christmas Eve of 1961, but Walter wasn't going to receive any presents.

"I screwed up. At first, I was com-

An *estatuario.* (Photograph by Carmona.)

De la Brosse offers an elegant, right-handed chest pass. (Photograph by Estrada.)

pletely lost with that bull. I seemed to forget everything that Jaime had taught me. Then, I got off some really good right-handed passes, and the applause gave me confidence and determination. I switched to the left hand, although Jaime kept yelling that the bull was no good on that side. All of a sudden, I was flying through the air. The bull had driven a horn deeply into the inside of my left leg. And

Following a triumphant performance during a festival in Tijuana, Walter de la Brosse is carried upon the shoulders of his fans. (Photograph by Constantine Mengason.)

somehow, I had fractured my jaw. People ran out to carry me to the infirmary, but Jaime Bravo ordered them to leave me alone.

"'Get up and kill your bull, or I'll just let you bleed to death!' What could I do? I got up and killed the bull. Then, I passed out. When I awakened, I was in the hospital, and tubes were running out of my leg. The horn had bruised my femoral artery."

Three weeks later, Walter was back in the ring, showing no apparent emotional scars from the goring. For the next couple of years, he performed throughout Mexico and South America, registering more triumphs than failures. And, although he suffered several more injuries, he gained experience and confidence. Dr. Gaona began to speak of Walter's debut in La Plaza México.

However, first, the Yankee novillero took a couple of weeks off. Back in Hollywood, the freeways proved to be more dangerous than the bulls. He was involved in a terrible auto accident and was temporarily paralyzed. And, although he managed to survive without being confined to a wheelchair, the doctors told him that his days of bullfighting were finished, forever.

It was somewhat ironic that, a year later, in 1966, Walter's *maestro*, Jaime Bravo, was killed in an auto accident in Mexico.

Walter returned to college and obtained a master of science degree in animal serology and a Ph.D. in equine reproduction from Texas A & M.

Today, Dr. Walter de la Brosse is a professor of horse husbandry who teaches at two southern California colleges: College of the Canyons in Valencia, and Chaffey College in Rancho Cucamonga.

And, he is a heavily-sought judge for horse shows.

He has no regrets about his former occupation as a torero.

"I gave it my best shot. I gave up a rather glamorous Hollywood lifestyle for one about two degrees above absolute poverty. I tried very hard and did a certain amount of suffering in the process, but it didn't work out. *Así es la vida* [Such is life]. But, at least, I did it honestly. And, it was worth it," he said.

Chapter 19

David Moss, Novillero

"The bulls, the bulls that make
a life without par for the torero.
And, at times, they collect."
— *Garcia Lorca*
(Spanish poet)

Still another Hollywood kid who left his mark on the bullfight world is David Moss, who is, today, a highly regarded theatrical agent.

A product of Hollywood's fluffy '50s, David's father was a film editor. But, after becoming involved in bullfighting, David abandoned the Hollywood scene.

"I saw my first corrida in Tijuana, around age 15. And, frankly, having no preparation or involvement in the bullfight culture, I was stunned. But, later, while serving with Squadron #155, on the aircraft carrier *Princeton*, we docked in Manila for some R and R. I saw a corrida, in a portable plaza, featuring Portuguese bulls and toreros, and I loved every minute of it!"

In 1955, after returning home from Korea, where he had served with an attack squadron on the aircraft carrier *Princeton*, Moss went to work in the mail room at MGM. His parents owned a restaurant, The Cattleman's Steak House, in West Los Angeles. Moss and his group of Hollywood aficionados, including Rory and Lita Calhoun, Gilbert Roland, Robert Stack, and Jeff Hunter, often attended the corridas in Tijuana. He began learning the disciplines of toreo while working out with amateur toreros in Roxbury Park.

"Even James Dean joined us in prac-

David Moss offers a statuesque *estatuario* to a bull in Avila, Spain.

tice, and he showed some aptitude with the capote."

Thereafter, David's parents allowed him and his brother to convert a storeroom at their steak house into a Spanish motif hangout for aficionados. It attracted fans and visiting toreros, including Carlos Arruza, Antonio Velásquez, Alfredo Leal, Luis Miguel Dominguín, Cayetano Ordoñez, Carmen Amaya and her dance troupe, and flamenco dancer José Greco. Eventually, the hangout even influenced the steak house, which became El Matador.

Living around toreros and attending corridas in Tijuana had a heavy impact on young David. Assisted by matadors Jaime Bolaños and Antonio Velásquez, David began appearing as sobresaliente for those two famed toreros. He went to Mexico City, where he shared a room with *aficionado práctico* (amateur torero) and budding film director Tony Brand, who had been the main guitarist at El Matador. The two trained together and attended tientas at famous Mexican *ganaderías.*

But the land of real opportunity for toreros was Spain. So, in November of 1957, David — with only a few hundred dollars in his pocket — traveled to the Iberian Peninsula. After spending the winter in Madrid, he moved to Sevilla, where he met John Fulton. Walking, riding third class buses, and sleeping on the ground, he and other *maletillas* starved while participating in tientas throughout Andalucía.

Alongside Dominguín and another matador, Antonio Borrero, "Chamaco," he ran with the bulls in Pamplona's *Feria de*

Holding his ground, David Moss accepts the bull's return attack with this splendid *pase por alto.*

San Fermín. (Later, Dominguín and Chamaco fought those very bulls.) He began to absorb the complicated techniques of dealing with brave bulls. His talents grew. He began to feel like a torero.

To feed his new passion, he worked in a few American films, including *King of Kings,* playing the Apostle Philip, opposite Jeffrey Hunter's Jesus. And finally, in 1960, his first genuine opportunity in the ring was presented. One of the novilleros who was scheduled to perform in a novillada in Murcia was injured, and David was offered the opportunity to fill in for him. He was applauded for his efforts to his first bull. Then, with his second bull, he cut the first ear of his new career, and left the ring on shoulders.

Thereafter, through 1964, David performed in 30 novilladas, in Castillón de La Plana, Soria, Ávila, Badajoz, Tafalla, Arevalo, and other provincial towns.

Then, on July 16, 1964, in San Sebastián de Los Reyes, he suffered his first taste of the horns. His first novillo nearly ripped off David's right leg. The goring had two trajectories. The first, of 30 centimeters, entered from the rear, passing completely through his leg. The second trajectory ripped into the femoral triangle. The injury was pronounced "*muy* (very) *grave.*" But his life and leg were saved by the one-legged Dr. Máximo de La Torre, who had helped attend Manolete when that great star was killed in Linares.

But David wasn't discouraged. Only two and a half weeks later, he performed in a novillada in Arenas de San Pedro. His

In a festival in Toledo, Spain's "Plaza Antigua," David gives a right-handed chest pass to a young bull from the Doña Rosa ranch. (Photograph by Mateo.)

first bull tossed him, reopening his wound. But, he continued and cut two ears from his second bull, before retiring to the infirmary. He reappeared in Arenas de San Pedro, the next month, again cutting an ear.

But, his life as a torero would quickly come to an end. While training on a ranch, he was thrown to the ground and suffered the rupture of a disk in his back. He never totally recovered. In 1965, limping and emotionally devastated, he returned to Hollywood and opened his talent agency. Twenty-five years later, he had recorded still another triumph, this one representing stage, film and television stars.

He returns, as frequently as possible, to Mexico and Spain, to reflect upon his days in the arenas and to watch other young men deal with the bulls of brave blood. As anybody else who has ever faced the horns, only to be forced into premature retirement, David's gusano still bites him, and he wonders if, indeed, *así es la vida.*

Chapter 20

The Sad Saga of Jeff Ramsey

Dr. Alfonso Gaona (on right, in sunglasses) gave Jeff Ramsey an opportunity.

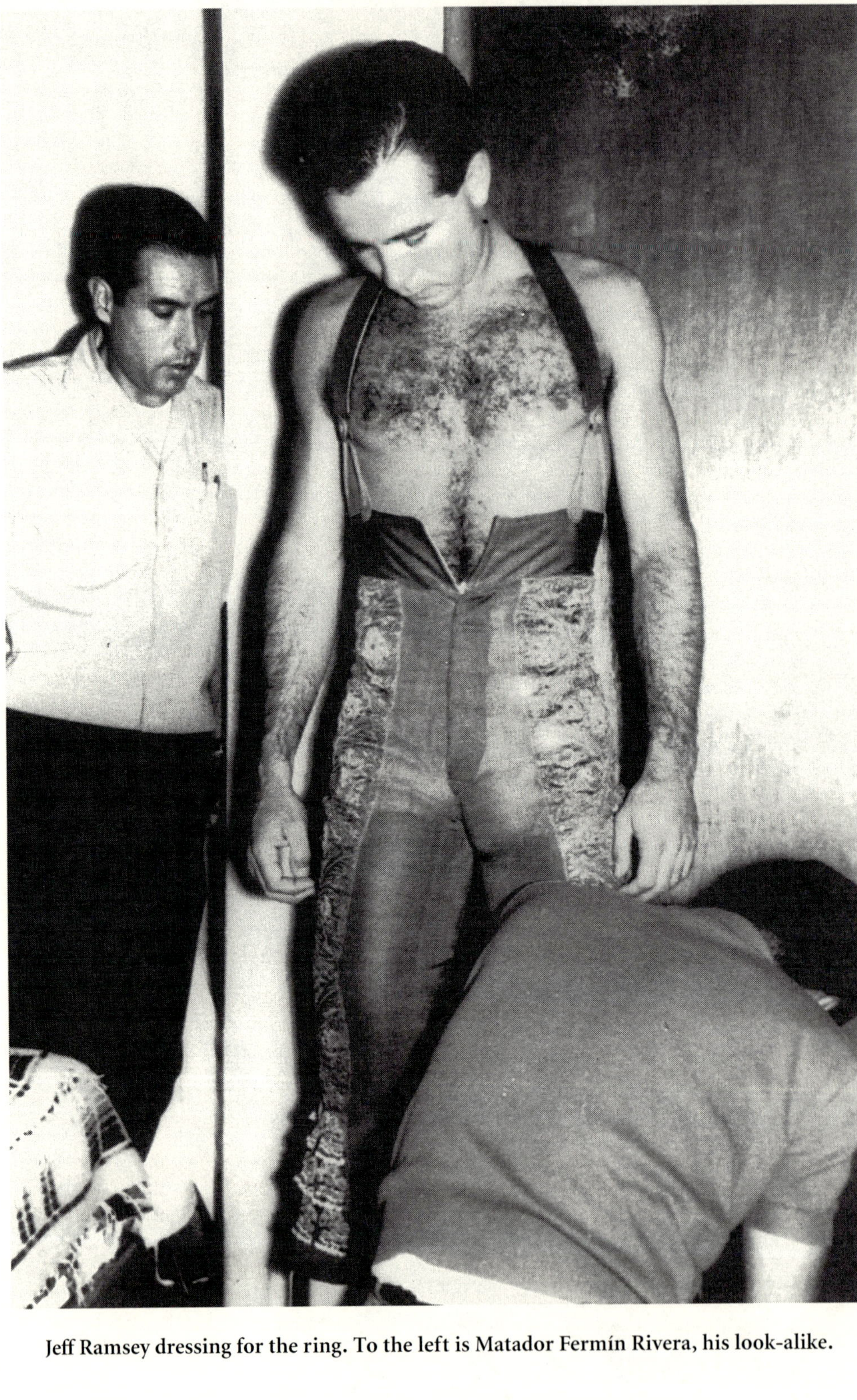

Jeff Ramsey dressing for the ring. To the left is Matador Fermín Rivera, his look-alike.

Jeff Ramsey's first suit of lights.

After graduating from high school in 1957, Jeff Ramsey was invited by his brother, Jay, to attend a bullfight in Tijuana.

"You'll experience something different and exciting," Jay promised. Little did Jay know that he was igniting in his brother a passion for bullfighting.

Jeff had worked as a wrangler on cattle ranches in Kingman, Arizona. He had even attempted a bit of rodeo. He had seen thousands of domestic bovines. But he had never seen animals such as those presented in the plaza de toros. He was overwhelmed by their strength and ferocity.

A ***natural*** **by Ramsey, in Acapulco.**

Only one of the afternoon's six bulls had been fought on that Tijuana afternoon when Jeff turned to Jay and said, "I'm going to do that."

Without any doubt that he would become a successful matador, and much to the consternation of his parents, Jeff went to Mexico City, where he met Antonio Toscano, brother-in-law of the great Mexican Matador Carlos Arruza. Jeff's first lessons took place in beautiful Chapultepec Park, where so many other aspirants had given so many imaginary, yet wonderful, performances, witnessed and applauded only by the trees and occasional passersby. Imaginary bulls always attack cleanly, and imaginary audiences always respond enthusiastically.

As with so many others who yearn for recognition, Jeff worked and trained, but found only closed doors. With the passing of time, the depletion of his money, and having realized no discernible progress in his adopted profession, Jeff returned, broke and disillusioned, to California. He moved in with Jay and worked as a gas jockey.

Realizing that it was probably a hopeless cause, Ramsey nonetheless continued practicing the disciplines of bullfighting. As fate would have it, he met future matador Robert Ryan, who arranged for an opportunity for Jeff to perform in a festival bullfight in Tijuana.

Although Jeff had virtually no actual ring experience, he jumped at the chance. And, on July 4, 1961, he demonstrated potential, albeit raw. In the stands that day was the famous Dr. Alfonso Gaona, the most important empresario of his day. As he also had done for Walter de La Brosse, Gaona saw the potential in Jeff and offered to assist him.

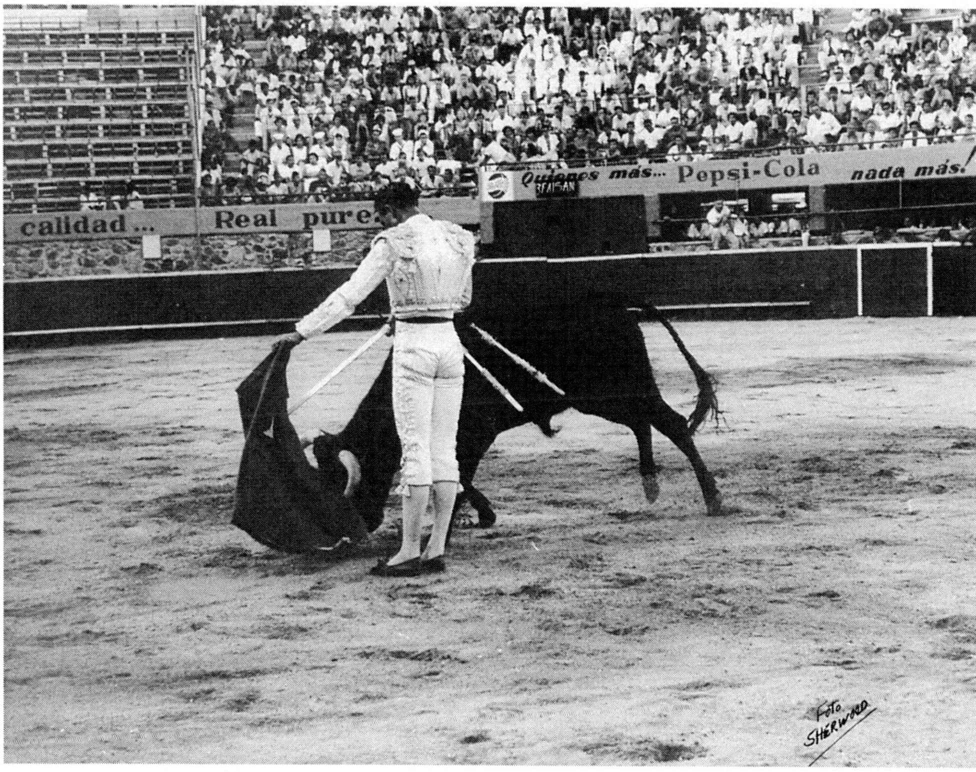

Jeff's first professional appearance was in Acapulco.

Less than a year later, Ramsey made his professional debut in Acapulco. Although he earned no ears, he tasted the sweet glory of being awarded a turn of the ring.

Before long, the taurine media began to notice an amazing resemblance between Ramsey and retired Mexican Matador Fermín Rivera, whose own son, Curro, was destined to become a top bullring star. After several stories appeared in the newspapers, Fermín agreed to manage Ramsey. He took him to bull ranches, where the Yankee was allowed to train with brave-blooded cows.

Thereafter came a series of novilladas. Ramsey's talent and confidence began to grow. And, for a few fleeting minutes, on one very special afternoon of 1963 in Orizaba, Veracruz, his dreams of success and glory were realized. Ramsey's ears-and-tail triumph was complete. He was on his way.

But then came a disastrous day in Puebla. Jeff was unable to kill either of his bulls. Each was returned, alive, to the corrals. It was a devastating failure, but one that many other professionals had suffered, and yet were able to continue and advance. But not Jeff Ramsey. Fermín Rivera refused to continue managing him. Most of the novillero's contracts were canceled. Ramsey's career was over before it had really gotten started.

But, one opportunity remained, one last chance to redeem himself. He had a contract for a performance in Villa Acuña. Ramsey fought well, but he also suffered a severe goring that barely missed the femoral artery. He began to wonder if he had made the right choice of careers. Thereafter, under the guidance of Romarico

Ramsey, performing *brega*, an opening, testing lance with the cape, in Villa Acuña, Mexico.

González, the empresario of the Villa Acuña bullring, the Yankee novillero went back to the ranches, where he trained hard and prepared himself for his return to the rings.

But, the failure in Puebla and the rejection by Fermín Rivera, combined with Jeff's own bitter, disillusioned attitude, were just too much. There are just so many opportunities, and so many young toreros seeking them. Ramsey had been pushed too hard, too rapidly. Without the benefit of enough training and preparation, he was cast into the fray, to either sink or swim. And, like a piece of raw meat thrown to the lions, he was devoured.

Looking back, Ramsey, who became a Hollywood movie stuntman, summarized the situation: "There were definite powers at play that kept me out of my rightful place as a novillero on-the-rise. There are forces in life that are beyond our abilities to control. On the bright side, possibly I was spared something ugly. Who knows? But, let's be honest. Nothing can replace the thrill of bullfighting. Nothing!"

CHAPTER 21

Others Worthy of Mention

Most rejoneadores kill with the *rejón de la muerte,* but Edith Evans preferred using a sword.

Edith Evans was a beautiful blonde and a fine rejoneadora, until a bull injured her badly.

Pat Cunningham, a good friend of Porter Tuck, was a legitimate novillero. Cunningham fought from 1953 through 1955, with 27 novilladas in Spain and Mexico. He registered initial success, but was seriously gored and was forced to give it up. Thereafter, he fought as a successful *aficionado práctico* (amateur). Thereafter, Cunningham concentrated on writing. His taurine novel, *A River of Lions*, was very successful.[1]

An English novillero, Henry Higgins, could apparently talk to the animals. He fought in Spain for a while, and apparently impressed the aficionados. Higgins died in a hang glider accident.

Little is known of Baron Clements, reported to have been a truck driver from Texas, who actually received an alternativa, of sorts, in 1959, in Tijuana. His sponsor was Sidney Franklin. However, the bestowing of the doctorate was never taken seriously and neither was Clements. He may have performed after that, but apparently without success. Efforts to make contact with him were not successful.

Southern Californian Robert Chipres, who fought under the name of Roberto de Grijalva, saw some action and had some success in Spain, in the '70s. Following an injury that had been afforded less-than-adequate medical care, Robert

[2]*Cunningham, Patrick,* A River of Lions, *Neville, Santa Barbara, Calif., 1991.*

Grasping a rejón in her right hand, Edith Evans and her horse charge toward the bull.

gave up performing. At this writing, Robert is a family man, living in Sevilla.

From 1970 through 1973, Morton Campbell aspired to be a professional, and even performed in Plaza Monterrey, one of the most important arenas in Mexico. When last heard of, he was living in Chicago.

Patricia Hays, Carolyn Hayward, Joan Ryan, and Rosita Barrios were novilleras of note, but they disappeared from the scene, apparently leaving no trace of their destinations.

In the '70s, Edith Evans, a beautiful blonde, enjoyed many triumphant afternoons as a rejoneadora. One of her horses was killed in a performance, while Evans suffered severe compound fractures that brought an end to her bullfighting career.

Later, she owned "The Kingdom of the Dancing Stallions" in Southern California. When that enterprise went belly-up, Evans returned to Mexico and other pursuits.

There is still another level of toreros, comprised of those who didn't quite make it as recognized novilleros, but were considered to be serious aspirants. Some of them later became active aficionados prácticos. Among them was this author, who fought throughout Spain from 1956 through 1959, but finally and painfully lost his teenage immortality and learned the

Robert Chipres, who peformed as a novillero using the sobriquet of Roberto de Grijalva, saw some action in Spain. Here, he performs in a festival in Tijuana, Mexico.

truth of the taurine axiom, "The brave blood flows first."

Others had more colorful histories.

Robert Buick worked in a few Mexican novilladas in the mid–'60s until authorities discovered that he was financing his bullfighting career by robbing 18 federally-insured banks in California.[2] He was arrested in 1966 by local authorities in Pecos, Texas. When last heard of, he was giving bullfight lessons to the inmates of a federal prison.

Kent Goodman, who may have been the only torero to wear a goatee, was seen in a few Mexican plazas de toros. Dressed in a suit of lights, he rode the Mexico City subway, carrying a sign that accused the management of La Plaza México of being anti–American. He finally got his opportunity in the world's largest plaza de toros, but due to his limited experience, he bombed, big time. Mexican taurine journalist Rosa Rivera told this reporter, however, that Goodman's march into the plaza, in the formal *paseillo*, was very impressive.

From 1949 to 1952, Jimmy Corbett performed as an aspirant novillero. From 1951 to 1955, Alexander Foster, of Connecticut, saw some action. From

[2]*Sabljak, Mark, & Martin H. Greenburg,* Most Wanted: A History of the FBI's Ten Most Wanted List, *Bonanza Books, New York, 1990.*

Fred Renk, stepfather of Matador David Renk, peformed along the Mexico-U.S. border in the '60s. Thereafter, Fred became an aficionado práctico. (Photograph by "Sol.")

1950 through 1954, Charles Patrick Scanlon, a genuine curmudgeon and a very knowledgeable aficionado, fought in several novilladas along the Mexican border. He then made his home in Sevilla, Spain. When last heard of, in 1999, Scanlon was hospitalized, in very poor health.

In 1955, Paul "El Indio Güero" (The Blond Indian) Elhert gained a bit of publicity, not so much for his work in the

Joan Ryan, killing a bull, along the Mexico-California border.

arenas, but for his reliance on a bicycle for all of his transportation. According to those who knew of him, he rode his bike from Monterrey, Mexico, to New York City, from where he somehow found his way to Spain. There, he saw a bit of action, but was reportedly jailed for performing without proper work or immigration

Opposite: **Robert Buick fought bulls in Mexico during which time he was also robbing 18 banks in California, some of them twice.**

No. 233 ROBERT CLAYTON BUICK

First Most Wanted Listing:
March 24, 1966
Apprehended:
March 29, 1966

In another era Robert Buick might have been called daring, perhaps even dashing.

Born in Pennsylvania, he spent much of his life in Mexico and even took up the sport of bullfighting. At the same time, however, Buick was also making a living robbing California banks. In 1966, he was named to the Most Wanted List, accused of robbing eighteen federally insured savings and loan associations in that area, some of them twice.

Buick was nearly brought down in February 1966 when a retired police officer, unaware Buick had just robbed a bank but suspicious of his actions, pursued him several miles before overtaking him for questioning. When the former officer attempted to detain Buick, he was bitten on the hand. The escapee sped away in his Buick station wagon.

The FBI release gave this description of the fugitive:

> Said to be a personal "playboy type" extrovert who likes attention and the opportunity to boast of his past bullfighting activity, Buick reportedly drinks expensive wines and liquors, frequents good restaurants, nightclubs and beach resorts and likes swimming, boating, dancing, television and jazz music. He is known to dress neatly and conservatively, to travel by air and private automobile, usually exceeding the speed limit, and to wear a diamond ring, a gold identification wrist bracelet and a gold religious neck medal. Buick reportedly smokes cigarettes, is especially fond of Italian and Mexican food and is fairly fluent in the Spanish language.

Buick offered no resistance when he was arrested by local authorities in Pecos, Texas.

Ed Byerly, who called himself "El Cóndor," spent a couple of years performing in Mexican novilladas. (Photograph by Fred Renk.)

papers. And, that's the last that anybody heard of Elhert or his famous bicycle.

Texas, home of two full matadors (three, if you include Baron Clements), seems to have had more than its share of toreros. In 1961, Charles Nixon, who owns a popular taurine bar in McAllen, fought several times a year for more than a decade in many Mexico/Texas border towns, and was known for his rather outrageous courage. In the '80s, Ed Byerly, who billed himself as "El Cóndor," enjoyed a certain amount of success as a novillero. Then, victimized financially in Mexico, he gave it up.

Texan Fred Renk performed as a novillero for a few years, along the Mexican-American borders, but lacked the stuff necessary for a career. He later became the stepfather of Matador David "El Texano" Renk.

There are a few others who made their marks, although not exactly indelibly, on La Fiesta Brava, and for whom there is little or no information.

In the '60s, Dixie Lee, of El Paso, fought in several novilladas. According to reports, she married an American astronaut, but NASA refused to either comment or to provide any information about her whereabouts, or even to confirm if *any* torera had ever married *any* astronaut.

Georgiana Knowles was an aspiring rejoneadora. Ernest Carleton Bass[3] is mentioned in 19th century accounts of Amer-

[3]*Hail, Marshall,* Knight in the Sun: First Yankee Matador, *pp. 5–6. Boston, Little Brown, 1962.*

Harry Fulsom fought as a novillero in Mexico and Spain. He is shown performing in Rota, Spain.

ican bloodless bullfights. Bong Way "Bill" Wong, "El Chino," was a Chinese American from San Francisco, a civil engineering graduate from Cal Berkeley, who fought for a while in Mexico and Spain. He was, according to reports, quite talented, at least with the cape. But, when not enough opportunities developed in Spain, he returned to Mexico, where he was killed in an automobile accident.

Other names that merit mention include: Harry Whitney, Bill Hedrick, Sam James, Tom André, Tony Cansino, Jim Conklin, Raúl Castro, Bob Evans, Harry Fulsom, John Munick, Mark Schwartz, Salvador Miliciano, Bill "Leon Camino" Cimino, Mike "Miguelito" Stumer, Luis Ross, Bill Lucidi, David Kunstler, and Dr. Tom Payte. There may be others.

There have also been a few characters who fraudulently claimed to be toreros, including Californian Steve Herlihy, who billed himself "Esteban Oleji" and managed to con many of the North American news media. He appeared, dressed in a suit of lights, on the *What's My Line* television show. He was also featured in *Gentlemen's Quarterly* magazine as "America's Youngest Matador."

When this author was hosting *Bullfight World* on a Los Angeles television station, I exposed Herlihy and charged that his membership papers to the Mexican Novilleros' Union were counterfeit; that the "scars" in his legs were placed there by a Mexican surgeon with whom he was living in Mexico City; and that, apparently, the only animal that Herlihy ever fought was a German shepherd named "Duke."

Following the TV exposé, Herlihy sued this writer and KLXA-TV, but following a meeting among lawyers from both sides, during which evidence of

Herlihy's deception was presented, the suit was quietly and abruptly dropped.

Aside from the phonies, all of those "also appearing" names shared deep afición that drove them into bullfighting. That their accomplishments might have been modest is of no importance. They experienced the impossible-to-describe emotion of overcoming their fear, while attempting to create beauty with a wild, deadly animal. And that is something that very few Americans can claim.

According to well-known aficionado Art Diaz, "in the early 1950s, Richard Evans, a novillero of African-American ethnicity, performed in U.S.-Mexican border plazas and other small venues in Mexico. In a career that spanned approximately 10 years, he killed some 180 bulls.

"Ernesto Pastor, born in San Juan, Puerto Rico, received the alternativa from José Gómez 'Gallito' in Oviedo, Spain, on September 19, 1919. He died as the result of a goring inflicted by the bull 'Bellotero' from the ranch of the Marqués de Villagodio, in Madrid, in the 1920s."

Chapter 22

The Strange Passion of Amateur Toreros

Los Muleteros was a club of amateur toreros. The members often participated in competitions with other amateurs.

Film director Budd Boetticher was a fine amateur rejoneador, performing in a variety of Mexican venues. Budd and his wife Mary frequently gave demonstrations of rejoneo on their horse ranch near San Diego, California.

It's easy to understand how men and women can be inspired to become matadors. Celebrity, excitement, money, glory. But, why would anybody fight bulls for fun? And, even pay for the opportunity to do so? That's the question often posed to those unique individuals known as aficionados prácticos, amateur toreros. But, they have no answer.

Some of these intrepid amateurs are pretty good toreros. A few attain special positions of respect, even from professionals. For the particularly talented ones, there is demand. They're invited to perform in festivals and charity functions. But, most are just everyday aficionados who really have no business as pseudo-toreros. They're usually too old, too far out of condition, and almost always too poor to engage in such an expensive and dangerous hobby.

In addition to costly capes, muletas, swords, and tailored trajes cortos—festival outfits of tightly-fitting, high-waisted pants; vests and short jackets, similar to those of male flamenco dancers; boots; and flat-brimmed Cordobés hats—these weekend toreros usually have to buy their own bulls, and almost always have to pay their own expenses. Their rewards are limited to painful bruises, broken bones, torn ligaments, a bit more experience, and once in a wonderful while, a small taste of glory.

Nevertheless, in city parks, backyards, and even living rooms from New York City to Pasadena, one doesn't have to look too

Author Barnaby Conrad performed in several formal festivals in Spain and South America. Here, he poses in front of a poster featuring the great Juan Belmonte, Conrad (Niño de California) and Roberto Mendoza, in Castillo de Las Guardas, Spain.

hard to find an aficionado práctico or two, practicing and dreaming of that special day when a perfect bull will allow them an historic performance.

Amateur bullfighting is a passion. Nothing else can compare to it. When things go well, it's the greatest feeling in the world. And, when things go poorly, the aficionado práctico wants to find a deep hole, jump into it, and cover his head.

In Southern California, Los Muleteros

Film director Tony Brand faced the horns in informal affairs. Here, he offers a cape lance to a 398-kilo bull in Quito, Ecuador.

Jim Verner, now a resident of Great Britain, performed in many festivals during his tenure in Quito, Ecuador. Here, he does a nice *Verónica* with an animal from Ernesto Gutiérrez, during Aficionados' Day. Verner won the trophy both times that he performed there.

Restaurateur Paul Dobson, of San Diego, enjoyed some fine afternoons in Baja México.

Women have also performed as amateurs. Over this torera's right shoulder is Matador Diego O'Bolger, while over her left shoulder is aficionado práctico Eddie Cohn.

Bill Torres Lira (Guillermo Torres Lira) has been one of California's best aficionados prácticos. Here, he gives a ***natural*** during a festival in Reynosa, Mexico.

Salvador Contreras, a member of Los Muleteros, was active for many years. Here, he gives a ***natural*** in Juárez, Mexico.

Dick Thieland, from northern California, had a few good afternoons in the arena.

Harry Conner was another very good aficionado práctico.

Southern California attorney Paul Gray, his pants only a shadow of what the tailor had in mind, smiles as he walks away from an animal that has just done the Mexican Hat Dance on his body.

Las Vegas blackjack dealer Anthony Galvez salutes the crowd.

Wally Burdge seems to be attempting to hypnotize his young bull during a performance in Tijuana.

Roy Badillo does a complicated lance during a festival in Ensenada, Mexico.

Fred Sayeg approaches his bull.

was an aficionados club whose membership consisted exclusively of male and female aficionados prácticos who got together to train and hone their talents. Club dues and fundraising activities helped its members to buy young bulls. Unfortunately, age does not discriminate. When most of the members became too old to continue fooling around with several hundred pounds of enraged pot roast, Los Muleteros disbanded.

They work hard, these amateurs, training, fine tuning their form and timing, and perfecting their techniques. And, several times per year, usually in 20th class rings in Mexico, Spain, France, and South America, groups of aficionados prácticos get together to compete for trophies and applause, and enjoy their special, albeit esoteric, camaraderie. As is the case with professionals, those final minutes that precede the sounding of the trumpets are sheer terror. They march slowly into the plaza, trying to look so brave and elegant, but feeling neither of those emotions.

The anxiety is in waiting. Standing behind a wooden *burladero*, waiting for your bull to come out, is pure mental anguish. Your heart beats so rapidly, you fear that it will burst from your chest. And, then, you're in the ring, and all of the responsibility hangs heavily upon your shoulders. Your feet feel so very heavy. Your throat is like sandpaper. Your voice cracks like that of a pubescent teenager. And, still, you find yourself holding out your cape, challenging a young bull that may have been fought before. You do it, in spite of everything, because this is why you're here.

For any torero—amateur or professional—the real fear is not of the animal, but of the crowd. The bull can damage you physically, but the fans can figuratively castrate you. They can humiliate you and leave emotional scars that manifest

Alex Sonek does a *Verónica.*

themselves in nightmares, until you have the chance to redeem yourself.

And another truth is apparent. There are many outstanding aficionados whose knowledge of the taurine arts is impressive. Yet, until they have actually stood on the sand, faced the horns, and put their personal honor and physical well-being on the line, they cannot truly understand the emotion of attempting to create something beautiful with an animal of killer blood and evil intentions.

The author gives a close chest pass to a novillo in Reynosa, Mexico. (Photograph by Renk.)

Don Joslyn displaying a pair of ears that he won during a festival in Tijuana.

Mike de Anda of El Paso competed in dozens of amateur festivals.

Jay Manrique was a very good aficionado práctico.

It doesn't matter whether it takes place in a formal presentation in a formal plaza de toros, or with two-year-old bulls in some obscure arena. As Mexican Matador Curro Rivera put it, "If it has horns and it attacks, it's a bull."

Even when amateurs are training, during tientas on some ranch, facing one- or two-year-old cows that couldn't do much more than give you nasty bruises or a few broken bones, the emotion is the same. The vaca, which may be the size of a large Great Dane, trots into the arena. The hairs stand up on her neck. You hear

Before taking up animals' rights, Stephanie Powers was known to occasionally flap a cape at a young animal of brave blood. (Photograph by Constantine Mengason.)

a collective exclamation, regarding how "cute" she is. She then proceeds to demonstrate how much fun it is to beat the living crap out of some poor aficionado práctico, then add insult to injury by doing the Mexican Hat Dance on the guy's head and body.

You pick yourself up, brush off the dirt, and doing your best to look at least somewhat dignified, retire to a convenient burladero. But, in most cases, after you catch your breath, you retrieve your cape or muleta, and go back for more.

Among some of the best known American aficionados prácticos have been, in no particular order: Guillermo (Bill) Torres Lira, Pete Rombold, Salvador Contreras, Roy Badillo, Ed Cohn, Fred Sayeg, Ray Michel, Tony Brand, Tracy Eaton, Dick Frontain, Sonny Galaviz, Paul Gray, Bruce Hutton, Phil Jongeneel, Fred Renk, Jay Manrique, Harry Conner, Rodrigo Zamora, Alex Sonek, David Clay, Mike DeAnda, David Morano, Jim Verner, Bill Lindsay, Hector Muñoz, Tony Galvez, Wally Burdge, Roy Shiflett, and the author of this book.

Former novillero Fred Renk occasionally performs as an aficionado práctico, usually in charity festivals with his stepson, Matador David Renk.

Barnaby Conrad, the outstanding author and artist from central California, is probably the only American to perform as an aficionado práctico in Mexico, Spain, and Peru. In spite of being only an amateur, he worked on cards with some very impressive professionals, including Carlos Arruza and Alejandro Montani, as well as with Montani's mentor, the great Juan Belmonte. In spite of receiving a large goring, Conrad continued to perform and to attract accolades for his efforts in the ring.

Aficionado práctico Juan Martinez.

And, Barnaby's brother, Hunt, is likewise an interesting story. At 16, Hunt was working as a cowboy on a Montana ranch when he entered the big Livingston rodeo. In a terrible horse accident, his leg was crushed and, subsequently, amputated below the knee. But, it didn't slow him down much. He continued to ride horses, fly an airplane, hunt pheasants, and play tournament golf.

And, he never lost his sense of humor. "How many people do you know who go into Brooks Brothers and order one garter and a thumb tack?" he asked.

Hunt Conrad became a businessman in Lima, Peru, where he met Carlos Arruza and Manolete. Over the years, Hunt became an ardent aficionado. "Someday, I'd like to try doing it," he said. But, nobody took him seriously.

When Hunt turned 30 and was rather portly, he took a trip to Sevilla, where he and the author called upon the immortal Juan Belmonte at the matador's beautiful ranch. Belmonte hosted a tienta for him, and, not realizing that Hunt had a prosthetic leg, invited him to fight a heifer. As they went down the steps to the little arena, Hunt said, "Well, Don Juan, I guess you've seen a lot of people fight for the first time."

Belmonte replied, "Sí, y por la última, también." (Yes, and for the last time, too.)

The matador gave a signal. The toril gate clanged open, and the heifer slammed into the ring.

As Barnaby tells the story in his book *Name Dropping*:

> A young matador lured the animal away and left it standing in the middle of the arena, its flanks heaving in anger,

Texas realtor Roy Shiflett has had his share of confrontations on the sand and has won a few trophies for his taurine efforts.

its tail twitching, as it looked around for something to charge. Behind the protective burladero shield, Belmonte showed Hunt how to hold the muleta and spread it with the sword. Then, he pointed to a place about twenty feet from the heifer.

"Now," he said, "over there."

Hunt stepped out from the burladero. He stood, straight, and tried to walk like

Well-known aficionado práctico/journalist/photographer/professor Dick Frontain has performed in scores of festivals and is a frequent guest of ganaderos in their annual tientas.

Eddie "Lalito" Cohn of Northern California has performed with young bulls throughout Mexico. Here, he prepares to give a ***natural***.

Manolete. "If I'm going to get it," he was saying to himself, "I'm going to go out like Manolete!"

The heifer charged, and Hunt froze, his eyes half closed, holding the muleta in the pase de la muerte (pass of death) position. Swoosh! It hurtled by, the horns missing his legs by a yard.

"It works!" Hunt exclaimed. "It actually wo..."

He never finished the sentence. The animal had wheeled, tightly, and its blunt left horn struck him a glancing blow in the midsection.

Hunt managed two more passes, but he got turned around and tried to make the heifer pass between himself and the fence, usually a bad move. The heifer drove a horn into his leg, luckily the wooden one. Belmonte stepped into the ring, in a flash, shoved his cape in the animal's face, and lured the heifer away from the fallen man.

Hunt got up, mad and frustrated. This time, when the animal charged, he decided to show the critter an old Montana trick. Tossing away the muleta, he grabbed the attacking heifer by the off horn with one hand and by the snout with the other. Wrenching its neck and falling backward, he neatly bulldogged, or cowdogged, the vaca brava.

Belmonte, who thought he'd seen everything that could happen in a bullfight, scratched his head, as he walked over to where my grinning brother held the animal helpless.

"Ya está muerta?" the great matador asked, between amazement and amusement. "Is it dead, yet?"[1]

Film director Budd Boetticher performed, on foot, as an amateur and could well have turned professional. Many years later, he accomplished grand things as an amateur rejoneador. And, the taurine-oriented films that he directed became classics.

Stephanie Powers fought a few times as an amateur before joining the ranks of the animal rightists. And, according to unconfirmed reports, Orson Welles also had a couple of afternoons on the sand.

Roy Shiflett, of Houston, performed in several festivals from 1964 to 1969, in benefit for a children's hospital, and one year even won the trophy as the best torero of the day. In 1968, Shiflett appeared on the *To Tell the Truth* TV show. The panel had no trouble identifying him.

Jim Verner, who currently lives in England with his wife, Felicia, was initiated to bullfighting in 1958, along the Texas, Arizona, and California borders with Mexico. With help from Matador Tomás Abaroa, he became an aficionado práctico, facing his first animal in 1961, when a group of disc jockeys from Tucson put together a bullfight festival in Nogales. But when the DJs saw the animals, they quickly changed their minds about the whole thing. Verner stepped in and showed them how it should be done.

Verner performed a dozen or so times in bloodless affairs in Baja California. In 1963, he killed a novillo in Nogales. Then he spent a year traveling with Mexican charro (cowboy)/movie star Antonio Aguilar and fighting the animals after the charros were done with them. He also performed as an amateur torero, facing some very large animals in Colombia, Spain, Puerto Rico, and Lima, Peru, sometimes with his twin brothers.

Amateur toreros are the real aficionados. It matters not that the animals that they face have blunted horn tips and are smaller and younger than those that are assigned to professionals, or that these ersatz toreros display their talents in modest rings, for meager crowds. Their animals

[1]*Conrad, Barnaby,* Name Dropping, *Harper-Collins West, San Francisco, Calif.*.

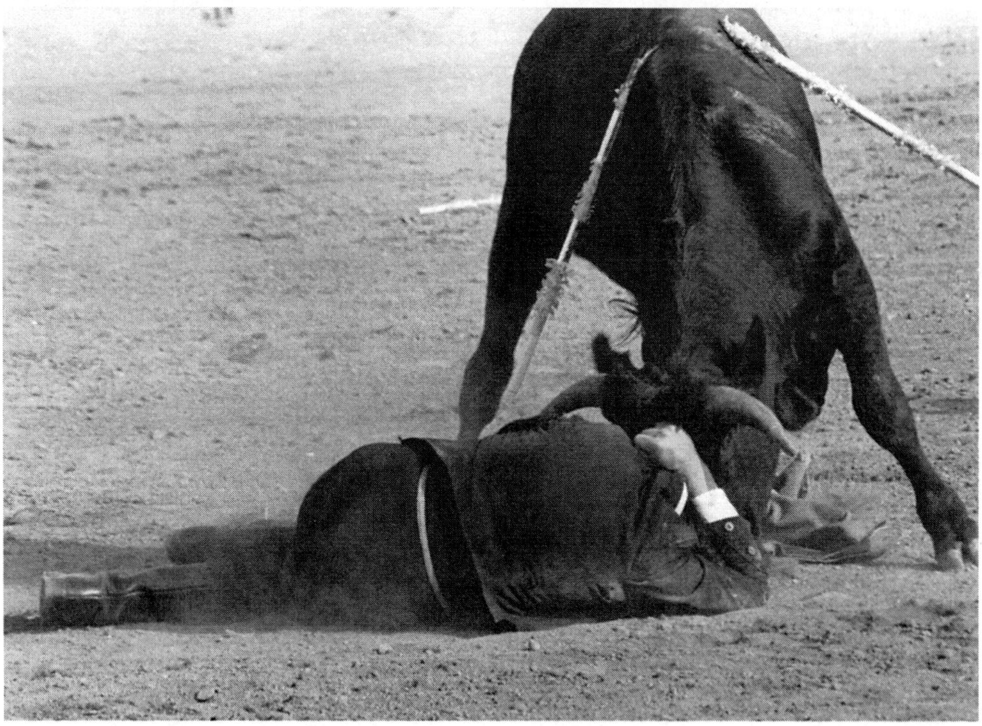

Don't ever imagine that amateur bullfighting isn't dangerous. More than one amateur has suffered injuries; some have been gored.

Sometimes the horns find their mark. Here, aficionado práctico Rodrigo Zamora is gored in the stomach during a performance in Tijuana.

are, nonetheless, products of brave blood, and the responsibilities of the amateurs are identical to those of the professionals. Theirs is honest afición, practiced for pure enjoyment. It's the love of the art, the emotion of the spirit, and the passion of the gusano, unencumbered by thoughts of economic reward.

When the fans are cheering and the music is playing ... when an ear is thrust into your anxious hand ... when you're hot, sweaty, exhausted and dirty ... when you've done it, in spite of your fear ... when somebody slaps you on the back and says, "Congratulations, torero!" ... when you take that delicious turn of the ring and you know that, by tomorrow, your whole body will ache like hell — it's then that you truly understand why La Fiesta is always celebrated, rather than merely staged.

To aficionados prácticos everywhere: Congratulations, toreros!

Afterword

There have been many Yankee men and women who have demonstrated enough courage, artistry, intelligence, and athletic ability to enjoy successful careers in bullfighting, were they allowed to do so. For toreros/as of any country to develop their talents, they must perform, frequently. But, few Yankees have been able to penetrate the obstacles of xenophobia and politics long or often enough to obtain the necessary experience and exposure.

Nevertheless, some Yankees have been tenacious enough to eventually receive their professional doctorates. But even after making it their alternativas, the political doors have been shut, firmly, in their faces.

Therein lies a conundrum that is difficult in Spain, but dramatically pronounced in Mexico, where, except for the sons of well-connected matadors or bull breeders, nearly every novillero must "purchase" his/her opportunities. Not only are most not paid for putting their lives on the line, they usually have to buy their own bulls, as well as pay for their own expenses. Novillos can cost as much as $2,000 apiece. Add the costs of transportation and lodging, and each performance involves a sizable investment.

In some cases, a torero of exceptional, natural talent is "discovered" by a group of wealthy investors who will finance his apprenticeship in exchange for a large percentage of his future earnings as a matador. A decent career as a novillero can cost hundreds of thousands of dollars. As a result, merely because most aspiring toreros can't afford to finance their internships, they're forced to quit, long before they ever get started.

In Spain, novilleros initiate their careers by honing their talents with cows of brave blood on bull breeding ranches, where they hope to attract the attention of some benefactor who will give them opportunities to perform in the off-season económicas, in which they face two-year-old novillos. After a few years of toiling in the económicas, and with enough celebrity, they graduate to novilladas picadas, with three-year-old animals. Only after they have faced hundreds of young bulls on the novillada picada circuit and have generated enough favorable press coverage — and thus, crowd appeal — do they seek their alternativas. When a Spanish novillero becomes a Matador de Toros, he's worthy of the title. He's a professional, in name and in fact.

But, with few exceptions, foreigners aren't allowed to perform in the Spanish económicas, and Mexico doesn't even offer them. For them, there is no such thing as a level playing field.

Neophyte novilleros in Mexico are forced to initiate their careers with the larger, less forgiving, more mature novillos, animals that are usually beyond their experience and knowledge. Thrown to the sharks to either sink or swim, most of them fail. Many of them are terribly gored. Some of them die. There are no scholarships to the university of hard knocks.

But, let's suppose that some brilliant, young torero is able to overcome those seemingly impenetrable obstacles and is able to gain a certain degree of celebrity on the novillada picada circuit. Those who control the destinies of such aspiring kids aren't willing to grant them the necessary time to fully develop their talents; they want to begin receiving returns on their investments as quickly as possible. In Mexico, mañana is merely the name of a song. The only thing that counts is today.

So, some kid who, in the beginning, may have represented great promise for the future, may have only 30 or 40 novilladas under his sash before being shoved, prematurely, into his alternativa. He becomes a Matador de Toros in name only, not by the professionalism that the title is supposed to represent.

And, in far too many cases, "professional" doesn't necessarily translate to experience, technical excellence, or even natural talent, but to market value, the numbers of ticket buyers that the greenhorn matador can attract. If that means performing as a suicidal tremendista in order to thrill the easily-deceived, thrill happy crowds in the provinces and frontiers, that's exactly what he'll have to do.

To most empresarios, toreros aren't human beings — they're slabs of meat hanging in their lockers to be consumed at will. And, to some, a bullfight is merely a vehicle for the sale of beer.

It's impossible to calculate how many young toreros have failed because they were pushed too hard, too quickly. And, when they're finally presented in the important interior rings, the crowds demand that they triumph, no matter what problems they may encounter. If the bulls are difficult, if high winds attempt to blow them out of the plaza, or rain storms threaten to inundate them, well that's too bad; it's back to the sticks. How many such kids have become jaded, disillusioned by their own dreams?

If that's the situation for Mexican toreros, imagine, then, how much more difficult it is for foreigners. Even after the aspiring Yankee novillero spends years on the circuit, always paying but never receiving, and in spite of that, becomes a full matador, what has he accomplished? Oh sure, as a matador he's paid for his labors. But, the empresarios in the important plazas — where he had previously paid for opportunities to triumph or fail as a novillero — aren't interested in paying him to perform as a matador. If he is afforded any contracts, they're exclusively in the frontier plazas de toros and seaside tourist venues, where, due to his Yankee heritage, he can attract ticket buyers from his own country. The empresarios don't consider the Yankee matador to be worthy of performing in the major rings, or of competing with front line, native matadors.

On the bottom line, with only rare exceptions, it hasn't been the lack of talent or potential, but a case of pure jingoism that has kept Yankee toreros from attaining greater success in the plazas de toros of the world. And, it seems that the situation will never change.

Bibliography

Acquaroni, J.L. *Bulls and Bullfighting.* Barcelona: Editorial Noguer.

Beamis, Huldine. *Cavaliers of Portugal.* New York: Bantam, 1966.

Belmonte, Juan, as told to Manuel Chaves Nogales. *Juan Belmonte, Killer of Bulls: The Autobiography of a Matador.* New York: Bantam.

Bitar, Alberto A., ed. *El Redondel.* 2a Epoca, Año 2, No. 25. México: Editorial La Tauromaquía, 1959.

_____, ed. *El Redondel.* 2a Epoca, Año 1, No. 9. México: Editorial La Tauromaquía, 1950.

Boetticher, Budd. *When in Disgrace.* Santa Barbara, Calif.: Neville, 1997.

Campos de España, Rafael. *ABC* (newspaper), June 11, 1972, Madrid.

Carrie, Douglas B. *Bulls, Bullfighting & Spanish Identities.* University of Arizona Press, 1962.

Cintrón, Conchita. *Memoirs of a Bullfighter.* New York: Holt, Rinehart and Winston, 1958.

Cintrón, Lola Verrill. *Goddess of the Bullring.* London: Frederick Muller, 1960.

Conrad, Barnaby. *La Fiesta Brava.* Boston: Houghton Mifflin, 1959.

_____. *Gates of Fear.* New York: Bonanza, 1957.

_____. *Name Dropping.* San Francisco: HarperCollins West.

Cossío, José María de. *La Fiesta de Toros.* Madrid, Dirección General de Turismo.

_____. *Los Toros.* Madrid: Dirección General de Turismo, 1960.

Cunningham, Patrick. *A River of Lions.* Santa Barbara, Calif.: Neville.

Daley, Robert. *The Swords of Spain.* New York: Dial, 1966.

Franklin, Sidney. *The Bullfighter from Brooklyn.* New York: Prentice-Hall, 1952.

Fraser, Allan. *The Bull.* Berkshire, England: Osprey, 1959.

Frontain, Dick. *How to Enjoy a Bullfight.* Phoenix, Ariz.: Hooper Press, 1966.

Fulton, John. *Bullfighting.* New York: Dial, 1977.

Gamboa, Fernando. *Mundo Taurino* (newspaper), Sept. 10, 1985, Madrid.

Hail, Marshall. *Knight in the Sun: The First*

Yankee Matador. Boston: Little, Brown, 1962.

Hemingway, Ernest. *Death in the Afternoon.* New York: Scribner's, 1932.

Kehoe, Vincent J-R. *Aficionado.* New York: Hastings House, 1959.

_____. *Wine, Women, & Toros.* New York: Hastings House, 1962.

Lera, Angel M. de. *The Horns of Fear.* New York: Dutton.

Llovet, Enrique. *Bullfighting/Tauromachy.* Paris: Art et Industrie, 1957.

Los Aficionados de Los Angeles taurine club (newsletter).

Luján, Néstor. *Historia del Toreo.* Oct. 1954, Ediciones Destino, Barcelona.

Macnab, Angus. *Fighting Bulls.* New York: Harcourt, Brace, 1959.

Marks, John. *To the Bullfight.* Alfred E. Knopf, 1952.

Montes, Serge. Article in *El Clarín de La Busca,* November 1995.

Shay Oag. *In The Presence of Death/Antonio Ordoñez.* New York: Coward-McCann, 1968.

Shorris, Earl. *The Boots of the Virgin.* New York: Delacorte Press, 1968.

Solana Verduguillo, Rafael, and Alexander Olyka. *Bulls and Their Fighters: A Guide to Bullfighting.* Mexico, Tourist Publications.

Index